BODIES

BODIES

SEX, VIOLENCE,

DISEASE, AND DEATH

IN CONTEMPORARY LEGEND

GILLIAN BENNETT

UNIVERSITY PRESS OF MISSISSIPPI / JACKSON

www.upress.state.ms.us

The University Press of Mississippi is a member of the
Association of American University Presses.

First edition

Library of Congress Cataloging-in-Publication Data
Bennett, Gillian.
    Bodies : sex, violence, disease, and death in contemporary legend / Gillian Bennett.—
1st ed.
        p. cm.
    Includes bibliographical references and index.
    ISBN 1-57806-789-8 (cloth : alk. paper) 1. Legends. 2. Body, Human—Folklore. I. Title
    GR78.B46   2005
    398.2'09—dc22   2005003925

British Library Cataloging-in-Publication Data available

CONTENTS

ACKNOWLEDGMENTS

In many respects this book is a joint effort. I am indebted to friends and family for finding many of the texts I quote. Special thanks go to my daughter, Kate; to Caroline Oates, the librarian of the Folklore Society; to Véronique Campion-Vincent for many of the French texts; and to Paul Smith, as always wonderfully generous in finding material for me. The library of the Folklore Society has been an invaluable resource, as has the Manchester Public Library (the best British public library outside London), and the library of Manchester Metropolitan University. Special thanks, too, to Bill Ellis for a thoughtful reading of an earlier draft.

Thanks also go to my teacher, Michèle Phillips, and my nephew, Mark Gray, for help with some of the French translations, and to Adrienne Mayor, Ruth Richardson, and Véronique Campion-Vincent for allowing extensive quotation from their work.

Finally, as always, I thank my husband, Andrew, for his unfailing patience and support.

PREFACE

I am a folklorist by profession and inclination. There are many ways of being a folklorist, but my own interests have led me to the branch of folklore that examines alternative ways of looking at the world and all that's in it and to the narratives through which these alternatives are explored and communicated. So for the past twenty years my chief interest has been in legends—in particular, contemporary legends (or, as others might call them, "urban" or "modern" legends or, in some circles, "belief" or "rumor" legends). All these terms refer to the same type of story, but they have acquired their names through a sort of negative definition, as folklorists have sought to distinguish them from so-called traditional legends.

For a traditional folklorist the term *legend* implies a long-lived story about the past told by elderly people living in remote rural places, told as true but inherently fictional. From the 1960s onward, these assumptions were challenged by a new breed of researchers who were collecting stories that defied this sort of categorization but also could not be fitted into any other recognized folk narrative category. Many conventional researchers simply discarded these stories, but other researchers recognized that the stories couldn't be entirely idiosyncratic because they were being collected again and again. The storytellers were young, urban, and often professional people. Their stories were not about saints or giants, fairies or monsters; instead, the tales relied on all the paraphernalia of modern city living and seemed to reflect an entirely untraditional way of looking at the world. They were often told as "news" or "real events" and seemed to be passed on in the same way as rumors, beginning in a small way and then spreading rapidly in surges of intense interest and committed belief before dying away, only to surge up again in a different time or place. The new breed of folklorists wanted these stories recognized as genuine folk narratives, intrinsically interesting, traditional in their own way though different from the sorts of stories researchers had previously been collecting as legends.

DEFINING A CONTEMPORARY LEGEND

At this point in an introduction, it is customary to set about trying to define the term *legend* itself. In the past, I was very interested in such discussions and anxious to engage in debate. However, I no longer find these questions particularly intriguing—and I suspect many of my colleagues feel the same. Over the years I have studied this sort of material I have arrived at a working definition that satisfies me and allows me to go on doing the sort of work I do. Many people might disagree with this definition—and I am aware that my orientation to "contemporary legend" in particular differs a little from the norm—but these definitions underpin my work and this book, so I think it will be best to revisit these debates and to spell out my approach. What follows is less of a reasoned argument and more of a personal declaration. It is designed to do no more than allow readers to see where I'm coming from and why I have chosen the six subjects that make up the case studies for this book.

For me now what makes a legend a "legend" is the difficulty of assigning fixed characteristics to it or placing it forever and always in one category. This is in part because legends can be told in so many different modes and media. But it is also partly because legends are situated somewhere on a continuum between myth and folktale at one pole and news and history at the other, moving along this continuum depending on the individual story and the whims or objectives of the individual storyteller who relates it. Myths are sacred narratives supporting a particular worldview and teaching the truths of a particular religion, and folktales are traditional secular fictions relating the (mis)adventures of fantastical protagonists (superheroes, superfools, kings and queens, supernatural beings, talking animals, magic objects, and so on) in a "once upon a time" world and epoch. In contrast, news presents as itself as fact. It informs us about real people and real events in the time and place in which we actually live; history makes the same claims about the past. For both news and history, factuality is part of the definition: untrue news and mistaken history are not news or history at all.

Legends, as it were, mix the genres and confuse the categories. Legends may be either sacred or secular: they may tell of fantastical people and events, as myths and folktales do, or of people and events that seem real enough. But—and here is the crunch—however fantastical the protagonists and events, the scene is always set in the world as we know it, and the stories seem to be giving information about that world. For this reason, readers or hearers are sooner or later faced with a challenge: where on the continuum between folktale and news, myth and history, should these stories be placed? Are they true, like news and history, or true in some symbolic way, like myths, or fictional, like folktales? Here another problem surfaces. *Legend* is not actually a scientific term, though scholars attempt to use it as if it were or to make it scientific by complex definitions. It is an evaluation, not a description—this is why we are so often asked "Is it true, or is it a legend?" But the content is ambiguous enough and important enough to warrant a continuous (re)assessment and (re)evaluation. So, in an ironic way, the question of whether or not a story is a legend is critical to recognizing it as a legend.

This is particularly so because the information (or misinformation) contained in the legend is challenging in some way; it creates what psychologists call "cognitive dissonance," a mental conflict or confusion arising from simultaneously holding two contradictory understandings of a single situation or concept. It creates this dissonance by juxtaposing the world as we know it with something very different or by melding two cultural categories we think of as quite separate. The first sort of clash gives us tales of ghosts, devils, saints, and monsters. The second—by juxtaposing, for example, safety and danger, love and death, children and cruelty—gives us stories of hatchet men, castrated children, parents who kill their children, women who kill their lovers. Broadly speaking, the first clash tends to result in "traditional" legends, and the second type of clash tends to give "contemporary legends." Though there are, of course, numerous exceptions, the characters and events in contemporary legends more often tend to be bizarre, scary, and macabre than overtly supernatural and are presented as topical and newsworthy reports from the everyday world, not the otherworld.

Nevertheless, contemporary legends are not new or modern in any meaningful sense and cannot be regarded as a distinct genre. This is because, like other legends, contemporary legends are traditional narratives. By that I mean that they are "stories" of some sort; they are not something vague, diffuse, and formless like a rumor, or a statement of folk belief, or a popular fallacy. They have structure (a beginning, middle, and end, though not necessarily in that order); they are texts rather than shapeless bits of discourse. They are also "traditional," which for me means that they are recognizable because they have been widely disseminated in

Handwritten margin notes (top):

legend → contemporary/recorded time
myth → before recorded time, sacred
→ sacred, no judgement on truth
→ origins or explanations abt things are

numerous times and places. Though subject to continuous adaptation to suit the varying circumstances of their (re)tellings, their core nevertheless remains constant. It follows that I would not consider the majority of what can be found on the Web or in popular compilations necessarily to be legends at all. Some may be or may become so: only time will tell. My interest is in the contemporary legend canon—those stories that have been around long enough to be instantly recognizable, to have acquired a history, to echo folkloric themes and motifs, and to be indubitably legends.

My preferred term for the genre has always been *contemporary legend*. The terms *modern* and *urban legend* are misleading because there is little intrinsically "urban" or "modern" about these stories. The other terms, *belief* and *rumor legend*, haven't made it into common usage and simply reflect the scholarly orientation of those who pioneered the terms' usage in the past. I think *contemporary legend* is the most informative available term. It has the advantage of highlighting the topicality of the genre without limiting its applicability to a specific place or time; for example, a story such as the Blood Libel legend (see chapter 6) was contemporary in twelfth-century England as well as in twentieth-century Germany. Having said that, I do not concur with the common view that these stories are also contemporary in the sense that they reflect the fears and anxieties of a particular age or are cautionary tales warning of modern dangers. I do not think that this contention has yet been satisfactorily proved. The arguments that seek to maintain this position are usually completely circular: it is alleged that the stories reflect the fears and so forth yet simultaneously the fears of the age are deduced from the content of the narratives. This is not to say that the stories are not best understood in the context of the cultures in which they flourish (as shown in legends about organ thefts discussed in chapter 5). In other words, one needs to know something about the culture but (1) one cannot deduce the nature of that culture from the legends, or vice versa;

Handwritten margin notes (right):
legends are told not if they're true but there's veracity alsief based = historic event but not even content may not be fully but rumour not a full narrative legend if fully fleshed out narrative

Handwritten note (bottom): Legends – specific time & place

and (2) there are other powerful forces at work apart from fear and anxiety (in the case of the stories I look at in this book, sexual, medical, and intergroup politics, for example, play a large role).

"TAKING A LINE FOR A WALK"

The stories in this book have been chosen with these sorts of things in mind. All of them have interesting histories, and at least two of them have very long lives. Most of them have existed in many different media—in literature, journalism, and theater as well as in the oral tradition—and their themes and motifs are reflected in traditional legends. The stories are sometimes interesting because of their history or the multiplicity of the media through which they have been presented; at other times they are interesting for cultural, social, or psychological reasons. I take whatever approach is most productive. All six case studies are of stories in the contemporary legend canon. The sources I have used—both texts and commentaries—are in either English or French. This does not mean, of course, that other peoples have not transmitted these stories or that other scholars have not studied them; one can find texts and first-class scholarly work all over the world, especially in Scandinavia and Germany. But I am a native English speaker and can read French reasonably competently (all the translations from French are my own unless otherwise stated), so limiting myself to these languages is a convenience and helps control the potential mass of information. Furthermore, because each chapter is fairly self-contained, rather than providing a single bibliography for all of the legends at the end of the book, as is the usual practice, I decided it would be more useful to give the references cited for each one at the end of the relevant chapter and to single out a short list of key texts.

The approach I have taken in each of these case studies is similar to Paul Klee's approach to painting. Klee famously was supposed

to have said that he "took a line for a walk": just so, I have started
with a familiar contemporary legend and have let it lead me on a
winding trail through folklore, legends, literature, history, and
current events, hoping to end where I originally began and to have
thrown light on the familiar story by setting it in a variety of contexts. The stories I have chosen to study are all examples of the
cultural clash of discordant categories and concepts I spoke of as
characteristic of contemporary legend. That clash is represented
in the chapter titles—"Animals Inside" (animals should be outside); Poison and Honey; AIDS Aggressors (the sick should be
patient and passive); "Killing the Prodigal Son" (the Prodigal Son
should be welcomed with love); "Dispossessed" (one should own
one's own body); and "Blood and Babies."

Finally, a word about the content. I had originally intended to
divide the book into four separate sections—one for sex, one for
violence, and so on. But this proved not to be practical since the
themes of many or most of the stories I came across—and especially the ones I eventually chose to present—fell into two if not
three of these categories. The legend of the Bosom Serpent with
which I begin, for example, involves disease and death; stories of
poison and honey feature sex, violence, and death; stories of AIDS
Aggressors feature all four themes. These are all grisly stories, the
stuff of nightmares, not bedtime reading. The view of human life
and nature they portray is not kindly or optimistic. There are no
jokes and no romance here. They are winter's tales, not suitable
for children or those of a nervous disposition. But they are potent
and, I think, important. Above all, they give the lie to those who
think that contemporary legends are just trivial stories to be told
after dinner, laughed at, and dismissed.

BODIES

ANIMALS INSIDE

BOSOM SERPENTS AND ALIMENTARY AMPHIBIANS

A . . . monstrous mouth, always avid, always devouring. . . . A mouth thirsty for blood
which destroys the springs of life, drinks them, and dries them up.

—RAOUL GIRARDET, "L'EMPIRE DES TÉNÈBRES"

In this chapter I shall be looking at the complex of old medical
beliefs, religious and secular prodigy stories, and sensational stories of today that is generally referred to as the legend of the
"Bosom Serpent." The name given to this classic of the contemporary legend genre is taken from a short story entitled "Egotism;
or, The Bosom Serpent," by American writer Nathaniel Hawthorne,
who uses the legend as an allegory for the destructive effects of
selfish pride.[1] This name does not actually provide a very accurate description of the legend's contents; nevertheless, it has
caught on since the earliest scholarly discussions came about as
the result of a consideration of Hawthorne's sources.[2] The legend
of the Bosom Serpent is as variable and subject to contemporary
fashions and storytellers' whims as any other, but the core story

remains pretty constant. A man, woman, or child is said to have a creature growing inside the body—not only reptiles, as in Hawthorne's story, but also amphibians. The creature has taken up residence in a vital organ, occasionally in the heart but more frequently somewhere in the gastrointestinal tract. Once it has taken up residence there, it moves about the body and steals the host's food, causing great suffering and sometimes even death.

In June 1990, *FOAFtale News*, the newsletter of the International Society for Contemporary Legend Research, printed a report said to have been contributed by "Dr. Bruno Gosse" that had recently appeared in the sensational U.S. *Sun* newspaper. The story was that a twenty-nine-year-old French woman, Marianne Koss, "began suffering from an odd illness." No matter how much she ate, she got weaker and weaker, as if she was being deprived of food. "Meanwhile," she reportedly said, "I was getting a very unhealthy looking paunch and hearing strange growling sounds from my stomach. All day long, I'd have a terrible queasy feeling as if something was wriggling round inside of me." Her doctor decided she must be operated on and the surgeon, "Dr. Lebideux," got to work. According to the report, "Stunned, the surgeon watched in horror as the largest frog he ever saw leapt out of Marianne's stomach onto the operating room floor" (Gosse, "Docs"). The frog is now said to be at the Arles zoo. French colleagues tell me there is no zoo at Arles and that neither Dr. Lebideux nor Dr. Bruno Gosse appear on any medical register.

The *Sun* had earlier reported the cases of a man with an eel in his intestines and of a four-year-old girl who had coughed up a snake. The *Fortean Times* had also carried similar reports: a fifteen-year-old Turkish girl was said to have "suffered mysterious stomach pains for five years." Her intestines were found to contain three water snakes "slightly thicker than string and nearly a foot long." Similarly, a Syrian woman was discovered to have a six-foot snake inside her which " 'cheeped' like a chicken when it was hungry." It is not only the fringe press that carries such reports: in 1987, sober newspapers including *Pravda*, the *Guardian*, and the *Scotsman* reported the case of an eleven-year-old girl who vomited up a twenty-five-inch Caucasian cat snake after a mysterious illness.[3]

Similar stories had turned up in newspapers in earlier times and different places. On 22 July 1901, for example, the *New York Herald* printed this story:

Bullfrog in the Stomach

Edward Blazier, a farmer in Dock Watch Hollow, a hamlet nestled among the Watchung Mountains, about 5 miles from Bound Brook, New Jersey, had been ailing for some time. His symptoms baffled doctors, who one by one gave up the case as incurable. Unable to work, and slowly wasting away, Blazier was nevertheless the possessor of a ravenous appetite, being particularly fond of meat.

Then Dr. Fred Wild took up Blazier's case. He was impressed by the fact that the man's appetite remained good, whereas the opposite would be expected to be the case. When questioned, Blazier said he often suffered stomach pains, and experienced sensations as if something animated was moving about. It was also discovered that the family was in the habit of drinking from a nearby stream.

An operation was performed, and Dr. Wild removed a full grown bullfrog more than five inches long. It was similar to an ordinary bullfrog, except that examination showed that it had never had the use of its eyes.

Blazier became a center of attraction for all the neighborhood and preserved the frog in a jar of alcohol. He later recalled that about five years previously he had taken a drink from the spring and later complained of having swallowed something of a foreign nature, although he did not know what it was. He is convinced that at the time he swallowed a tadpole which, in the course of natural events became a full grown frog, undergoing the different changes in his stomach. (Mangiacopra)

My interest in this curious tradition has extended over several years.[4] Since 1990 I have collected texts of more than 120 legends of bodily contamination with reptiles and amphibians. The list stretches from the twelfth century to the last five years of the twentieth century, but I have no doubt that it is still only a very partial one. It was compiled from books, journals, magazines, broadsides and newspapers, correspondence, and conversation and can be consulted in table form in the appendix to this chapter. All these stories are told in contemporary legend mode (that is, their focus is not on magic and the supernatural but on remarkable and newsworthy events of the here and now). The stories were told in places as far apart as Azerbaijan and Australia; 90 of them come from the United States, the United Kingdom, or Ireland, though that probably is merely a reflection of the dominance of English-language sources in the collection. There are several subsets according to how the creature is thought to get in and how it is removed: the animal may have been swallowed in water, crept in while the victim was asleep, or developed from an egg or larva that was accidentally ingested; it may be removed by surgery, when the victim vomits or excretes, or it may be tricked out. The creatures are usually said to be toads, frogs, newts, snakes and serpents, lizards, or "worms," and the organs where they have taken up residence are chiefly said to be the stomach or the intestines.

Within this general framework, stories from different places feature different animals. In Ireland, for example, there seems to have been a particular dread of newts, perhaps because they are rare there, and West Yorkshire in the United Kingdom has a tradition of creatures known as "waterwolves," which are probably also newts.[5] Changing times have also produced changing emphases. For example, snakes lodged in the heart appear only in the older stories; "worms" appear most regularly throughout the seventeenth and eighteenth centuries; and amphibians turn up particularly frequently in nineteenth-century stories. Special circumstances have also produced distinct variations over time. For example, since the Western world became obsessed with fear of obesity, there have been persistent rumors that diet pills contain tapeworm eggs that hatch inside the victim;[6] similarly, from the 1920s onward, the fashion for ocean bathing, combined with the expansion of the overseas vacation market, seems to have produced fears of accidentally swallowing octopus eggs; and the increasing importation of foodstuffs from abroad would appear to have caused various food panics, including a rumor in the 1920s that a batch of particularly large eggs were crocodile eggs that would hatch inside people who ate them.[7]

I shall discuss these accounts in the section headed "The Bosom Serpent as Medical Folklore," but first I want to situate the contemporary stories in their historical context by looking at some precursors and parallels. Though all the stories I have collected are contemporary legends, like most contemporary legends they have equivalents in older traditions.

ANIMALS INSIDE: MEDICINE, MAGIC AND MORALITY, 1100–1830

The belief that animals, especially reptiles and amphibians, can survive in the human body plainly is not new. There is a fascinating story about the Emperor Nero in *The Golden Legend*, compiled by Jacobus de Voragine in the fourteenth century. Though it is not really a Bosom Serpent story, it does indicate that from early times it was thought possible for a frog to survive (even thrive) in the human body:

> The same apocryphal story tells us that Nero, obsessed by an evil madness, ordered his mother killed and cut open so he could see how it had been for him in her womb. The physicians, calling him to task

over his mother's death, said: "Our laws prohibit it, and divine law prohibits a son to kill his mother, who gave birth to him with such pain and nurtured him with so much toil and trouble." Nero said to them: "Make me pregnant with a child and then make me give birth, so that I may know how much pain it cost my mother!" He had conceived the notion of bearing a child because on his way through the city he had heard the cries of a woman in labour. They said to him: "That is not possible because it is contrary to nature, nor is it thinkable because it is contrary to reason." At this Nero said to them: "Make me pregnant and make me give birth, or I will have every one of you die a cruel death!"

So the doctors made up a potion in which they put a frog and gave it to the emperor to drink. Then they used their skills to make the frog grow in his belly, and his belly, rebelling against this unnatural invasion, swelled up so that Nero thought he was carrying a child. They also put him on a diet of foods they knew would be suitable for the frog, and told him that, having conceived, he had to follow the diet. At length, unable to stand the pain, he told the doctors: "Hasten the delivery, because I am so exhausted with this child-bearing that I can hardly get my breath!" So they gave him a drink that made him vomit, and out came a frog horrible to see, full of vile humours and covered with blood. Nero, looking at what he had brought forth, shrank from it and wondered why it was such a monster, but the physicians told him that he had produced a deformed foetus because he had not been willing to wait the full term. He said: "Is this what I was like when I came out from my mother's womb?" "Yes!" they answered. So he commanded that the foetus be fed and kept in a domed chamber with stones in it. All this, however, is not contained in the chronicles and is apocryphal.[8]

The belief in infestations of animals persisted into the seventeenth century. In his *History of Four-Footed Beasts and Serpents* (1658), British naturalist Edward Topsell stated that "Serpents do

sometimes creep into the mouths of them that are fast asleep . . .
and then is the poor man miserably and wretchedly tormented"
(quoted in Arner). Also from the seventeenth century there is a
story from volume 3 of the *Ephemerides of the Curious* for the
year 1675 about a shoemaker who had suffered from intense
abdominal pain for ten years and in despair of a cure or any relief
stabbed himself in the stomach and died: "preparations were
made for the funeral . . . when a person wishing to examine the
wound, removed the [coffin] lid, and found beside the body a
serpent of the length of a man's arm, and as thick as two
fingers. It had crept out of the wound, and lived for days afterwards."[9] A later text is a fully formed Bosom Serpent legend
and attests to the existence of the tradition in the eighteenth century. It may be found in the Dawson Turner Collection in the
British Museum, Department of Natural History, in London.[10]
This November 1780 letter from the Reverend Samuel Glasse
to Sir Joseph Banks (1743–1820), a well-known naturalist and
explorer who accompanied Captain Cook on a round-the-world
voyage in 1768–71 and who served as president of the Royal Society beginning in 1778, contains a deposition from a man named
Thomas Walker:

Borough of King's Lynn in Norfolk

Thomas Walker, late servant to
Archdale Wilson Taylor

of King's Lynn in the County of Norfolk Esq., maketh oath and saith
that some time in the last Spring he attended his said Master to
Matlock in Derbyshire, where they continued about five Weeks and
in their return to Lynn staid at Nottingham about a fortnight; and
that during their stay at Matlock, he in general eat Water Cresses
twice a day; and for some days before he left that place he had pains

in his Stomach, which pains continued with frequent inclinations to vomit until the fifteenth of October last, when, (after having complained to several Persons of having something alive within him) his Stomach swelling and his pains increasing to a violent degree, he was advised by Doctor Davison of Nottingham (at whose House he then was) to take an Emetic, which he accordingly took in the presence of the Doctor's Servant, who was with him the whole time of the Operation; and that after several strains he found something stick in his Throat, which this Deponent, thought would have suffocated him; but on pulling the same out and throwing it into a Pail (which was placed for him to vomit in) it proved to be a living Toad of about two inches and a half long and an inch and a half broad, which was afterwards laid upon the floor, and crawled towards the fire in the presence of the Doctor and several other Persons, and was then thrown therein by one of the Servants present.

Thomas Walker
Sworn in the Borough
aforesaid the nineteenth
day of November 1780

Before me Samuel Brown, Mayor

The belief that animals, especially reptiles and amphibians, could enter and be nourished in the body and cause disease seems to have been medical orthodoxy at one time. From the ancient world—from Greece, Syria, and Rome—come accounts of disease caused by infestations by animals. Hippocrates, the "father of modern medicine," for example, described the case of a young man who drank too much and passed out; while he was lying on the ground, a snake slithered down his throat, and he died from an apoplectic seizure. The fourth-century Syrian bishop and medical practitioner Aëtius gives a long list of the symptoms arising from the presence of amphibians in the human stomach. And in his famed *Natural History*, also written in the fourth century, Pliny the elder lists snakes and frogs as parasites of the human gut (Bondeson 27). Nearer our own time, extant medical works from fourteenth-century England list remedies to cope with such emergencies as "gif an addere oþere eny ouþer evel worme be y-cropyn in-to a manys body, oþer to breyde þer-in [if an adder or any other evil worm has crept into a man's body to breed therein]" (Henslow 18). In 1639 celebrated surgeon Edward May treated the existence of animals, especially snakes and frogs, in the body as fact and published a drawing of a dissection he had undertaken on the body of a young man after his death from heart disease. The left ventricle of the heart is cut away, revealing a tubular object with a divided tail and what May insists is a head. A second illustration folds out to show the "serpent" as it was when laid out flat (S. Bush 92–93).

An enlightening medieval medical perspective on Bosom Serpent traditions is provided in Marie-Christine Pouchelle's book about Henri de Mondeville, court surgeon to Philip the Fair of France (r. 1268–1314). Pouchelle tells us that Mondeville, in common with many others of his age, imagined the body in two dominant ways: as a fortress and as a series of containers nested one inside another. Regarded as a fortress, the body has thresholds between the different parts and doorways and windows to the outside. The task of the medical man is to safeguard the doors and windows, the orifices that expose the body to the outside world. The chief of these doors into the body is the mouth (Pouchelle 147). The parts of the body are thought to be nesting one inside the other: when the body is viewed as a fortress, the parts are imagined as precincts within the building; when the body is viewed as a container, the parts may be coffers, chests, or pots, and those in the depths of the body might be bags or purses. Other popular metaphors are drawn from the natural world, especially when the body is diseased. So a bubo is imagined as an owl, an ulcer as a crab, blackheads as woodworms, and a small tumor as a frog. The sufferings caused by disease are dominated by metaphors drawn from the movements of animals: a cancer is said to "gnaw," an ulcer to "crawl," a whitlow to "suck" or "bite" (Pouchelle 212–16).

The imagery of the body as a fortress that should be guarded from the ravages of the outside world permitted moral as well as medical interpretations. In Pouchelle's words, "Medical and religious concepts converge on these apertures opened by the senses in the human body. For its windows and doors deliver the body, and the whole being, of man up to the outer darkness, allowing it to be invaded by sin" (150). The nature of the animals said to inhabit the human body aids these sorts of interpretations, of course. Snakes and scorpions are a perennial symbol of sin. Throughout the Old Testament, the venomous animal is a surrogate demon, and the same association of snake and moral evil continues into the New Testament and into medieval literature and sermon stories.[11] In Chaucer's "The Parson's Tale," imagery of the venomous animal embodies sexual deception: lustful glances are said to kill "right as the basilcock [basilisk] sleeth folk by the venym of his sight," and lecherous contact with women is said to be like handling a scorpion "that styngeth and sodenly sleeth thurgh his envenymynge" (quoted in Hallissy 95–96). In English witchcraft accusations in the early modern period, toads were as commonly thought to be witches' familiars as the black cat of fictional representations.[12] Even if not directly associated with sin and evil, these creatures might be seen as primeval, problematic, or threatening in some way. They are all interstitial (that is, they do not belong unambiguously to a single category of creature but either cross boundaries or fall between them); they are thus both defiled and dangerous according to Mary Douglas's persuasive analysis.[13]

These creatures may therefore be used as forceful symbols of the evil within. This is, of course, how the image was used in Hawthorne's short story that gave the legend its name; here, the serpent is a metaphor of spiritual or moral sickness.[14] Similarly, the toad that Nero fosters in his gut is a potent representation of his spiritual loathsomeness. Jacques Berlioz has studied the medieval exemplum of *"l'homme au crapaud* [the toad man]" and is particularly insightful about the connections between disfigurement, parasites, and sin in medieval exempla. In this story, an ungrateful son is punished by having a toad fix itself to his face; the toad either steals the man's food or covers his mouth so that he cannot eat. Berlioz follows the theme of bodily infestation with toads and serpents through medieval literature, concentrating on toads and snakes as more or less interchangeable symbols of cupidity, greed, and luxuriousness. The same association between snakes and toads and moral evil may be found in classical and medieval literature[15] and in popular folklore, especially in the character of the venomous woman.

Alternatively, of course, the sensational events may be variously interpreted as examples of miraculous portents sent by God or as evidence of witchcraft (see Kittredge 134–35, 180–84, 456–57n). One of the witches executed in the United Kingdom in the southeastern county of Essex in 1645 as a result of the activities of notorious witch-hunter Matthew Hopkins was accused of threatening a neighbor by saying that she could send one of her imps down his throat if she chose to and then "there would have been a feast of toads in his belly" (Kittredge 135). Similarly, evidence presented at the trial of Julian (modern-day Gillian) Cox for witchcraft in 1663 included the following testimony in which a toad suddenly appears between the legs of her accuser as if by magic. This is not a Bosom Serpent story, but it does indicate the forceful connection between certain categories of animal and evil. Some of the effect of the first part of the testimony seems to be that Julian Cox is unnatural in not shrinking from the toad in horror, as the accuser does:

> Secondly, another witness swore, that as he passed Cox at her door, she was taking a pipe of tobacco upon the threshold of her door, and invited him to come in and take a pipe, which he did, and as he was smoking, Julian said to him, "Neighbour, look what a pretty thing there is": he looked down and there was a monstrous great toad betwixt his legs staring him in the face: He endeavoured to kill it by spurning it, but could not hit it: Whereupon Julian bade him forbear, and it would do him no hurt; but he threw down his pipe and went home . . . and told his family what had happened, and that he believed it was Julian Cox, one of her devils.
>
> After, he was taking a pipe of tobacco at home, and the same toad still appeared: He endeavoured to burn it, but could not: At length he took a switch and beat it; the toad ran several times about the room to avoid him, he still pursuing it with Correction. At length the toad cried, and vanished, and he was never after troubled with it.[16]

Alternatively, rather than being the work of the devil, Bosom Serpent–type incidents might be taken to be miraculous portents sent by God to impress humans with his power over nature. Several such stories turn up in the literature of "remarkable," "illustrious," or "divine" "providences," especially the compilations of Cotton and Increase Mather, a father and son who were early American colonists and devout Puritans. Increase Mather's *Remarkable Providences* of 1684, for example, contains a story about a woman "who having drunk stagnating water out of a pond where frogs used to keep, grew cathartical and swelled so that she was thought hydropical. One evening, walking near the ponds where the frogs croked, she perceived frogs to croke in her belly." After taking a strong emetic, she "cast up two living frogs, pretty large, green on their back, and yellow under their bellies, and voided three dead by siege." [17]

Such "providences" in the hands of other writers soon fade into "prodigies." One of the fullest Bosom Serpent stories presented in this mode comes from the Euing ballad collection. Though it is contained within a religious envelope, the real focus of the story is on its wondrous and uncanny aspects. In August 1664, so the ballad says, a servant girl named Mary Dudson fell asleep in a garden, and a snake entered her body through her mouth while she slept. The story was presented as

> A warning fair to those that sleep
>   upon the ground or in the grass
> Lest serpents into them do creep,
>   as to this maid it came to pass.[18]

It goes on to tell how:

> Her torments they grew very strong,
>   her body was exceeding weak,
> It seemed unto her great wrong
>   to sit, to lye, to speak.
> Her thirst it was exceeding strange,
>   she did drink so abundantly,
> Her body all coal black did change,
>   which seemd a wondrous Prodigy.
> . . . .
> But God, that brings all truths to light,
>   where means was wanting did supply,
> Before the neighbouring people's sight,
>   that all might praise his majesty.

At time as I do understand,
*   fourteen young adders from her came,*
By Vomit, and the Lord's command.
. . . .
The fourteenth day of August last,
*   the old adder by Vomit came,*
Quite through her throat, and out was cast,
*   the standers by admir'd the same.*

This hideous sight put them to flight,
*   They judg'd her fourteen inches long:*
Her body thick, and colours bright,
*   With seeming legs exceeding strong.*
She hist, and back strove to return,
*   into her mouth with eager speed,*
Being withstood, away she run,
*   for they had destroyed all her breed.*
. . . .
Thus have you had this Story true,
*   which hundreds [there do] testify:*
God knows what to us may ensue,
*   For who knows when that we shal die?*
Thus to conclude and make an end,
*   Of what to you I here do tell,*
To heaven I you all commend,
*   And so I bid you all farewel.*

Thirty years after Mary Dudson had been vomiting snakes in England, the twelve-year-old son of a pastor in southern Germany was taken very ill with fits and stomach cramps. He subsequently vomited a wood louse. Medical experts were called in but failed to cure him. During the following three weeks, he vomited 162 wood lice, 32 caterpillars, 4 millipedes, 2 worms, 2 butterflies,

2 ants, and a beetle. Then he started vomiting amphibians—21 newts, 4 frogs, and a few toads. Jan Bondeson, who has studied Bosom Serpent stories as medical curiosities, says,

> These macabre and uncanny happenings soon attracted notice among the clergy. Many German parsons came to visit the house . . . and they concluded, of course, that the boy was possessed by the devil. It particularly impressed them that when the suffering boy was led to take some fresh air near a pond with croaking frogs, his stomach frogs croaked loudly in reply. When the local doctor was somewhat skeptical about the possibility that a multitude of frogs might be living inside a human being, the clergyman reminded him that if Jonah could have survived within the whale, the reverse should also be possible.[19]

The medical men were dismissed and the exorcists took over. The boy then began vomiting even stranger objects: eggshells, knife blades, a link from a chain, and some nails and tacks.[20] On one occasion, the onlookers thought they saw a large snake put its head out of the boy's mouth. "In the meantime," Bondeson reports, "a physician had dissected one of the vomited [frogs]. It had several half-digested insects in its stomach, evidence that the frog had been alive outside the boy's body shortly before it was vomited. The boy's attendants . . . made no such deduction. They merely concluded that the frogs were supernatural and did not obey the ordinary laws of physiology" (360). A cure was finally effected by strong doses of horse's urine and threats of more to follow.

The literature from the seventeenth and eighteenth centuries contains many more of these sorts of exotic displays. Some of them were accepted as genuine wonders of the natural or the supernatural world, but others were exposed as frauds. Indeed, there had been dissenting voices and forceful denunciations of Bosom Serpents as medical reality from as early as the sixth century. Bondeson tells us that the learned Alexander of Tralles, who lived in Lykia in the sixth century, "was once consulted by a woman who was sure she had a snake in her stomach. He soon understood that she was an hysteric, the snake existing only in her imagination. He asked her to describe exactly what she thought the animal looked like and then procured a similar specimen, which he put in her bowl of expectorations! The woman was completely cured" (27).[21]

In the sixteenth century, celebrated French physician Ambroise Paré related how a "fat wench from Normandy" was working the fairs in 1548, begging alms and letting people feel the snake she said she had in her belly. Paré thought she was just churning her stomach muscles and set out to prove she was a fraud. He subjected her to a number of undignified procedures including vaginal examinations and, finding no snakes, got her hustled out of town (83–84). Then there was the famous case of Frau Catharina Geisslerin, "the toad-vomiting woman of Altenburg." In 1642 she started vomiting toads and lizards, which she claimed to have swallowed as spawn. They had grown in her intestines, and she could feel them "running and sporting" there, "especially after she had drunk milk." Her physician admitted that he was defeated by her case, and several eminent men were called in, including the physician to the elector of Saxony. In 1648, after all the medical men had retired defeated from the scene, Catharina again started vomiting. This time, she threw up no fewer than thirteen toads during the course of only two weeks. One of these toads was sent for dissection, and its stomach was found to contain more than thirty winged insects. Since the animal could not have eaten insects if it had spent its life inside Catharina eating the food she ate, she was denounced as a fraud. At the autopsy performed when she died in 1662 after a lifetime of vomiting amphibians, no foreign bodies were found anywhere in her gastrointestinal tract. She had died of liver failure (Bondeson 33–34).[22]

Despite these and other demonstrations, however, the idea that animals might get into the human body and be the cause of disease and dysfunction remained a respectable hypothesis in some medical circles until well into the nineteenth century.

A recently discovered Bosom Serpent text, apparently from the eighteenth century, tells the story of Sarah Mason, age twenty-three, who was "opened" before "a great Number of the most eminent Physicians and Surgeons" in Hyde Park Hospital London to remove "a surprising Monster" that had been growing in her for three years.[23] It shows the classic structure of Bosom Serpent legends—that is, an explanation of how the creature got in, a description of the animal and the symptoms it caused, and an account of how it was gotten out of the body. Sarah's stomach swelled enormously and, although she had a ravenous appetite, she wasted "to an Anotamay." Frightful noises were heard in her belly, and she could feel the "monster" crawling about. Many of "the most learned Men by whom she had been attended for a Twelvemonth past" were of the opinion that she must have swallowed the eggs or spawn of some animal. They decided that it was too dangerous to give her emetics or enemas and that the only possible course of action was surgery. When the frightful operation was over, "they took full view" of the creature and "acknowledged that they had never seen or heard of the like":

It was in Form much like a Lizard, and of a nasty greenish colour.

It had four Legs, and had feet like an Eagle's talons, having three Claws on each Foot; its mouth was very wide, but had four Teeth, and those very small; its length from head to tail measured full 23 Inches, was 16 inches round.

When it was put in the Machine which was prepared to hold it in, it flew about and beat itself with such Voilence [sic] that it died in about an Hour after it was taken out.

The account then goes on to discuss other cases of "worms" and the strange sizes and shapes that they could come in. "[S]everal animals were produced, which had been brought away from Persons all which were of different Shapes, one of which was exactly like an Elf but much larger, another like a Toad, and there was hardly an Animal that could be nam'd, but some of these Creatures bore some Resemblance of."

Dr. Moor, a famous "worm doctor," was said to have "a very large Collection of these creatures which he had taken from his Patients, some of which had four, others six Legs, and in Form notmuch [sic] unlike that terrible Creature we are speaking of." Dr. Moor believed that "all Bodies are liable to breed Worms, specially persons who have bad Digestion [and that] the Egg or Spawn of these Creatures which are so common in the Food and vegetables that we eat, being enlivened by the Heat of the Stomach, they grow to an extraordinary Size, by the great Quantity of Nutriment they find there." [24]

According to Bondeson, the first "full frontal assault" on "this age-old medical doctrine" did not come until 1834, when a German general practitioner became suspicious of a patient who claimed that she had suffered an epileptic attack in a marsh and had accidentally ingested polluted water containing frog spawn. Since then, she said, she had been troubled with a number of unpleasant intestinal symptoms and had recently vomited two frogs, which she presented as evidence (Bondeson 39). The doctor dissected the frogs and, as in Catharina Geisslerin's case, found that their stomachs were full of half-digested insects, including an almost-intact beetle. He concluded that the frogs could not have been in her body very long before being "vomited," if at all. He bullied the woman into a confession. Ironically, she said that she had pretended to vomit the frogs because no one would believe that she did indeed have live frogs in her gut. However, the doctor's somewhat rash conclusion was that not only did his patient not have any frogs inside and never had had but that all other cases of "animals inside" were hoaxes, too.

A vigorous defense of the old belief was quickly mounted. No less a medical personage than the Russian court physician announced that he had recently cured a poor peasant by delivering him of a twelve-inch adder that had entered his mouth when he was sleeping out of doors. The case was widely publicized throughout Europe in the medical literature and the newspapers, and the proof of the story was a picture of the snake itself, its body rather broken by the force of the emetic used to dislodge it. The debate continued to rage in German medical literature throughout the 1830s and 1840s (Bondeson 1997, 40).[25] In 1849, experiments were conducted on some of the exhibits in German pathological collections to see what was in the stomachs of the frogs and other animals supposedly vomited or excreted by humans and on show in the museums. Most of these creatures were found to have partially digested insects in their stomachs, indicating that they had been outside the body and feeding on their usual prey very shortly before they died. Similar experiments were conducted by an American physiologist fifteen years later, with similar results. The physiologist also conducted experiments in which live slugs and newts were fed to dogs, which were killed and dissected an hour later: all the slugs and newts were found to be already dead and partially digested (Bondeson 41–42). These continued demonstrations of fraud finally put the theory to rest as a respectable medical hypothesis.

Bondeson suggests that belief in "animals inside" as a cause of disease did not survive in Europe after the early 1880s but was transported to the United States and thrived there until the end of the century (42–43). As the table in the appendix to this chapter shows, this is not quite accurate: of the fifty-one Bosom Serpent accounts collected after this date, twenty-six come from the United Kingdom, Ireland, or elsewhere in Europe, and though the events in some of the stories may have occurred well before the time they were recorded, many others are said to be contemporaneous. Again, although many of the stories are presented as folklore, some are presented as medical fact. It seems, too, that debates among medical persons did continue in the United Kingdom at least until the first decade of the twentieth century.

However, it is true that there is an increase after the mid-1800s in the number of accounts showing the characteristics that to my mind distinguish the Bosom Serpent when told as contemporary legend. To recap: I think that one can distinguish between Bosom Serpent stories when told as instances of witchcraft, providences, and prodigies and when told as contemporary legends. When the focus of the story is on the animals, it is most likely being told as a providence or prodigy. In this case, the voiding or vomiting of the animal is always a theatrical display of no mean proportions: one animal never suffices. In contrast, when the tellers are as keen on symptoms, diagnosis, and cure as on the strange and exotic creatures thought to be responsible for the patient's sufferings, then I think the stories are being told in contemporary legend mode. In this case, they are rounded medical accounts covering causation, symptomatology, diagnosis, treatment, and outcome. In both instances, the stories are weird and/or monstrous in some way, but in contemporary legend mode they are not stories of magic or the supernatural and carry little or no religious weight.

THE BOSOM SERPENT AS MEDICAL FOLKLORE: EXPLAINING WHY WE GET ILL AND HOW WE CAN CURE OURSELVES

In view of the typical emphasis and structure of Bosom Serpent stories told in contemporary legend mode, one way of understanding them may be to treat them as survivals of older medical orthodoxy.

Unfortunately, however, this is impossible to prove. As in any search for origins, it is possible to prove that a modern tradition resembles an older one, but it cannot be proved that there is a causal link between the two or even a transmission link.

An alternative, more productive, approach is to think of Bosom Serpents as a sort of "folk illness" that functions as a "language" that enables people without formal knowledge of disease to understand and communicate what is wrong with them. One of the advantages of this is that it fits in well with popular understandings of the nature of the body. As we have seen, in medieval times the body was visualized either as a fortress with doorways that must be guarded against attack or as series of containers, pots, sacks, and purses. I think people today still visualize the body in similar ways. If you were to ask people today how they would describe the gastrointestinal tract, I think you would find that many people still visualize it as a series of winding watercourses and pondlike sacs (literally the "alimentary canal"). Given this image and the dominant metaphors through which patients describe pain to their physicians ("gnawing," "shooting," "stabbing," and so on), it is easy to see why some people think or have thought in the past that semiaquatic creatures might be able to live in the gut and make them ill. Second, whether or not one accepts that living creatures may invade the body and take up residence there, it has to be admitted that the stories do provide a comprehensive picture of the progress of disease from causation to cure. At their fullest, these tales have three elements—a description of the animal and how it got in, what suffering resulted, and how the patient was cured. They may be framed as an explanation of a death, or narrators may say that the protagonist was "attacked by various complaints" or "gradually sickened" or some such expression, or the events may be contextualized in terms of hospitals, doctors, and remedies. Though all of the stories obviously appeal to the human appetite for the incredible, the accounts show a concern with the etiology and symptomatology of disease and feature authentic folk cures. This suggests that they were intended to be medical discourses and that the victims/narrators may possibly therefore be talking about genuine medical conditions though in unconventional/unfamiliar language (unconventional and unfamiliar to us, of course; the language makes good sense to those who use it).

So let us look at what they have to say about the course of disease—the way the creature got in, the patients' symptoms, and the way they were cured. Many versions of the legend are circumspect about how the animal got into the body, but the general consensus in the others would seem to be what it was in earlier times—that reptiles and amphibians and similar creatures can run down the throat of persons sleeping out of doors or can be accidentally swallowed either as adults or as eggs. Principal among the symptoms is intense pain, victims being said to have "died in agony" or to have "suffered terribly." Dramatic weight loss, enfeeblement, and exhaustion are the next most common complaints, together with chronic dyspepsia, a sensation of movement in the body, and audible noises in the belly or chest cavity. Other symptoms often mentioned are, in order of frequency, bloating; insatiable hunger; choking or a sensation of something rising into the throat; nausea and vomiting; fainting; and convulsions. Other symptoms mentioned are coughs, headaches, fevers, thirst, disfigurement, discoloration of the skin, itching, and diabetes. Finally, after the creatures are in, the patient is cured—very logically—by getting the creatures out. In about 10 percent of cases, the animal is shown to be a fraud or delusion, but in three-quarters of the accounts, the animal emerges (usually alive) to prove the diagnosis correct. In some—mainly modern—accounts, the creature may be found during surgery or an autopsy or when the patient's stomach is pumped. In older accounts, the creature often is vomited, is "voided," "comes up," or "comes out." In these cases, the poor patient has usually been given life-threatening doses of laxatives or emetics that would dislodge an elephant.

An undated story from *Northamptonshire Past and Present* shows all these features. It also incidentally shows how one should not take the nature of the creature too much on trust. The story is called "When the Woman Swallowed an H'Alligator":

a Mrs Sarah Ann Smith was a carrier who used to journey to and from Northampton with a horse van two or three days a week—this was a hard occupation, and Mrs Smith one day complained to the landlady of an inn which she used to visit, saying, "I have a terrible pain in my innards, missus; I feel as if I have swallowed something and it's moving about inside me." As a result of further complaints from Mrs Smith saying she was sure there was something alive and moving inside her, she was advised to go to Northampton hospital, which she did, and was given an emetic which made her violently sick, and it was then discovered she brought up a small newt which was still alive.

How to account for this strange sickness? On investigation it was found that Mrs Smith had eaten watercress in which the newt was concealed and remained unnoticed. So she had swallowed it alive, and alive it remained until she brought it up again.

Mrs Smith was given the newt in a specimen bottle which she used to produce for inspection when relating the story. "Yes, my dears," she would say, "I swallowed an h'alligator and am still alive and (producing the bottle) here is the little gentleman!" (V.A.H.)

The most interesting stories, though, are those in which the creature is tempted out in search of food or drink. If the Bosom Serpent is a sort of "folk illness," then the cures may be a sort of "folk medicine," though a strange sort. There is no evidence that they were ever tried, let alone that they ever worked, yet variations of these techniques for dealing with invading animals may be found from the Middle Ages to the present day. The picture of the traditional approach to therapy appears in some detail in twenty-five stories and in comments on two others. The remedies rely on somehow getting the creature out of the body. Perhaps the simplest expedient is that contemplated by Henry Thoreau in his diary for 17 August 1851. It is not clear whether he had actually ingested snake eggs or whether the passage is an extended metaphor for the creative process. Nevertheless, the remedy is clear—what has been ingested has to be forcibly pulled from the depths. In the case of snakes, the process of getting them out relies on the assumption that the creature has come from water and therefore can be encouraged to return to water; the patient should therefore be taken to a noisy stream and wait there with open mouth until the creature comes out to investigate. It can then be grabbed by the tail and thrown away. In Thoreau's words,

> The rill I stopped to drink at I drink in more than I expected. . . . Ah, I shall hear from that draught! . . . How many ova have I swallowed? Who knows what will be hatched within me? The man must not drink of the running streams, the living waters, who is not prepared to have all nature reborn within him, to suckle monsters. . . . Is there not such a thing as getting rid of the snake you swallowed when young, when thoughtlessly you stooped and drank at stagnant waters, which has worried you in your waking hours and in your sleep ever since, and appropriated the life that was yours? Will he not ascend into your mouth at the sound of running water? Then catch him boldly and draw him out, though you may think his tail be curled about your vitals.[26]

To make sure the snake responds to the sound of running water, however, it is usual to make it thirsty by depriving its host of water. According to the *Flaterjarbók*, a fourteenth-century

Icelandic compilation, King Harald Hårdråde of Norway advised a distraught father how to rid his daughter of a serpent she had accidentally ingested in egg form: "She must thirst for several days without being given any water; after that she was to be taken to a waterfall and there open her mouth wide so the thirsty snake could hear the streaming water. When it slithered up her gullet and stretched its head out between the girl's jaws, her father was to strike it with his sword" (Bondeson 26).

Snakes are, of course, traditionally known to be inordinately fond of milk. (There is another legend complex in which a child pines away though apparently having enough to eat; it is then somehow discovered that a snake has been stealing the child's milk [see, for example, Satchell].) This fondness is sometimes exploited to trick the snake out of the victim's body. The effect of the trick is reinforced by getting the patient to eat a huge meal before thirsting. The food is usually strong tasting, strong smelling, and/or salty—bacon is the prime favorite, but salt beef, salt herring, and toasted cheese are also frequently mentioned. A "pound of salt" and "a strong solution of salt and water" are advised in two stories; roasting meat and fried onions are also recommended. This is a surprisingly old idea. A woodcut from Hieronymous Brunschwig's *Cirurgia* of 1497 shows a serpentine creature being extracted from a patient by suspending him upside down on a sort of pulley over a bowl of milk.[27] A reference to the milk treatment also appears in Rabelais's *Quart Livre* (c. 1548?), where the giant, Bringuenarilles, "fell ill with convulsions of the heart so horrific and dangerous, as if serpents had entered his stomach via the mouth." The giant's brother recalls that he has "heard said that a snake, having entered the stomach, suddenly emerges back out if one holds the patient by his feet and places a bowl of milk near his mouth" (my translation from Le Quellec 65).[28] In his *History of Four-Footed Beasts and Insects and Serpents* (1658), Edward Topsell glumly announces that there is nothing one can do to alleviate the misery of having a serpent in one's body "unless it be by feeding this unwelcome guest in his guest-chamber, with good store of milk, and such other meats as serpents best like of" (quoted in Arner 104). He says nothing, though, about using milk or meat to trap the creature.

Sometimes, as in the story about King Harald Hårdråde, the victim is then taken to a stream to await the effects of the remedy; sometimes the cure takes place at home, the patient going to bed with a basin of milk or water at hand or holding his/her head over a bowl. It is taken for granted that the creature will realize it has been tricked and try to get back again. Great care must be taken to shut the mouth promptly so that the creature doesn't jump back in again: alternatively, it can be grabbed or lassoed as it comes out of the mouth. A few examples from Bosom Serpent legends in my collection will show some variations on the technique.

A "worm with legs" ran down a man's throat as he slept in a field, and he pined away [that is, became very thin], with an ever-increasing appetite, until he was persuaded to consult a "wise person." He was kept from drinking for two days by the expert, and then fed on bacon and taken to a stream. The patient's mouth was fastened open, and a freshly toasted piece of bacon put near it. The thirsty "worm" heard the running water and came out into the man's mouth, where it smelt the meat and sprang on it, fixing its claws in it. The "wise man" then threw the bacon into the water, and the man rapidly recovered. (Westropp 454)

Now snakes adore fresh milk, and the only way to save somebody suffering from a snake inside, is to bend the sufferer's head over a bowl of new milk and at the same time to hold a strong band tight against the person's mouth like a noose. When the snake puts its head out to drink the milk, the noose must be suddenly drawn tight behind the snake's head until it is throttled. Then the snake can be drawn out of the sick person's mouth. (comment following story in Hughes 46)

A young woman was ill, and the doctor said she had consumption. As he could not do her any good, they consulted a herbalist, who said . . . it was an askard [newt] egg that she had swallowed some time when drinking cold water. . . . He advised that she should stand with her mouth open over a piece of roasting meat when it began to smell, and said that then the askard would come out to get the meat. But as soon as this happened she was to shut her mouth directly or the askard would "laup" back again. The askard did come out, and tried to run away, but the mother and daughter pursued it, the one with the poker and the other with the tongs, and it looked "right wicked" at them. ("Animals in People's Insides," *Notes and Queries* 9, no. 7: 222)

[I] heard a tale about a bloke who was eternally hungry and yet grew thinner and thinner. His parents were told it had to be a "giant tapeworm" and he was starved for a couple of days, then tied to a chair while a large plate of food was placed in front of him. A noose was made with a violin string rubbed with resin, and this was placed in front of his mouth. The tapeworm's head emerging was success-fully lassoed with the violin string, the resin preventing the animal slipping from the noose.[29]

The most complex story about a cure comes from the oldest text in my collection, a twelfth-century Irish tale, "The Vision of MacConglinne" (Meyer[30]). An episode in this long story tells how the king of Munster, Cathal mac Fionghuine, was poisoned by his sweetheart's brother, who contaminated one of her love gifts with parasites. One of the parasites grew into a "demon of gluttony" and caused Cathal to have such a ravenous appetite that all of Munster was threatened with starvation as the people tried to keep the king satisfied. By means of a dream, the nomadic scholar and poet MacConglinne was identified as the man who could cure the king. MacConglinne came into the king's presence and enter-tained him with jokes and juggling and prevailed on him to spend the night fasting with him. In the morning, MacConglinne tied the hungry king to the wall of his fortress with strong ropes and began to cook and eat huge quantities of delicious food in front of him but just out of reach. The king was driven frantic with hunger and greed, his bosom demon even more so. MacConglinne waited, and the demon gradually began to appear in the king's mouth. MacConglinne then increased the temptation even more by recounting a dream composed entirely of references to food (this witty and inventive narration in prose and poetry takes up almost twenty pages of the printed text). Driven wild with frustration and desire, the demon jumped out of the king's mouth, fixed its claws in one of the juicy morsels MacConglinne had cooked and tried to run away. In vain—he was caught and thrown in the cauldron.

The most grotesque account of a cure comes from the United States:

The doctors' treatment involved having the patient eat nothing for five days, thus hoping to starve the animal enough to make it come up out of the esophagus in search of food. The patient, in "intense" pain, was given a heavy dose of opium and rendered unconscious. . . . [H]e was then held in a recumbent position, with the face downwards and the body inclined to an angle of forty-five degrees, the head being lowest. In about ten minutes, the cause of the difficulty was manifest, a snake, of dark brown color, and large size, protruded full eight inches from the mouth, with its eye bright and glaring with every manifestation of rage. One of the physicians immediately seized it by the neck with the intention of drawing it out, but suddenly fell flat on the floor without sense or motion, as if struck by lightning! . . . [T]he snake was electric. (S. Bush 185–86)

It is surprising that more failures aren't recorded, but there are only three. In one a nurse is bitten by a hungry snake inside her

(Dale 74–75). (I assume that she was starving the snake before trying the standard folk remedy.) In another, a sick girl is taken to hospital as an emergency and diagnosed as being infested with a tapeworm. Her mother waits outside but cannot resist peeking into the treatment room. She sees a doctor dangling a piece of meat in front of her daughter's mouth and a tapeworm squirming out to get at the meat. The mother screams, and the daughter chokes to death (Bishop 37). The third story takes place "early in 1916," when it

> was being much talked about and I heard it from several sources. A woman had lately swallowed a frog, or a frog's egg, which lived and grew inside her. She was taken to Stroud hospital. "And they tried to open her, but they couldn't open her, because it moved about. And she was in such agony that she asked them to give her poison and put her out of her misery. So they wrote to the King to ask if they might poison her, but the King wrote back to say No, they mustn't. Then the doctor put a piece of cheese on her tongue, and the frog smelt it and came up, but as it came up it choked her. And they do say that frog weighed half a pound. (Enquiries at Stroud Hospital failed to discover any foundation for the story). (Partridge 313)

The latest instance of a similar cure I have come across is the one that the U.S. government was said in 1982 to recommend to people suffering from tapeworm infestations after swallowing "diet pills." The patient first had to starve for several days. "Then they set a bowl of hot milk in front of the person. He had to keep his mouth open. After a while the tapeworm began to come up his throat 'cause he smelt the milk. They kept moving the bowl further away until the tapeworm was completely out" (Baker 226).

Maybe it is unlikely that a snake could or would slither down a sleeping person's throat, but could it be possible that the victims of "Bosom Serpent attacks" really were suffering from some medical condition? This is an interesting question, especially in the light of definitions of "contemporary legend" that state or imply that legends are intrinsically false. Is it possible that, buried inside the story with its lurid details, there may be descriptions of bona fide illnesses? Given the degree of medical ignorance even among educated people today, and given that many of the stories were collected in times when education and health care were not universally available, surely it would not be surprising if people suffering a mysterious ailment used legends such as the Bosom Serpent to describe and explain what they thought was wrong with their body? If this is the case, we might be able to "translate" Bosom Serpents into the language of modern medicine. To see how this might work, in my essay about medical aspects of the Bosom Serpent (Bennett, "Medical"), I analyzed a selection of 112 of the fullest narratives from times and places not too dissimilar to our own[31] and explored the possibility that the symptoms described in the stories were consistent with a number of (mainly gastrointestinal) conditions, some of which have only recently been identified. As we have seen, the symptoms featured in Bosom Serpent stories include intense pain, weight loss, enfeeblement and exhaustion, chronic dyspepsia, a sensation of movement in the body, and audible noises in the belly or chest cavity. Elsewhere, the stories mention vomiting, convulsions, bloating, fever, and coughing.

The first group of symptoms seems to me to present a convincing picture of gastrointestinal distress. Here, for example, is a story from the *Deseret News* of 31 August 1883:

A Living Creature in the Stomach of a Lady for Fifteen Years.

One of the rarest cases ever brought to the notice of the medical faculty has transpired in this city. About fifteen years ago, Mrs. Jane Carrington Young, wife of Apostle Brigham Young, was suddenly awakened from sleep by a feeling caused by some creature running into her mouth and down her throat. She was naturally alarmed at the incident and swallowed different things to cause vomiting.

No great subsequent inconvenience ensued until four years ago, when the lady was greatly alarmed by a sensation of a living thing moving about in her stomach. The feeling increased accompanied by a pain of something gnawing or biting at the left side, especially at times when there was not much food in the stomach. In addition to the sensation was the fact that she could plainly hear the sound of the creature when it was in the act of drinking.

Leading physicians in the city were consulted, but all, or nearly all, attributed the symptoms described by Sister Young to imagination, some going so far as to claim that no living creature could exist in the human stomach. The patient read medical works for satisfactory information and swallowed any amount of nostrums, but all to no avail until recently she took some preparations given by a couple of gentlemen of this city. The desired result was attained, as the creature ceased to live and was vomited by Mrs Young on Monday last. Although somewhat disfigured and broken up by the action of the medicine its form is still traceable, being evidently of the lizzard species. It was emitted in fragments, the main portion being several inches long. It is preserved in two bottles of alcohol, and a large number of people have called and examined it. The many friends of the esteemed lady will congratulate her on getting rid of such an unwelcome intruder. We are pleased to state that she feels remarkably well considering her terrible experience. (Poulsen 83)

Putting aside the somewhat gaudy details and looking at the symptomatology alone, I would be prepared to bet that Jane Young had a gastric ulcer. The "gnawing" pain suffered in the left side, particularly acute when the stomach is empty, is typical; so are the loud gurgles in the chest, which she interpreted as the lizard coming up to drink. Again, the acid reflux and flatulence typical of gastritis or gastric ulcers really do feel as if a living thing is moving about (K. Taylor).

Audible noises are mentioned in a handful of stories and a sensation of something moving in the body in twenty others. In many the pain, sensation of movement, and audible noises are often linked to weight loss (which is again consistent with gastric problems but is interpreted as the creature feeding on the body or stealing the human host's food). The organs given as the resting place of the creature confirm the impression of digestive disorders. The terms *stomach, intestines, bowels, abdomen,* and *insides,* all of which laypeople commonly use to suggest the gastrointestinal tract, between them occur in fifty-seven stories, and the term *belly* appears in three more.

Various motility disorders also show a similar pattern of symptoms to those described in Bosom Serpent stories. It is possible, for example, that the child in the following account was suffering from a hiatal hernia: "Last summer a little girl . . . drank some water out of a ditch, and, it appears swallowed some kind of reptile in it. Since then the poor child has periodically experienced incredible pains in her chest, from the increasing bulk and movement of the reptile, which at times ascends the throat in search of food, causing intense agony. On these occasions warm milk and water is poured down her throat; and, when the reptile has imbibed the nourishment it descends to its place of lodgement, just above the diaphragm" ("Newspaper Folk Lore," *Notes and Queries* I, no. 6: 221).

There are less common diseases of the gastrointestinal tract that may be consistent with some or all of the symptoms described in various Bosom Serpent stories: these include Zemker's diverticulum, small bowel diverticula, Crohn's disease, ulcerated colitis, irritable bowel syndrome, gall bladder disease, bowel tumors, celiac disease, and amebic dysentery.[32] A very rare condition, intussusception of the colon, is also consistent with the sorts of symptoms described in a couple of Bosom Serpent stories. A case is described by Leitch Wilson in the *British Medical Journal* in 1910. Dr. Wilson's patient was in great pain, vomiting, constipated, and passing blood. He was given enemas for five days, after which he "felt something move at the painful spot, accompanied by a shooting pain and a 'feeling of hollowness.'" He then evacuated twenty-four inches of his own gut (which, no doubt, to an inexperienced eye would have looked not unlike a snake or very large eel).

Then there are various parasites that cause disruption to the human system, including nematodes, threadworms, whipworms, roundworms, and tapeworms. (Bill Ellis has also suggested a connection with parasites [Ellis, "Sushi"].) The symptomatology of these infestations fits another group of symptoms particularly well: weakness, pain, vomiting, convulsions, bloating, fever, cough, anorexia combined with hunger, and even the sensation of movement in the body. All may be found in the parasitological literature as well as in descriptions of symptoms in Bosom Serpent stories. The strongest correlation, however, is with liver fluke infestation (*fascioliasis hepatica*). This is a very unpleasant condition similar to the tropical disease bilharzia (schistosomiasis). It is caused by a fluke normally parasitic on sheep and cattle.[33] It was not until 1911 that it was recognized that humans could host this fluke. Outbreaks have been recorded in the United Kingdom in Kent in 1911 (Ward), Devon in 1955 (J. P. Bush), Hampshire in 1958,[34] Monmouthshire in 1968 (Hardman, Jones, and Davies), Scotland in the 1970s (J. P. Bush), and Shropshire in 1970 (Ashton et al.). Fifty-three cases have been documented in France.[35]

Fasciola hepatica has a complicated life cycle. Its primary hosts are cattle and sheep, where the adult fluke lays its eggs in the gall bladder or bile duct at the rate of three thousand a day. The eggs leave the animal's body in feces and, in streams or marshy ground, hatch and seek an intermediate host, a small semiaquatic snail, *limnaea truncatula*. Within six or seven weeks, when the weather is wet and mild, the creatures are in the next larval stage, ready to leave the snail's body. They then encyst on water plants and wet pastures, especially wild watercress, and wait to be devoured. When they find a suitable host, they encyst in the intestine, pass through the intestine walls, and reach the liver in two or three days. "They bore into the liver, wandering and feeding on its substance for 5 to 6 weeks before entering the bile ducts and maturing" (Seaton 126). They start to lay eggs three months after ingestion. The symptoms, as recorded in the medical literature, seem to be quite variable. However, the most common ones—severe weight loss, anemia, raised temperature, exhaustion, coughing, bouts of severe gastric pain, intestinal disorders, and occasional rigors (medical terminology for the folk expression spasms)—will be familiar to readers of Bosom Serpent stories. "An infinite variety of catastrophes" follow the migration of the flukes as they journey on in search of the liver: 10 percent of flukes are found in the lungs, for example, and they have also been found in the eye, the scalp, the sole of the foot, and protruding from a ruptured vein in a man's leg (Ward 931). Here, it would seem we really do have a mystery illness in which a creature wanders around the body feeding on its host.

As it happens, the fullest Bosom Serpent account in the folkloristic literature can also be read as a case history of fascioliasis (though a fanciful one). In this tale, a wealthy Irish farmer falls asleep in the field where his laborers are cutting the hay. When he wakes up, he finds he has a pain in his side and begins to feel very strange. In the morning he is worse, complaining that "there's something inside of me running back and forwards" and that "there was a pain on him, but that he did not know rightly what place the pain was in." During his six-month illness, "the poor man that was stout and well-fed before [became] bare and thin, until at last there was not an ounce of flesh on him, but the skin and bones only." He became so weak that he was unable to walk, he lost his appetite, and "it was a great trouble to him to swallow a piece of soft bread or to drink a sup of new milk, and everyone saying that he was better to die." He had, of course, exhausted the skills of all the medical men in the neighborhood. However, when a beggar man appeared on the scene, he encouraged the sick man to describe his symptoms. The story goes on:

> The beggarman listened to him carefully, and when he had finished all his story, he asked him: "What sort of field was it you fell asleep in?" . . . "Was it wet," says the beggarman. . . . "Was there a little stream or a brook of water running through it?" said the beggarman.
>
> "There was," says he.
>
> "Can I see the field?"
>
> "You can, indeed, and I'll show it to you." . . .
>
> The beggarman examined the place for a long time, and then he stooped down over the grass and went backwards and forwards with his body bent, and his head down, groping among the herbs and weeds that were growing thickly in it.
>
> He rose at last and said: "It is as I thought," and he stooped himself down again and began searching as before. He raised his head a second time, and he had a little green herb in his hand. "Do you see this?" said he. "Any place in Ireland that this herb grows, there be's an alt-pluachra near it, and you have swallowed an alt-pluachra. . . . Didn't you say that you felt the thing leaping in your stomach the first day after you being sick? That was the alt-pluachra; and as the place he was in was strange to him at first, he was uneasy in it, moving back-wards and forwards, but when he was a couple of days there, he settled himself, and he found the place comfortable, and that's the reason you're keeping so thin, for every bit you're eating the alt-pluachra is getting the good out of it, and you said yourself that one side of you was swelled; that's the place where the nasty thing is living." (Hyde)

The beggar man, it seems, was a pretty good diagnostician. Though he had mistaken a liver fluke for a newt (an "alt pluachra" is a rare and distinctive newt, *lissotriton punctatus*), using only experience and observation, he seems to have successfully identified one of the rarest and most unpleasant parasitical conditions.

Cases such as this lead me to wonder whether at least some Bosom Serpent stories may be accounts of unusual but real illnesses, embellished, storified, and traditionalized in the language of legend. The significant thing is that in all but a small minority of the tales, where the creature is identified it is said to belong to an egg-laying species—that is, a creature that begins life as a small object that may easily be ingested accidentally. Among these, creatures that lay their eggs in or near water are mentioned in a substantial proportion of the stories. Furthermore, in more than half of the Bosom Serpent stories we have explored, the victim is specifically said to have done something that modern medical knowledge associates with a danger of disease or parasitic infection.[36] More than a third of the victims are said to have drunk water from wells, troughs, bog holes, drains, ditches, ponds, springs, streams, or, in one case, a garden hose before the onset of the disease. In the past, polluted water was a very real danger to the rural poor. "No wonder that people think they sometimes swallow frogs," said a correspondent in *Notes and Queries* in 1880, "there is no doubt that they often do, for the kind of water which poor people are obliged to drink in many country places . . . is dreadful—liquid mud out of ponds trampled up by cows I have seen standing in tubs to settle, preparatory to being boiled for drinking. Some never drink water in summer, but beer and cold tea" (R.R. 392). Other victims have been sleeping outside in a field, forest, or boggy meadow: I would suggest that if you fall asleep outside in summer, there is a strong likelihood that you'll be thirsty enough on waking to take a drink from any source available, so the water connection may be stronger than at first appears. Others have eaten unwashed watercress or salad vegetables from streams or boggy fields. In short, water, sleep, fields, bogs, and/or unwashed salad leaves appear in more than half the 112 texts I studied in 2000. Finally, the victims/patients in the stories are just the sort of people who, for one reason or another, one would expect to be most liable to these sorts of diseases. They belong overwhelmingly to the less affluent strata of society (they are described as "women," not "ladies," and as "men," not "gentlemen"), and more than three-quarters live in rural areas. In other words, they are too poor and too badly educated to have the luxury of being fussy about personal or food hygiene, and they live in areas remote from what passes for civilization (Bennett, "Bosom").

In suggesting that many of Bosom Serpent stories may contain descriptions of diseases recognized by modern medicine, I am not undertaking a pseudoscientific reductive exercise. I am not trying to explain the legend away, to suggest that it makes a logical medical whole, or to propose that every story can be thus translated. All I want to propose is that if there is a popular tradition about animals existing in the body and causing mystery illnesses, and if one is suffering from a mystery illness, then the tradition has immediate explanatory power. It may provide a template onto which sick people, picking and choosing which features of the legend to highlight or suppress, can fit a wide range of diseases to their own satisfaction, so they are able to explain their sickness to themselves and describe it to others. The tradition thus provides a "language" for sickness, which may be why it has persisted for so long.

BOSOM SERPENTS: THE DIALECTIC

As well as being a way of talking about sickness, Bosom Serpent stories have often been used as tools in an ongoing dialectic between "regular" and "irregular" doctors. The debate would center on the crucial question of whether the bizarre cures promoted in Bosom Serpent stories actually worked and whether the traditional healers who proposed them were superior to the upstart scientific doctors who opposed them. If Linda Dégh and Andrew Vázsonyi are right about the presence of a dialectic about truth being the principal definitional criterion of the legend genre, here we have a superb illustration of the nature and processes of legend. Told by some people, Bosom Serpent stories were adapted to show the ignorance and incompetence of regular doctors; told by others, they were used to show the folly of consulting any but the "real professionals" and to demonstrate that popular ideas of sickness and health were nothing but ignorance and superstition.

We cannot be sure, of course, that the traditional remedy was ever tried, but if the Bosom Serpent legend was indeed a language for talking about sickness and healing alternatives, one thing is certain—the folk procedure had a considerable advantage over regular medicine in that it addressed itself to the problem as seen by the patient. Rather than dismissing the patient's version of the cause of the illness, the folk cure took that description at face value and worked with it rather than against it. According to British medical historian Roy Porter, quack medicine offered certain advantages in eighteenth-century Britain. It offered "visions of health, sickness and recovery, which made sense from the sick person's point of view—verbalizations and visualizations of the body's workings, telling plausible stories, accounting for pains and perturbations, and permitting some degree of co-operation on the part of the sick person in working towards recovery" (132).

This is something the regular medical profession often signally failed—and still fails—to achieve. In particular, the traditional procedure would have worked potently with the folk belief that "disease is an entity which is 'in' until it is brought 'oot,' " as David Rorie has so succinctly put it (Buchan 100). The more recalcitrant the disease, the more obdurate the entity within, so the more complex the procedure for getting it out. The theatrical show put on for or by the patient—the starvation, the tying up, the lassoing, the trek to the stream, and so on—is all expertly geared to this conception of sickness and cure.

This may be why, in the mid-nineteenth century, stories about Bosom Serpents became the vehicle for some very lively debate among members of an increasingly professionalized medical establishment and their rivals in the United Kingdom. The sturdy independence of patients who chose to prescribe their own treatments on the basis that they knew their bodies best became anathema to an increasingly regularized medical profession, whose position, stated or implied, was that its practitioners alone were authorized to arbitrate on matters of sickness and health (Porter 201). Within this context, tales about invading creatures became propaganda tools for both sides.

An English perspective on this dialectic can be seen in the columns of the long-running magazine *Notes and Queries*. Between 1852 and 1854—just before the establishment of the General Medical Council, a time of great contention between regular and irregular practitioners—there was a lengthy correspondence on the subject of "Newspaper Folk Lore." This had been initiated by a person calling himself "A Londoner" who, deploring the inhumanity of an age that could allow a child to suffer so, had sent in the story quoted earlier about the little girl with a snake lodged "just above her diaphragm." Two correspondents replied to "A Londoner's" letter: the first remarked that he had often read such stories in the provincial press and had always thought them "to be emanations from the brains of that highly imaginative class of persons, the village correspondent." The second response came from a Birmingham surgeon who regarded all such cases as hypochondria ("Newspaper Folk Lore," *Notes and Queries* 1, no. 6: 338, 466). Two years later, "A Londoner" revived the subject, enclosing a newspaper account of the "Escape of a snake from a man's mouth" ("Newspaper Folk Lore," *Notes and Queries* 1, no. 9: 29–30). A correspondent promptly wrote to correct his account: the creature was a worm, not a snake, and was swallowed in the East Indies where "such things are common enough" ("Newspaper Folk Lore," *Notes and Queries* 1, no. 9: 84). Five other correspondents now joined in: three people sent factual letters discussing the phenomenon and whether any creature could survive in the environment of the human stomach; two people sent in amusing little dismissive anecdotes ("Newspaper Folk Lore," *Notes and Queries* 1, no. 9: 276, 523).

During this debate (indeed, into the next century) it was a popular pastime to swap "well-known medical stories" about popular ignorance. Many of these depended on puns or near homophones. One such concerned a man who thought he had swallowed a cobbler (a type of eel) and was convinced he was cured when he was deceived into thinking that he had vomited up the tools of the cobbler's (shoe mender's) trade. Another was about a poor woman who, when told her husband had an ulcer in his stomach, thought he must have swallowed an "ulster," a heavy overcoat or blanket worn as a shawl ("Animals in People's Insides," *Notes and Queries* 9, no. 7: 333). Telling "well-known medical stories" about credulous patients thus demonstrated the superiority of the narrator and asserted the rights of the regular medical profession to arbitrate on medical matters. Sometimes, however, the patient (and the tradition) struck back. One story in *Notes and Queries* told of an old woman who went to the hospital complaining about pain in her bowels, caused, she said, by a "nowt" (newt) lodged there. The doctor gave her a placebo and told her it would dislodge the creature, but

> Not long afterwards again she was shown up to the doctor, when the following colloquy ensued:
>
> Dr J: Well, my good woman, I suppose the draught I gave you soon killed the reptile.
>
> Woman: Lord bless you, no, Sir. The nowt has had young ones since! ("Newspaper Folk Lore," *Notes and Queries* 1, no. 6: 466)

If laughing at human ignorance bolsters the confidence of the regular doctors, telling stories where the patient's assessment of the situation is triumphantly vindicated gives patients the confidence to defend their right to know what is wrong with them. No matter how many times they have been told that their sufferings are imaginary, "a plain case of hysteria," or rampant hypochondria, in the end the scoffers are confounded and the patient is vindicated. The legend is then shaped into a dramatic demonstration that doctors are incompetent know-nothings. In nineteen stories from the period 1820–1920, the narrators repeatedly assert that the "doctors could do nothing for" the patient or that the patient's malady had "completely set at nought all medical attention" or "the doctors could not help him." In some cases, the story tells how the patient's family or doctor did not believe that there was a creature living in his/her stomach, but when he/she consulted an irregular practitioner or used the traditional remedy, the creature was found and the patient was cured.

A good story from this particular angle is the case of a young man in Wales who fell ill of a mysterious complaint ("Animals in People's Insides," *Notes and Queries* 9, no. 8: 391). When the regular doctors confess themselves unable to do anything for him, he consults a quack, who advises him to poison the creature by taking up smoking. Appalled by this advice, the young man turns again to his regular doctor, who advises him that, in his present state of health, smoking would kill him. So the young man declines to do as the quack suggests. He dies, of course. The quack then performs an autopsy, with the regular doctor as witness. The regular doctor can see nothing abnormal, but the quack points out a worm still alive in the dead man's heart. The quack, who has been smoking throughout the post mortem, blows a mouthful of smoke at the creature, and it shrivels up and dies.

Two well-told stories exemplify the difference between the scientific and the traditional approaches and show the dialectic at its liveliest. The first, the story of the wealthy Irish farmer we looked at earlier, is presented in folktale form in an 1890 collection of Irish Gaelic stories (Hyde 47–73 no. 49). The farmer's description of his symptoms and the beggar man's diagnosis are framed within a potent critique of regular medicine. When the farmer first starts to feel ill, he sends for the doctor:

> The doctor stripped him and examined him well, but saw nothing out of the way with him. He put his ear to his side and to his back, but he heard nothing, though the poor man himself was calling out: "Now! now! don't you hear it? Now, aren't you listening to it jumping?" But the doctor could perceive nothing at all, and he thought the man was out of his senses, and there was nothing the matter with him. . . . The poor man got no relief from all that the doctor had given him, and when he came again he found him to be worse than before, but he was not able to do anything, and he did not know what sort of sickness was upon him. . . . The woman of the house could hardly keep in her anger. . . . "That doctor *braduch*," says she. "He's not worth a *traneen*; . . . he said himself he knew nothing about anything. . . . [H]e'll cross this threshold no more."

So the couple seek the advice of doctor after doctor in their search for a diagnosis and cure; eventually, "there was not a doctor in the county . . . that they had not got and they had lost a power of money over them, and they had to sell a portion of their cattle to get money to pay them." At this point, the beggar man makes his entrance and diagnoses the farmer's trouble as being due to his swallowing an "alt pluachra." He advises the sick farmer to consult Mac Dermott, Prince of Coolavin, "the best doctor in Connacht or the five provinces." The prince confirms the beggar man's diagnosis and gives the farmer a huge meal of salted beef. After that, in due sequence, come the trip to the stream, the open mouth, and the emergence of a dozen alt pluachras and their old mother. The story ends with the farmer giving thanks: "He was for three hours before he could speak a word; but the first thing he said was: 'I am a new man.' . . . As long as he was alive he never lay down on green grass again; and another thing, if there was any sickness or ill-health on him, it isn't the doctors he used to call in to him." Thus, the story is not only entertaining but also offers a powerful advertisement for traditional ways of dealing with health problems.

Its mirror image, the "antilegend," as Linda Dégh would term it, is a tale taken from the notebooks of a country physician in the United States at roughly the same time (1870) and later published by a fellow doctor (Sawyer). This story is framed as a polemic against traditional medicine and in favor of the new scientific approach to disease. As a young man, the country physician over-hears a "horse doctor" telling how his fourteen-year-old daughter was "drinking out of a . . . spring in the back lot and accidentally swallowed a very tiny snake." The family finds an "old Indian doctor" who begins "dosing her with all sorts and kinds of nos-trums and concoctions." The physician becomes one of the new breed of scientific doctors and makes "an exhaustive study" of "anything pertaining to living creatures in the human organs." Twenty-five years later, having moved back to his hometown, he is called to a mysterious case and finds it is none other than the horse doctor's daughter. "Her twenty-five years," he says, had been spent in bed "telling people of her condition." "No doubt," he observes, "during all the strenuous treatments to which she had been subjected, her life had been put to the test and even laid low from the harsh remedies which had been employed without doing her a particle of good." His treatment is to persuade her to get up from her bed and return to normal life. The patient is not convinced, asking, "Yes, but what about the snake? How will you get him?" "Martha," he says. "You haven't any snake"—at which point she becomes angry and rebellious, and when the doctor insists that she has no snake in her "she [throws] a hysterical fit": "It was a case [he concludes] that didn't need medicine. . . . Instead of whimsical notions from her father, she should have been told the truth about her hysterical condition. This would have saved her twenty-five years of suffering and a fortune spent on her without help or relief." The patient gradually recovers some of her strength and marries her childhood sweetheart. She dies shortly thereafter, and when an autopsy is performed, tuberculosis is shown to have "almost entirely consumed" her lungs.

The second story is thus a negation of the first one: the failure of the regular doctors in the Irish story is matched by the failure of the "old Indian doctor" and a host of other empirics in the U.S. story; the family is almost bankrupted by the expense of the regulars in the Irish story and is almost ruined by the irregulars in the U.S. story; in the Irish story, all the regulars fail, and in the American tale all the irregulars fail; in the Irish story, traditional concepts of illness are triumphantly justified when no fewer than twelve little alt pluachras and their mother come from the patient's body, and in the American one scientific medicine is justified when the autopsy proves that the only thing wrong with the patient is a familiar disease.

CONCLUSION

The Bosom Serpent story is a fine case study in the nature of contemporary legends. It shows that they are not just silly tales that can be automatically dismissed as trivial and untrue. Good stories though they are, embellished with fantastic details and even at times with fairy-tale characters, they are nevertheless functional. They can be and often are "discourses of knowledge and power" (Emke 1). As Brian Turner has said, disease is a language, the body is a representation, and medicine is a political practice (209). Medical historians and folklorists can use Bosom Serpent stories as documents, not only demonstrating a folk view of the body and the way it is constructed but also preserving a traditional cure for a traditional condition.

Since the mid-nineteenth century, many tellings have exemplified and debated the vital question of medical authority—who knows best what is wrong with the body, the patient or the professional? And who knows best what is the cause and what the cure? Folklore has been called the "games of the powerless" (Holbek). The legend of the Bosom Serpent, as told by the dissenting voices of the ordinary folk, is a classic example.

APPENDIX

In this table the dates given are, where possible, the supposed date of the occurrence. If this date is not available, then I have given the date when the story was published. With the exception of the Irish "Demon of Gluttony," which I have referred to in the text, I have included only reports of worms, amphibians, and reptiles that have taken up residence in some vital organ, so that we are in the heartland of the legend of the Bosom Serpent. I have come across many similar accounts of "insects inside" and some of mammals or unspecified creatures "inside," but I have omitted them from this list.[37]

Table 1. Place, Date, and Nature of Reported Animal Infestations

PLACE	DATE	CREATURE	ORGAN
?United States	1995	snake	stomach
Malaysia	1993	snake	stomach
Malaysia	1992	snake	womb
France	1989	frog	stomach
United States	1988–9	lizard	stomach
Azerbaijan	1987	snake	?

(Continued)

Table 1.   (Continued)

PLACE	DATE	CREATURE	ORGAN
United Kingdom	1984	snake	intestines
United States	1984	snake	stomach
United Kingdom	1984	snake	stomach
United Kingdom	1983	snake	stomach
Syria	1982	snake	intestines
Turkey	1979	snake	stomach
Ireland	1972	newt	?
United States	1971	snake	intestines
United States	1970s	snake	vagina
United Kingdom	1968	snake	?
United Kingdom	1964	frog	stomach/throat
United States	1963	snake	?
United Kingdom	1960s	newt	?
United States	1956	snake	womb?
United States	1944	serpent	intestines
United States	1943	snake	stomach
India	1943	snake	womb
United States	1940s	snake	stomach
United States	1926	reptiles & amphibians	stomach
United States	1926	salamander	stomach
United States	1926	snake	penetrates skin
United States	1926	lizard	penetrates skin
United States	1924	snake	stomach
United Kingdom	1920	crocodile	?
United Kingdom	1916	frog	?
Ireland	1916	newt	stomach
Ireland	1911	"worm with legs"	?
United Kingdom	1909	newt	stomach
United Kingdom	1908	frog	throat
Ireland	1904	newt	?
United Kingdom	1904	worm	?
United States	1901	frog	?
United Kingdom	1901	newt	?
United Kingdom	1901	frog	?
Ireland	1900s	newt	?
United Kingdom	1900s	newt	?
United Kingdom	1900s	newt	?

PLACE	DATE	CREATURE	ORGAN
United States	1899	snake	stomach
United States	1897	snake	stomach
United States	1896	newt	stomach
Ireland	1894	newt	?
United Kingdom	1892	lizard	stomach
Ireland	1890	newt	?
United Kingdom	1890s	newt	?
Germany	1890s	snake	penetrates skin
United States	1883	lizard	stomach
Austria	1882	frog	abdomen
United Kingdom	1880s	newt	?
United Kingdom	1878	toad	breast
United States	1870	snake	stomach
United Kingdom	1868	snake	?
United Kingdom	1855	newt	?
United Kingdom	1854	newt	head
United States	1854	snake	stomach
United Kingdom	1854	worm	?
United Kingdom	1854	toad	?
United Kingdom	1854	snake	stomach
United States	1854	snake	?
United Kingdom	c. 1854	amphibians	stomach/throat
United Kingdom	1854	snake	stomach
United Kingdom	1854	worm	?
United Kingdom	1854	worm	?
United Kingdom	1854	newt	?
United Kingdom	1854	worm	"insides"
United Kingdom	1852	reptile	"just above the diaphragm"
United Kingdom	1852	newt	bowels
United States	1851	water snake	stomach
United Kingdom	c. 1850	toad	?
United Kingdom	c. 1850	worm	heart
United Kingdom	c. 1850	frog	stomach
United Kingdom	1850s	newt	bowels
United Kingdom	1846	reptile	?
United Kingdom	1846	lizard	?
Ireland	1840	snake	stomach

(Continued)

Table 1.   *(Continued)*

PLACE	DATE	CREATURE	ORGAN
United Kingdom	c. 1840	toad	stomach
United States	1837	electric snake	stomach
United States	1837	snake	stomach
United States	1836	snake	stomach
United States	1836	snake	?
United States	1828	snake	stomach
France	1822	snake	stomach
United Kingdom	1813	"small lizard"	stomach/ intestines
Germany	1811	crayfish, leeches, & worms	?
United Kingdom	1799	newt	?
United Kingdom	1790	snake	stomach
United Kingdom	1780	toad	stomach
United Kingdom	1765	"an animal like an evet"	belly
Lapland	1732	"three live frogs"	stomach
United Kingdom	1721	worm	?
Sweden	?18th century	lizards & amphibians	?
United Kingdom	?18th century	"monster" lizard	belly/stomach
Germany	?18th century	snake	stomach
?	1684	frog	belly
France	1680	hairy worm	?
?	1675	snake	stomach
Polish Prussia	1667	"3 living toads"	stomach
United Kingdom	1664	snake	stomach
?United States	1658	snakes	stomach
Denmark	1648	amphibians	?
?	1647	toads & other creatures	abdomen
United Kingdom	1639	snakes/eels/frogs	stomach
United Kingdom	1637	snake	heart
France	1618	snake	stomach
United Kingdom	1612	"2 toads and a serpent"	?
Italy	17th century	"hairy worm"	?

PLACE	DATE	CREATURE	ORGAN
United States	1574	snake	?
France	1561	snake	belly
France	1548	snake	stomach
France	1519	worm	heart
Poland	1494	snake	womb
Norway	?	serpent	stomach
India	1339	snake	entrails
Europe	13th century	snake	stomach
(Ireland	12th century	"demon of gluttony"	stomach)
Balkans	? (traditional tale)	snake	stomach
Balkans	? (traditional tale)	snake	stomach

Notes:

Some caution must be exercised about the term *worms*, which was often used in medieval texts to signify putrescence (Pouchelle 170) or lice. Cowan 196, 197, comments on the "vague classification" prevalent in the classics and Middle Ages of bugs, fleas, and lice as "worms." He quotes from a sixteenth-century translation of a fifteenth-century text, "a louse is a worm." However, here I have taken the description at face value.

Efts, evets, asks, askers, askerds, (dry) askards, alp luachras, dark lookers, mankeepers, and *man leppers* are all folk names for varieties of newt. The majority of these terms may be found in dialect dictionaries or have been identified by correspondents in the magazines from which the stories were taken. See, for example, Hyde; Westropp.

Waterwolves present more of a problem. The *English Dialect Dictionary* simply notes that the term is used in West Yorkshire and that waterwolves are thought to be swallowed and to live and grow in the human stomach, which, of course, is what we know already! (see P. Smith and Smith 12). However, they do sound like newts, so I am assuming for the purposes of this analysis that that is what they are.

There is one story about a creature called a "water dog." I'm not sure what that is. Dictionaries of British English say it is a water vole, but that seems unlikely. In Australia, so I am told, this creature may be called a "mud puppy" and is a sort of amphibian. I have not included this creature in the list.

There are very similar tales about tapeworms, eels, centipedes, and octopuses, which, like insects, have not been included in this list. There are single stories featuring a scorpion and a slug, which again in every other respect are similar to Bosom Serpent stories. There are even narratives, again similar in all other respects, which feature mammals: there are two stories about dogs and two about mice and several about "wolves" being found in the body (though perhaps the term *wolf* should not be taken literally, as it is possible that "the wolf" was a folk name for herpes). (Pouchelle 168 says that in French folk speech, herpes was called *le loup* [the wolf]). Accounts can also be found of a "beast," "live animals the size of a sixpence," "something alive and black," "two uncommon creatures," "something wick [alive]," "something . . . like a monkey," "animals," and "live things." None of these has been included in the list.

NOTES

1. Hawthorne's story is not the only work of fiction to employ this motif. Barnes and Smith draw attention to several more, including Marjorie Walker's short story, "The Summer of the Serpent" (1971); Hortense Calisher's short story, "Heartburn" (1951); and an episode in Willa Cather's novel, *O Pioneers!* (1913).
2. Arner; Barnes, "Physical"; Barnes, "Bosom"; S. Bush; Harding; Monteiro; Shroeder; A. Turner.
3. See Gosse, "Man"; Gudden; Rickard; "Sleeping Girl."
4. "The Bosom Serpent" 1991; Bennett, "Bosom"; Bennett, "Medical."
5. See Dewhirst, "Haworth"; Dewhirst, "Search"; Mortimer; for a very fine "waterwolves" story, see Barnes and Smith 138–42.
6. See Tucker; Baker.
7. See "Sorry"; "Crocodile Scare." For swallowing an octopus, see also Barnes and Smith 146–47, which draws attention to Roald Dahl's 1979 story, *My Uncle Oswald.* Chapter 8 of Dahl's tale contains an account of Oswald's old nanny, who suffered pains for many years due to having ingested an octopus. The "Crocodile Scare" item was sent to me by Michael Goss; for this and several other similar stories, I owe him many thanks.
8. De Voragine 347–48. My thanks to Jacqueline Simpson and Jennifer Westwood for this text.
9. See also *FOAFtale News* 6 (July 1987).
10. Quoted in Rickard; also appears in Kirby.
11. Hallissy 90; Marchalonis 174.
12. Kittredge 182–83. The intimate connection between witches and toads, Kittredge says, was maintained into the nineteenth century. As late as 1857 a Shropshire "witch," Nanny Morgan, was said to have kept a box of live toads in her cottage and a modern wizard from Somerset "kept toads on hand in pots" (182–83).

13. See also Clements. The same range of creatures frequently turn up as ingredients of poisons, and curiously—but perhaps not unexpectedly—as cures; see, for example, Kittredge 181.

14. This aspect of the legend has been usefully explored by Poulsen in his study of Puritan and Mormon versions of the legend.

15. Hallissy 90; Marchalonis 174.

16. Kors and Peters 306, from Joseph Glanvil's *Sadducismus Triumphatus* [1681].

17. Preface; quoted in Ross 13.

18. Rollins 132–38; see also Barnes and Smith 128.

19. 34–35, from Georg Abraham Mercklin's *De Incantamentis* [1715].

20. The ability to cause victims to excrete or vomit strange objects was also, of course, common in witchcraft accusations. Kittredge has a long and impressive list of objects supposedly vomited or voided by bewitched persons from 1574 to 1701, including bones, pins, nails, needles, bits of lead, coins, whetstones, nutshells, rushes, and balls of wool or hair (134, 456 n.78).

21. A very similar trick was played by a physician in a "well-known medical story" from the first year of the twentieth century. His patient "imagined" she had a frog in her stomach:

    Her doctor, after trying vainly to persuade her that it was only imagination, considered a little deception justifiable. . . . [H]aving administered an emetic, he managed adroitly to introduce a frog into the basin, as if it had just arrived from the old lady's stomach. The patient's joy was great, as there was proof positive that she had been right all along as to the cause of her illness. Her joy was soon overclouded, as the idea struck her that, although there was the old frog, there might be little frogs left behind. The doctor, however, was equal to this sudden emergency, for on a rapid examination of the frog he immediately assured the patient that her fears were groundless, as her late guest was a *gentleman* frog. ("Animals in People's Insides," *Notes and Queries* 9, no. 8: 391)

22. Kirby gives a more sympathetic account. Here called Catharine Geilerin, the woman is said to have symptoms very like standard Bosom Serpent ones ("pains in the abdomen, accompanied with extraordinary movements"). The list of the creatures she vomited is very long and includes "two living green frogs and . . . a large dead toad with very sharp claws." She attributes her symptoms to drinking polluted water and "lived on bread soaked in milk, and could drink nothing but water. She had an invincible dislike to meat, and whenever she tasted it, she experienced very great agitations in her stomach" (363–64).

23. Newcastle antiquarian John Bell gave Sir Walter Scott a number of bound volumes of broadsides, chapbooks, and garlands. This is item 101 in volume 2 of a multivolume set of "garlands" (shelf P.5.2) in Scott's library at Abbotsford. Courtesy of Paul Smith.

24. The reference to Dr. Moor, the famous worm doctor, helps to date this item. In 1735, a satirical verse (usually attributed to Alexander Pope) was published in the *Gentleman's Magazine*. Entitled "The Worm Doctor's Harangue," it is preceded by two lines of verse from an "Old Ballad" referring to "Moor of Moor Hall." We can therefore deduce that the verses were directed against Moor, the famous worm doctor. For a copy of "The Worm Doctor's Harangue," see Barnes and Smith 132–34.

25. Bondeson does not give his sources, so I have not been able to track any of this literature down.

26. 2:392–93; see also Barnes and Smith 136–37.

27. My thanks to Matthew Ramsey for this reference. The woodcut is reproduced in Guthrie, facing p. 129.

28. The same trick based on the same folklore reappears hundreds of years later in 1982 in a story about "tapeworm diet pills"; see Baker 226.

29. Bill Scott, personal communication. The story comes from his seafaring days.

30. Text by courtesy of Patricia Lysaght.

31. That is, nineteenth- and twentieth-century United States, Australia, and Western Europe; 39 of the narratives come from the United States, one from Australia, and the rest from Western Europe, principally the United Kingdom and Ireland.

32. List courtesy of Dr. Gareth Roberts.

33. Maurice; Seaton 1979; Muller and Baker; Ashton et al.; Jones and Smith; A. Taylor; J. Bush; Facey and Marsden; Tee.

34. Jones and Smith; A. Taylor; Facey and Marsden.

35. A. Taylor; Hardman, Jones, and Davies.

36. Fascioliasis is not the only disease connected to polluted water and/or inadequate hygiene. Whipworms are transmitted by eggs laid on salad vegetables that are eaten unwashed. The eggs of roundworms (*ascaris lumbricoides*) can be swallowed in contaminated water or food or when eating with dirty hands. They have a worldwide distribution, particularly among settled communities with poor hygiene or sanitation.

37. The mammals include mice. Mice issuing from the body are also a feature of stories found in the witchcraft literature. Kittredge, for example, records a story from 1634 in which a sick man complained that a witch had caused him to feel as if a mouse was inside his body, and in 1665 it was reported that one could be cured of bewitchment by "boiling certain herbs over a pot and holding one's head over the pot. This was done to a [quack?] doctor's patient at [Market?] Harborough [United Kingdom] and [something] like a mouse leaped forth out of her mouth, and she was absolutely freed." See Kittredge 135.

KEY TEXTS

"Animals in People's Insides." *Notes and Queries* 9, no. 7 (1901): 222–23, 332–33.

"Animals in People's Insides." *Notes and Queries* 9, no. 8 (1901): 89–90, 346, 390–92.

"Animals in People's Insides." *Notes and Queries* 9, no. 9 (1903): 467–68.

"Animals in People's Insides." *Notes and Queries* 9, no. 12 (1903): 414–15, 471.

Barnes, Daniel R. "The Bosom Serpent: A Legend in American Literature and Culture." *Journal of American Folklore* 85 (1972): 111–22.

Bennett, Gillian. "Bosom Serpents and Alimentary Amphibians: A Language for Sickness?" In *Illness and Healing Alternatives in Western Europe*, ed. Hilary Marland, Hans de Waardt and Marijke Gijswijt-Hofstra, 224–42. London: Routledge and Kegan Paul, 1997.

———. "Medical Aspects of the Bosom Serpent." *Contemporary Legend*, n.s., 3 (2000): 1–26.

Berlioz, Jacques. "L'Homme au Crapaud: Genèse d'un *Exemplum* Médiéval." In *Tradition et Histoire dans la Culture Populaire*. Grenoble: Centre Alpin et Rhodanien d'Ethnologie, 1990.

Bondeson, Jan. "The Bosom Serpent." In *A Cabinet of Medical Curiosities*, 26–50. Ithaca: Cornell University Press, 1997.

"The Bosom Serpent" (special issue). *Dear Mr Thoms . . .* 22 (August 1991).

Cattermole-Tally, Frances. "The Intrusion of Animals into the Human Body: Fantasy and Reality." *Folklore* 106 (1995): 89–92.

"Newspaper Folk Lore." *Notes and Queries* 1, no. 6 (1852): 221, 338, 466.

"Newspaper Folk Lore." *Notes and Queries* 1, no. 9 (1854): 29–30, 84, 276–77, 523–24.

Renard, Jean-Bruno. "L'Animal Avalé Vivant." In *Légendes Urbaines: Rumeurs d'Aujourd'hui*, ed. Véronique Campion-Vincent and Jean-Bruno Renard, 28–44. Paris: Payot, 1992.

REFERENCES CITED

"Animals in People's Insides." *Notes and Queries* 9, no. 7 (1901): 222–23, 332–33.

"Animals in People's Insides." *Notes and Queries* 9, no. 8 (1901): 89–90, 346, 390–92.

"Animals in People's Insides." *Notes and Queries* 9, no. 9 (1903): 467–68.

"Animals in People's Insides." *Notes and Queries* 9, no. 12 (1903): 414–15, 471.

Arner, Robert D. "Of Snakes and Those Who Swallow Them: Some Folk Analogues for Hawthorne's 'Egotism; or, The Bosom Serpent.'" *Southern Folklore Quarterly* 35 (1971): 336–46.

Ashton, W. L. G., P. L. Boardman, P. H. Everall, and A. W. J. Houghton. "Human Fascioliasis in Shropshire." *British Medical Journal* 5721 (July–September 1970): 500–2.

Baker, Ronald L. *Hoosier Folk Legends.* Bloomington: Indiana University Press, 1982.

Barnes, Daniel R. "'Physical Fact' and Folklore: Hawthorne's 'Egotism; or The Bosom Serpent.'" *American Literature* 43 (1971–72): 117–21.

Barnes, Daniel R., and Paul Smith. "The Contemporary Legend in Literature—Towards an Annotated Checklist, Part 4: The Bosom Serpent." *Contemporary Legend,* n.s., 4 (2001): 126–49.

Bennett, Gillian. "Bosom Serpents and Alimentary Amphibians: A Language for Sickness?" In *Illness and Healing Alternatives in Western Europe,* ed. Hilary Marland, Hans de Waardt and Marijke Gijswijt-Hofstra, 224–42. London: Routledge and Kegan Paul, 1997.

———. "Medical Aspects of the Bosom Serpent." *Contemporary Legend,* n.s., 3 (2000): 1–26.

Berlioz, Jacques. "L'Homme au Crapaud: Genèse d'un *Exemplum* Médiéval." In *Tradition et Histoire dans la Culture Populaire.* Grenoble: Centre Alpin et Rhodanien d'Ethnologie, 1990.

Bishop, Amanda. *The Gucci Kangaroo.* Hornsby, New South Wales: Australian Publishing, 1988.

Bondeson, Jan. *A Cabinet of Medical Curiosities.* Ithaca: Cornell University Press, 1997.

"The Bosom Serpent" (special issue). *Dear Mr Thoms . . .* 22 (August 1991).

Buchan, David, ed. *Folk Tradition and Folk Medicine in Scotland: The Writings of David Rorie.* Edinburgh: Canongate Academic, 1994.

Bush, J. P. "Liver Flukes in the Common Bile Duct." *British Medical Journal* 5285 (July–December 1962): 1147.

Bush, Sargent J. R. "Bosom Serpents before Hawthorne: The Origins of a Symbol." *American Literature* 43 (1971–72): 181–99.

Clements, William M. "Interstitiality in Contemporary Legends." *Contemporary Legend* 1 (1991): 81–92.

Cowan, F. *Curious Facts in the History of Insects.* Philadelphia: Lippincott, 1865.

"A Crocodile Scare. An Amusing Hoax over Egyptian Eggs." *I. P. News,* 15 April 1920, 8.

Dale, Rodney. *The Tumour in the Whale: An Hilarious Collection of Apochryphal Anecdotes.* London: Allen and Universal Books, 1978.

Dégh, Linda, and Andrew Vázsonyi. *The Dialectics of Legend*. Bloomington, Ind.: Folklore Preprints Series 1.6., 1973.

Dewhirst, Ian. "The Haworth Water-Wolf, and Others." In *The Howarth Water-Wolf and Other Yorkshire Stories*, 10–11. Driffield: Ridings, 1967.

———. "In Search of the Water-Wolf." *Lore and Language* 1 (1971): 12–14.

Douglas, Mary. *Purity and Danger: An Analysis of the Concepts of Pollution and Taboo*. London: Routledge and Kegan Paul, 1966.

Ellis, Bill. "Two Reasons Not to Eat Sushi." *FOAFtale News* 14 (June 1989): 4–5.

Facey, R. V., and P. D. Marsden. "Fascioliasis in Man: An Outbreak in Hampshire." *British Medical Journal* 5199 (July–December 1960): 619–25.

Fenwick, W. Soltau. "Existence of Living Creatures in the Stomach as a Cause of Chronic Dyspepsia." *British Medical Journal* 2563 (January–June 1910): 371–75.

Girardet, Raoul. "La Conspiration." In *Mythes et Mythologies Politiques*, 25–61. Paris: Seuil, 1986.

Gosse, Bruno. "Docs Nearly Croak When 4-lb Frog Is Removed from Woman's Stomach." *Sun*, 12 December 1989, 15.

———. "Man Has Eel Living in His Intestines." *Sun*, 13 June 1989, 25.

Gudden, George. "Girl, 4, Coughs up a Live Snake." *Sun*, 19 July 1989, 44.

Guthrie, Douglas. *A History of Medicine*. London: Nelson, 1945.

Hallissy, Margaret. *Venomous Woman: Fear of the Female in Literature*. New York: Greenwood, 1987.

Harding, Walter. "Another Source for Hawthorne's 'Egotism; or, The Bosom Serpent.'" *American Literature* 40 (1968–69): 537–38.

Hardman, E. W., R. L. H. Jones, and A. H. Davies. "Fascioliasis: A Large Outbreak." *British Medical Journal* 5721 (July–September 1970): 502–5.

Henslow, George. *Medical Works of the Fourteenth Century*. London: Chapman and Hall, 1899.

Holbek, Bengt. *Games of the Powerless*. Copenhagen: Institut for Folkmindevidenskab, 1977.

Hughes, Martin. "Strange Tales of Lincolnshire: The Adder." *Lincolnshire Life* 8, no. 7 (1968): 46.

Hyde, Douglas. *Beside the Fire: A Collection of Irish Gaelic Folk Stories*. London: David Nutt for the Folk-Lore Society, 1890.

Jones, Idris, and Peter Smith. "Liver-Fluke Infection in Man." *Lancet* 7293 (January–June 1963): 1241.

Kirby, R. S. *Kirby's Wonderful and Scientific Museum*. 6 vols. London: Kirby, 1803–20.

Kittredge, George Lyman. *Witchcraft in Old and New England*. Cambridge: Harvard University Press, 1929.

Kors, Alan C., and Edward Peters. *Witchcraft in Europe, 1100–1700: A Documentary History*. Philadelphia: University of Pennsylvania Press, 1972.

Kumar, Devinder, and David L. Wingate. "The Irritable Bowel Syndrome: A Paroxysmal Motor Disorder." *Lancet* 8462 (October–December 1985): 973–77.

Le Quellec, Jean-Loïc. *Alcool de Singe et Liqueur de Vipère—Plus Quelques Autres Recettes.* Mougon: Geste, 1991.

Mangiacopra, Gary. "Bullfrog in the Stomach." *INFO Journal* 43 (1984): 8.

Marchalonis, Shirley. "Three Medieval Tales and Their Modern Analogues." *Journal of the Folklore Institute* 13 (1976): 173–84.

Mather, Increase. *Remarkable Providences Illustrative of the Earlier Days of American Colonization.* Boston: Green, 1684.

Maurice, John. "Is Something Lurking in Your Liver?" *New Scientist*, 19 March 1994, 26–31.

Meyer, Kuno, ed. and trans. *Aislinge Meic Conglinne: The Vision of Mac-Conglinne: A Middle-Irish Wonder Tale.* London: Nutt, 1892.

Monteiro, George. "A Nonliterary Source for Hawthorne's 'Egotism; or, The Bosom Serpent.'" *American Literature* 41 (1969–70): 575–77.

Mortimer, Nigel. "Yorkshire's Water Wolf." *Fortean Times* 51 (1988–89): 48–49.

Muller, R., and J. R. Baker. *Medical Parasitology.* Philadelphia: Lippincott, 1990.

"Newspaper Folk Lore." *Notes and Queries* 1, no. 6 (1852): 221, 338, 466.

"Newspaper Folk Lore." *Notes and Queries* 1, no. 9 (1854): 29–30, 84, 276–77, 523–24.

Paré, Ambroise. *On Monsters and Marvels.* Trans. Janice Pallister. Chicago: University of Chicago Press, 1982.

Partridge, J. B. "Notes on English Folklore." *Folk-Lore* 28 (1917): 311–15.

Porter, Roy. *Health for Sale: Quackery in England, 1660–1850.* Manchester: Manchester University Press, 1989.

Pouchelle, Marie-Christine. *The Body and Surgery in the Middle Ages.* New Brunswick, N.J.: Rutgers University Press, 1990.

Poulsen, Richard C. "Bosom Serpentry among the Puritans and Mormons." *Journal of the Folklore Institute* 16 (1979): 176–89.

R.R. "Frog Folk-Lore." *Notes and Queries* 6, no. 1 (1880): 392.

Rickard, Bob. "Embeddings." *Fortean Times* 40 (1983): 17–18.

Rollins, Hyder Edward, ed. *The Pack of Autolycus; or, Strange and Terrible News . . . as Told in Broadside Ballads of the Years 1624–1693.* Cambridge: Harvard University Press, 1927.

Ross, Morton L. "Hawthorne's Bosom Serpent and Mather's *Magnalia*." *Emerson Society Quarterly* 47 (1967): 13.

Satchell, Thomas. "The Child and the Toad." *Folk-Lore Record* 1 (1878): 237.

Sawyer, Donald J. "The Lady with the Snake in Her." *New York Folklore Quarterly* 25 (1969): 299–305.

Seaton, D. R. "Cestodes and Trematodes." In *Parasites and Western Man*, ed. R. J. Donaldson, 114–32. Lancaster: M.T.P., 1979.

Shroeder, John W. "Hawthorne's 'Egotism; or, The Bosom Serpent' and Its
Source." *American Literature* 31 (1959–60): 150–62.

"Sleeping Girl Swallows Snake." *Fortean Times* 50 (1988): 4.

Smith, Marian W. "Musings on Folklore, 1943." *Journal of American Folklore* 57
(1944): 70–72.

Smith, Paul, and Georgina Smith. "In Search of the Water Wolf." *Lore and Language* 1, no. 4 (1971): 12.

"Sorry about That, Myth!" *Daily Mirror* (15 April 1986).

Taylor, A. W. "Liver-Fluke Infection in Man." *Lancet* 7216 (July–December
1961): 1534–36.

Taylor, K. B. "Gastritis." In *Oxford Textbook of Medicine*, ed. D. J. Weatherall,
J. G. G. Ledingham, and D. A. Warrell, 12: 77–86. Oxford: Oxford University
Press, 1987.

Tee, George. "Fascioliasis." *Lancet* 7597 (April–June 1969): 778.

Thoreau, Henry D. *Journal of Henry D. Thoreau.* Ed. Bradford Torrey and Francis
H. Allen. 14 vols. 1906; Boston: Houghton Mifflin, 1949.

Tucker, Elizabeth. "The Seven-Day Wonder Diet: Magic and Ritual in Diet
Folklore." *Indiana Folklore* 11 (1978): 141–50.

Turner, Arlin. "Hawthorne's Literary Borrowings." *Proceedings of the Modern
Language Association* 51 (1936): 545–50.

Turner, Brian. *The Body and Society: Explorations in Social Theory.* London:
Blackwell, 1984.

V.A.H. "When the Woman Swallowed an H'Alligator." *Northamptonshire Past
and Present* 4 (1969–70): 238.

Voragine, Jacobus de. *The Golden Legend: Readings on the Saints.* Trans.
William Granger Ryan. Princeton: Princeton University Press, 1993.

Ward, Gordon. "Hepatic Distomiasis (Sheep Rot) in Man." *British Medical Journal* 2625 (January–June 1911): 931–35.

Westropp, Thomas J. "A Folklore Survey of County Clare." *Folk-Lore* 22 (1911):
49–60, 203–13, 332–41, 449–56.

Wilson, Leitch. "A Case of Intussusception of the Transverse Colon in an
Adult." *British Medical Journal* 2563 (January–June 1910): 375–76.

POISON AND HONEY

And it shall come to pass, that instead of a sweet smell there shall be stink; and instead of a girdle a rent; and instead of glossy hair there shall be baldness; and instead of fine embroidery there shall be sackcloth; and burning instead of beauty.

—ISAIAH 3:24

A large number of rumors and contemporary legends are preoccupied with the possibility that the pleasures, comforts, and necessities of life may somehow be rendered harmful. Some of these are concerned with "dirt" of various forms—out of place bodily excretions (usually blood and semen), mind-altering substances, and so on.[1] Among these are stories of drug-laced transfers or tattoos that circulated widely in the late 1980s and early 1990s.[2] Others concern chemical and biological warfare.[3] Among these we may count rumors of the poisoning of wells or foodstuffs, the presentation of "smallpox blankets" to Native Americans during the opening up of the American West, rumors of government or medical involvement in cholera outbreaks in European cities in the mid-nineteenth century, and rumors of the contamination of foodstuffs in the United States by right-wing groups to sterilize

African American men.[4] The stories I shall discuss in this chapter show another aspect of this preoccupation with poison, contamination, and disease. They share a concern with dirt, biological warfare, and bodily invasion, but here the dangers come directly or indirectly from much nearer home, from clothing and from the bodies of those we love or lust after. In these legends, beautiful and desirable things are contaminated; honey becomes poison by being touched by death, disease, hatred, and/or sexual warfare.

I shall be looking at stories of poisoned garments, snake women, and poisonous brides. In some stories, the transformation of honey into poison comes about via the body's outer skin, its clothing; in others, the transformation comes about via the inner flesh, a woman's sexual parts. In the first group, the victim is killed by a garment impregnated with poison. In legends from the classics, the poisoned garment is sent either knowingly or unknowingly as a gift to a faithless lover. In modern versions, the garment is impregnated with poison as a result of carelessness or cupidity, and a marriageable girl is consequently killed. In the second group, it is the marriageable woman herself who is poisonous, either because it is her nature to be so or because she has been fed on poison. In all of these stories, the promise of beauty, love, and sex brings death, often quite literally fulfilling Isaiah's prophecy that beauty shall be turned into burning.

POISONED GARMENTS

Modern Redactions: "The Poisoned Dress"

In the 1930s a story began to circulate in the United States concerning the death of a young girl. The tale was later recalled by a correspondent to *Hoosier Folklore Bulletin*:

> It so happened that a young girl was out dancing [in Chicago] one evening when she felt faint, and later in the evening she collapsed and

died. Since the death was so sudden, the authorities investigated every detail. They traced the department store from which the evening gown which she was wearing was purchased. The store was Marshall Field and Company. Through their records they were able to tell the authorities that a Negress had bought the dress, and sometime after the dress was returned. Further investigation led to the story behind the dress.

It seemed that the young Negress bought the dress for her bridal gown. Prior to the wedding she died. The family decided to bury the girl in the dress, but after some consideration, they thought the dress was too expensive an item to clothe a corpse. (From what I remember, the family was in the low-income bracket.) The dress was returned, after it had been taken off the body of the corpse, and placed on display. Evidently the first girl mentioned purchased the gown. (Hochsinger 33)

The letter had been written in response to an appeal by the *Bulletin*'s editor, Ernest Baughman, who had begun to collect versions of the story. To stimulate discussion, he printed a story that had been sent to him in 1942 and was reportedly "spreading throughout the entire Mid-West," taking everyone "by storm." In this story a girl had been invited to a banquet at "a prominent hotel in a certain city" and had decided that she had to have a new dress to grace the occasion. At a local department store, she bought "a simple but exquisite gown." During dinner, the girl began to feel faint, and her escort noticed that the dress had a peculiar smell. She went to the cloakroom and took the dress off, thinking that perhaps the dye was coming off and giving rise to the smell and the faintness, but nothing seemed to be wrong with the garment, so she went back to her table. Before long she passed out, and her escort took her home and called the doctor. She died before the doctor got there, but he thought he recognized the smell. "He ordered an autopsy and they discovered that the girl had formaldehyde in her veins. The drug had coagulated her blood, and had stopped the flow. They investigated the department store where she had bought the dress and learned that the dress had been sold for a corpse and had been returned and sold to the girl. When she perspired and her pores opened, she took in the formaldehyde which killed her." [5]

This story had probably been circulating as a student horror story since the early 1930s. In a 1952 article, J. Russell Reaver recalled having heard a version circulating in the Cincinnati area "at least from 1933 to 1937," when he was an undergraduate (217). As he recalled the story, "a pretty girl . . . had just been engaged to be married." Shortly after the engagement, she bought a white satin gown at "one of the leading department stores" and wore it to "a country-club dance," with the usual fatal consequences. This time, the death was said to have been caused by embalming fluid. "When the officials of the store where she had bought the dress were threatened with the police, they finally admitted that they had allowed a wealthy family to rent the dress for the funeral of their daughter, after which it had been returned to the store and sold." [6] According to Reaver, virtually the same story appeared in Bennett Cerf's 1944 collection of *Famous Ghost Stories*. The ingredients of Cerf's story are beautiful girl, white satin dress, formal dance, dress rented (from pawn shop), collapse. So far, so ordinary, but Cerf added a twist to the story, a motif very common in adolescent ghost lore: "it was then, possibly in her delirium, that she heard a woman's voice whispering into her ear. It was harsh and bitter, 'Give me back my dress,' she said, 'Give me back my dress! It belongs to the dead!' The next day the lifeless body of the young girl was found stretched out on her bed." The story then returns to the usual legendary structure: an autopsy is ordered; the girl has been killed by embalming fluid; the dress has been sold to the pawnbroker by an undertaker's assistant "who had taken it from the body of a dead girl just before the casket was nailed down for the last time" (quoted in Reaver 219).

In another student version published in *Hoosier Folklore* in 1946, the story is again located in Cincinnati. Here, an undertaker's error leads to a woman being dressed for her burial in the wrong dress. Her daughters demand that the dress be changed, and the wrong dress is taken back to the store where it was purchased and is later bought by a girl who wears it to a dance. The story unfolds like the earlier versions, and again embalming fluid kills the girl (Hartikka 78–79). As far as I know, the most recent version of the story is one from *Hoosier Folk Legends* (Baker 1982) that Jan Harold Brunvand quotes in his legend compilation, *The Choking Doberman* (1984). In this "a local woman shaved her armpits and went shopping. She bought a dress, and when she wore it the first time got terribly sick and died." As in the first of our examples, "a coloured family" had "bought the dress and used it on a dead relative." Embalming fluid, which had soaked into the dress, had gotten into the second woman's skin through lesions caused by shaving (114).

Commentators on these legends have each seen a different moral in the story. Gloria Hochsinger, one of the first to bring it to folklorists' attention, interpreted it as a mercantile legend. She suspects that "it is a part of a cycle of stories told to discredit well-known firms or prominent families" (32). After telling her version of the story, she adds a coda: "rumor had it that the store . . . paid . . . to keep the entire incident quiet" (33). Others think the story reflects on the competence or the honesty of undertakers. Brunvand's comments on it refer to an "unscrupulous mortician who was switching dresses on corpses and selling the better garments while burying his clients in inferior ones" (*Choking* 113). Paul Smith, too, footnotes the version in his *Book of Nastier Legends* (1986) with the comment that "perhaps one reason for its popularity is our apparently growing mistrust of the undertaking profession," and he points to legends about undertakers stealing jewelry and substituting cardboard coffins for solid oak ones (49).

There is no doubt that if the story is taken seriously, somebody—family, store, or funeral parlor—must be guilty of a serious breach of decency or professional standards, care for the dead, or good taste. Suggesting that the story is part of a cycle of legends about "dreadful contaminations" of the body, Brunvand says that in this legend the contamination comes by means of "unclean clothing" (*Mexican* 112). In two out of the ten stories I have consulted, this motif receives a racist cast, when the narrator stresses that the body from which the dress was taken was that of a black woman. However, I think Cerf probably comes closest to understanding the underlying nature of the contamination. In his non-traditional telling, he inserts a typical ghost story motif, the ghost who demands restoration of property or body parts. As Cerf tells it, the ghost demands the dress back with the words: "It belongs to the dead." I would suggest that the contamination in all these stories consists of the touch of the dead. The dress is the (flimsy) intermediary between the skin of the dead and the skin of the living. In this case, death is catching.[7]

Cerf's version has another passage that I also think is significant in understanding these stories. He says that "the legend maintained that a very lovely but poverty-stricken damsel was invited to a formal dance. It was her chance to enter a brand-new world. Who knew but that some rich young man would fall in love with her and lift her out of life in a box factory?" (quoted in Reaver 218). This comment brings us to sex, a dominant theme in these legends. In Cerf's version, the connection between the dress and sex is quite explicit: the girl has bought the dress in the hope of seducing a boy (hopefully, a rich one). The connection between the dress and sex is also there in all but the 1970s version that Brunvand quotes, albeit less overtly so. Of the ten versions I have looked at, one says the dress was originally intended to be a wedding dress, five describe it as a white satin gown (that is, like a wedding dress), and one says it was worn at a dance after an engagement.

So there is a more or less overt wedding motif in seven of the ten. Even the other three versions contain the suggestion of sex. In all but one (Brunvand's version), the dress has been purchased for a dance, and most times the narrator stresses the beauty or seductiveness of the girl who wears it. In the 1930s, 1940s, and 1950s, when these stories were collected, going to a dance was a principal way to meet a potential mate, so in almost all of these mid-twentieth-century stories, dancing and dresses are linked to sex and perhaps are symbols of sex. The stories then forge a double link between the dress and death—the first wearer wore it when she was dead and the second wearer wore it and died. So, via the intermediary of the dress, the promise of sex is touched by the hand of death.

Classical Redactions: The Deaths of Herakles and Glauke

In all of the modern stories, the links among dress, sex, and death are circumstantial, and the blame for the death is muted and focused on a third party. Older legends with the same motifs, however, are more direct; narrators shape these older tales into fables of deliberate betrayal, where death is the punishment for treachery or infidelity. I am not suggesting that the Greek myths were the source of the modern legends. (The time gap is too large for there to be a direct link.) But there are interesting similarities, and both groups show the fruitfulness of the themes. Two stories in particular from Greek literature—Nessus's shirt and Glauke's poisoned gown—share the central motif of the modern poison-dress legends.

The similarity between these classic stories and modern poisoned dresses was first noticed by another correspondent to *Hoosier Folklore* in the 1940s (Himelick) and was later pointed out by Jan Brunvand in his brief discussion in his 1984 compilation, *The Choking Doberman* (112–14).[8] The fullest discussions, however, can be found in the work of classical folklorist Adrienne Mayor.[9]

The examples that follow are taken from Mayor's work, though the commentary is my own.

Both of these stories were known to ancient Greeks as well as to the most casual readers of Hellenic mythology. The tales were retold in many versions in Greece and Rome, and artists painted scenes from them on vases (Mayor, "Fiery" 56). Nessus's shirt is probably the most familiar of these stories today. In Mayor's rendition of the myth,

> Herakles shot the centaur Nessus with a poisoned arrow for abduct-
> ing his wife Deianeira. The dying centaur told Deianeira to collect
> blood from the wound, mix it with oil, and preserve it in an airtight
> container. If Herakles ever strayed, said Nessus, Deianeira could win
> him back by treating his clothing with this magical mixture. Years
> later Herakles fell in love with a young woman, and Deianeira wove
> a tunic and anointed it with the potion. She sent the robe to Herakles
> with the message that it should touch no one's skin but his, nor
> should it be exposed to sun, heat or moisture. After the messenger
> had set off with the robe, Deianeira watched in horror as a bit of the
> treated wool that had fallen in the courtyard burst into flame. She
> realized too late that she had been tricked.
>
> Sophocles' tragedy The Trachinian Women (ca. 440–420 B.C.)
> describes what happened when Herakles donned the robe. The hero
> began to perspire, and the cloak exploded into flames, corroding
> Herakles' skin and boiling his blood. He tried to rip off the garment,
> but it clung so that the flesh tore away with it. He plunged into a
> stream, but the robe burned more fiercely in water. Finally, on
> Mount Oeta in Thessaly, Herakles threw himself onto an altar fire
> and was burned to death. ("Fiery" 55)

In this story, Nessus's revenge is achieved through a double betrayal of Deianeira: she is deceived first by Nessus and then by Herakles, and thus the death plot is consummated.

In the second story from the classics, faithlessness and betrayal are also the engines that drive the plot. Here, the sexual element is foregrounded by getting rid of the innocent intermediary and making revenge for infidelity the motive of the poisoning and the poisoner the betrayed wife. This point is underscored by the fact that the poisoned garment is a wedding dress:

> Euripides' tragedy Medea (431 B.C.) was based on well-known legends about the barbarian sorceress who helped Jason win the Golden Fleece near the Black Sea. Jason married Medea but later abandoned her to wed a young Greek princess (called Glauke or Creusa) at Corinth. Knowing of the girl's vanity, the distraught Medea poisoned a wedding gown, placed it in a sealed casket, and sent it to the bride-to-be, ordering that only Glauke should touch the gift. The princess immediately donned the finery. Pirouetting before a mirror, she suddenly cried out, staggered, and fled in panic as the gown began to burn. Her violent activity ignited more flames, and the clinging gown "melted the flesh from her bones." Consumed by an unquenchable "devouring fire," Glauke dashed headlong into a fountain outside, but water was no relief. Her father and all of the guests were also engulfed by flames and perished along with Glauke. (Mayor, "Nessus" 63)

The similarities between old and new variants on the theme seem plain, especially in the second story. In all of the versions, the poison enters the bloodstream via the body's second skin, its clothing; the poison burns or corrodes; there is a link to sex.[10] Further parallels are the motif of the poisonous touch of the dead. In the story of Nessus's shirt, the parallel is quite explicit because the poison is made from the blood of the dying centaur.

The Poisoned Robe in India

Very similar stories have also been collected in India, where they are part of historical traditions surrounding the Mughal Empire

(1526–1858).[11] The tales revolve around fears of symbolic harm and real contamination aroused by the ancient Iranian-influenced custom of presenting robes of honor (khilats) to friends and enemies as demonstrations of a social and political relationship. Gifts of clothing were part of every major life-cycle ritual in preindustrial India, symbolizing changes in status and forging alliances. In Iranian-influenced cultures such as Mughal India, gifts of fine garments bestowed in political contexts had extra ramifications— the giving and receiving of a khilat established a hierarchical relationship between the giver and the recipient. By giving, the donor claimed superiority; by accepting the gift, the recipient acknowledged and submitted to that claim (Maskiell and Mayor, "Killer Khilats," pt. 1, 24–25). A poisoned khilat was therefore not only a double demonstration of power (the power to compel submission and the power over life and death) but also a significant betrayal of a public political bargain. The dominant features of these stories closely resemble the classical ones. The garment is impregnated with a harmful substance, it is presented to an enemy, and the enemy puts it on and is consumed. In these stories there is an extra frisson in that etiquette and power relations demand that the gift is not only accepted but immediately put on. In only one of the tales does the victim avert his fate. Here, the intended victim is the son of the would-be poisoner, the tyrant Aurengzeb: Prince Akbar knows his father too well to trust the gift, invents an excuse to delay putting the khilat on, and makes a slave try it on first. The slave, of course, dies a day or two later.[12]

These stories were first collected by James Todd, Norman Chevers, Richard Carnac Temple, William Crooke, and other acknowledged Indianists of the time. On the whole, their informants simply assumed that the practice of poisoning khilats was well known and needed no explanation. The motives for the act were therefore suppressed, but they seem to be pride, greed, power, hate, and political chicanery. In several stories, it is not clear what exactly the garments had been impregnated with, whether poison or disease. Other common motifs are heat, water, perspiration, and fire (Maskiell and Mayor, "Killer Khilats," pt. 1, 27). In several tales, the victims are said to die or be taken ill soon after donning the garment; in others they "expire in great torture," are "burnt to ashes," or "develop a fever."

The story that offers the most interesting parallels with classical and modern Poisoned Dress tales is the legend of the poisoning of Dost Muhammad Khan by the rani of Ganore. Sex, war, and betrayal combine to create a powerfully traditional story akin to biblical and apocryphal narratives of avenging and murderous women such as Delilah and Judith. The story takes place against the background of territorial wars between Hindu Rajput clans and the founder of the Muslim dynasty that ruled Bhopal until 1947. The version below was recorded by the begum of Bhopal in her history of the state, written in the mid-1870s. It describes how, having defended five fortresses from the invaders, the queen of Ganore retreated to her last fortress but was soon overwhelmed by the Muslim forces under Dost Muhammad Khan:

> The beauty of the Queen of Ganore was an allurement only secondary to his desire for her country, and he invited her to reign over it and him. Denial would have been useless, and would have subjected her to instant coercion. . . . [S]he therefore sent a message of assent. . . . She told him to prepare for the nuptials . . . on the terrace . . . and demanded two hours for unmolested preparation, that she might appear in appropriate attire, with the distinction her own and his rank demanded. . . . At length the Khan was summoned to the terrace. Robed in the marriage garb presented to him by the queen . . . the Khan gazed at her beauty [and] they conversed for some hours. But presently his countenance fell—he complained of heat. Fans and water availed him not and he began to tear the bridal garments from his body. Then the Queen said, "Know, Khan, that

your last hour is come; our wedding and our death shall be sealed together. The vestments which cover you are poisoned; you left me no other expedient to escape pollution." While all were horror-struck by this declaration she sprang from the battlements into the river below. The Khan died in extreme torture and was buried on the road to Bhopal.[13]

In this story, marriage and poison again come together, blended with the familiar traditional motif of the virgin queen who would rather die than submit to sexual coercion.

POISON, WOMEN, AND SNAKES

Once having entered the dangerous realm of the female, will the hero emerge intact?

—VERRIER ELWIN

Biting and Stinging

An essential ingredient of the plot of the older stories is the gift of a shirt or gown, but these are not, of course, the only gifts that may be poisoned. In a fascinating little book, *Poison Mysteries in History, Romance and Crime*, C. J. S. Thompson, formerly honorary curator of the museum of the Royal College of Surgeons, London, discusses the "Curious Methods Employed by Secret Poisoners" and cites the case of King John of Castille, who was poisoned by means of a pair of boots given him by a Turk, and King Henry VI of England, who died from a poisoned glove. Thompson also lists examples of poisoned rings, poisoned flowers, and even a poisonous bed, all sent as gifts (199–203).[14]

In modern stories, the dresses are not gifts but they are second-hand—they have been touched or worn by somebody else. In each case, someone must give or sell and someone must receive or buy

the poisonous article, and the article is a visible physical intermediary between poisoner and victim. But in a further refinement of
the theme, many legends feature poisonings that are less overt
and that entail no visible intermediary. In these cases, there is
nothing to give the game away; the poison lurks in something
entirely hidden. When the queen of Ganore appeared to offer sex
but actually offered death to the khan, she had to achieve her ends
indirectly. But wouldn't it have been simpler if the poison could
have been more subtly and more invisibly administered? If sex
alone somehow could be sufficient to kill her would-be lover?

The fear that this may actually be so—that a man could be
harmed by sexual intercourse—is a commonplace of masculine
erotic folklore. In addition to the age-old belief that sex weakens
men and robs them of spiritual and physical energy,[15] legend holds
that men have been known to fear that women's sexual organs
might wound, damage, or entrap the male organ or lead to the man's
death. Hence, there are stories of vaginas lined with glass or razors,
penises severed or glued up by vengeful women, penises stuck in
women's vaginas, and, above all, stories of toothed vaginas.[16]

For interesting variations on this ubiquitous theme, let us
return to India. In a study in the *Journal of Medical Psychiatry*,
ethnographer Verrier Elwin presents the texts of twenty-three
stories from central India. All feature intemperate women, avid
for sex, three of them daughters of traditional Indian monsters.
All demand sex and all castrate any man who attempts to give
them what they want so badly. Some actually devour the man or
his penis. In one story, a man is literally turned into a girl, first
castrated, then decorated with bangles and cowrie shells, and sent
to live apart from the men. In some, the women are overpowered
and their vaginal teeth removed by force using sticks, tongs, or
iron dildos; in some the would-be lover wraps horsehair around
his penis and mutilates the woman's vagina; and in three others, the
biting vagina is matched with a killer penis that is also toothed,

has thorns growing out of it, or, after being severed from the body, goes on a rampage, raping men and killing women. All but one of these stories (an antilegend to which I'll return later) are exceptionally bizarre and cruel and show a great deal of medical ignorance.

Significantly for our theme, in four of these stories snakes—the symbols and essence of poison—living in the women's bodies threaten the man's life or virility. One of the most bizarre of these comes from the Mandla District of India:

> A Raja had two sons. When his wife died, he said to his sons, "Shall I get a wife for myself or for you?" The boys said, "Marry her yourself and we'll call her mother." The Raja then married a very beautiful girl. But as he kissed her on the mouth as if she was a child he died. It was as he was lying on her, lost in love and he kissed her as if she was a child. The sons thought, "This girl was really for us and our father took her and has died for his sin. Now which of us will marry her?" The younger boy said, "You marry her," thinking that he could still enjoy her.
>
> One day, as the elder boy slept with her, a snake small as a thread came out of the girl's mouth, then grew very big and swallowed up the boy. The younger brother was near by and saw what had happened. He cut the snake into three pieces with his sword. But in doing so he cut off one of his brother's legs. The brother was very angry and got out of the snake's body. He thrust the leg that had been cut off into the girl's vagina. She died, but the leg stuck on to the boy again. But now when he tried to pull it out of the vagina he could not. So the younger brother cut open the belly of the girl and took out the leg, and they ran away together very sad, to find other wives. (Elwin, story 14, p. 443)

Here we find some very strange as well as disturbing motifs. The snake comes out of the woman's mouth when the older man is kissing her "as if she was a child." I presume this means that he was kissing her tenderly on the mouth: the implication here is that only an old man would be so besotted as to make the mistake of showing affection to a woman with whom he was copulating. Anyway, for this mistake and the sin of taking a bride that younger men could have enjoyed, he dies. So the elder son takes the girl and is (literally) swallowed up in the act of love. Next comes a Red Riding Hood episode where the younger brother cuts the snake up to get the older brother out of its body. Unfortunately, one of the blows amputates his brother's leg. Even worse, when the older brother gets out of the snake he uses the severed leg as if it was a penis and (in revenge?) rapes his wife with it. She dies. But the leg sticks in her vagina, a sort of *"penis captivus* by proxy," and simultaneously it reattaches itself to the rest of the boy's body. His leg thus traps him in the dead body of his wife, and he cannot get free of her. Another Red Riding Hood episode finishes the tale: this time, it is the girl's body that is chopped up to release the boy. What this story says about sexual relations in this culture is best not imagined.

A second story in which snakes, not teeth, feature as the principal danger of sex comes from Surguja State. This is particularly interesting in that it brings these legends of sexual danger within sight of Bosom Serpent traditions.

One night the wife of Mansingh Gond went out to excrete near an ant-hill. As she sat there the ground broke and a small snake came out and entered her vagina. In her belly it grew fat. Her husband thought her pregnant. So twelve months passed. One day she went with her husband to the bazaar. As she sat in a bania's shop, the snake poked its head out from under her sari. The bania saw it and knew what danger the husband was in. He bade him get a crowing cock, tie his wife's hands and feet to four staves, open her clothes and run away. "Tie the cock near and when it crows the snake will come out and you can save your wife and yourself." All happened as the wise bania had said. This is a true story. (Elwin, story 16, p. 443)

All the usual elements of Bosom Serpent legends are here. A snake secretly enters into the body of a careless person, takes up residence, grows fat (in this case, as in many later Western legends, being mistaken for a pregnancy), and is forced out by a trick proposed by a wise man. The final comment, "This is a true story," marks it as a contemporary legend.

Elwin's article also includes an antilegend that suggests how and why such stories are told and shows the remedy. This story does not, of course, carry my argument further, but it seems fair to include it to redress the balance. It, too, comes from the Mandla District:

An old Baiga married a girl of only twelve years. He used to fondle her breasts and rub her cheek but that was all he could do. She consoled herself with a lover in the village. When the old man discovered this he took her away to another place. He called a Dewar [priest] and asked him to whisper a charm in the girl's ear. He was to say, "In this village every man has not one penis, but two, and if a girl goes to him her vagina bursts open." The girl was very frightened at hearing this, and the old Baiga also told the young men of the village that his wife had a tooth in her vagina which would cut off the penis of anyone who went to her. So for a long time the girl lived unsatisfied. Then one day by the well, she met a very handsome Baiga youth and they sat under a tree to talk. "I have heard," said the girl "that every man here has a double penis." "Well, I have only one," said the boy. "No, you must have two," said the girl. "No, I'll show you. But we all know you have a knife in your vagina and will cut off my penis if I give it to you." Then they began to laugh and they examined each other and when they saw there was no cause for fear they lay together. When the girl got home, the old man guessed

what had happened, and he declared that they would go to another
village where, he said, "the people copulate so violently that they
kill their wives." "We must certainly go there," said the girl. Next
day they set out. But it was very hot, and the old man died by the
way. The girl went back and married the handsome Baiga youth.
(Elwin, story 22, p. 445)

To continue with the subject of women with snakes in their
vaginas and to demonstrate that this gross idea is not confined to
the Indian subcontinent, we should add a few more examples
from elsewhere. There are several from which to choose. In his
well-known and useful book on *The Fear of Women* (1968), Wolfgang Lederer lists a number of cultures with traditions of heroes
being saved from dangerous maidens. In most cases, the dangers
involve one or several snakes or a dragon issuing from the maiden.
One such story comes from the Shuswap Indians: "The [hero] saw
a woman who cried and moaned: 'Who wants to sleep with me?'
Having placed in his mouth a leaf which he chewed, [he] went and
slept with her. He saw many human bones lying roundabout. All
men who had slept with her had died, because her intimate organs
were made of a serpent. . . . [H]e spat the leaf which he had chewed
on her organs and transformed them, saying 'From now on women
will no longer kill the men with whom they have sexual relations'"
(Lederer 48–49).[17] Similar stories have been reported from Bulgaria,
Serbia, Russia, Siberia, and Armenia and from Gypsy sources. In
Polynesia, where there are no snakes, voracious eels take their
place.[18]

Another example comes from fourteenth-century English traveler Sir John Mandeville's account of his journey to the East. In
one Indian island, ruled by the legendary Prester John, there is a
"first night" marriage custom. Specially employed men (with
nerves of steel) are engaged to spend the marriage night with new
brides. When Mandeville "asked them the cause, why that they

held such custom . . . they said to me, that of old time, men had been dead for deflowering of maidens, that had serpents in their bodies, that stung men upon their yards [penises], that they died anon: and therefore they held that custom, to make other men, ordained thereto, to lie with their wives, for dread of death, and to assay the passage by another, rather than for to put them in that aventure [risk]." [19]

Yet another variant appears in a collection of Irish Gaelic folktales. It forms an incident in the story of "The King of Ireland's Son" and appears to be linked to traditional fairy lore: "The couple were married then, and the short green man was to have the first kiss. The short green man took the wife with him into a chamber, and he began on her. She was full of serpents, and the King's son would have been killed with them when he went to sleep, but that the short green man picked them out of her" (Hyde 45).

Lamiae

> She dwells with beauty, beauty that must die
> And joy, whose hand is ever at his lips
> Bidding adieu. And aching pleasure nigh
> Turning to poison while the bee-mouth sips.

—KEATS, "ODE TO MELANCHOLY"

It is interesting to see how frequently creatures considered poisonous or polluting in biblical, classical, and medieval literature—toads, scorpions, spiders, snakes—not only are feared as potential invaders of the human body but also are associated with perilous sexual encounters. In Christian iconography, the serpent of Eden was often pictured with a woman's head: the concept of the serpentine woman, "the woman whose special relationship with a venomous animal makes her more fearful than either serpent or woman alone would be" (Hallissy 89) is an extension of this image.

One logical step further along the path that links women →
harm → poison → snakes therefore is the concept of the snake
woman. In these stories the snake is not *in* the woman, the snake
is the woman.

Such is the lamia of the classics, a shape-shifter who uses dangerous magic to appear irresistibly seductive. She seems to offer
wealth and comfort as well as beauty, but she is inimical to men.
Only a cold-eyed sage can see her real shape. Any man who marries her should be very afraid.

In his article, "The Holy Man and the Snake Woman," Nai-tung
Ting brings together a large body of stories on this theme (188–89,
190). In contrast to commentators, such as David Leinweber, who
have suggested that the lamia figure originated in Greek mythology and then developed into a kind of fairy tale figure to scare
children into good behavior, Ting traces the roots of this story
to "ancient beliefs and myths," possibly "a primitive ogre tale" ori-
ginating in Asian folklore. He suggests that it entered Western
folklore during the twelfth century; the story then developed in
two separate but ultimately related threads in the East and the
West (esp. 187–90). Pointing out that snake brides were a feature of
Chinese cultural traditions as early as the twelfth century, Ting
tells a lamia story that shares motifs with Bosom Serpent legends.
A holy man suspects that a woman living with the king is a lamia.
The holy man suggests a test: the woman is to be given very salty
food at dinner but not allowed to drink. At night he sees her resume
her serpent shape to search for water in a nearby lake (151–52).
Ting also discusses the well-known Chinese "Legend of the White
Serpent" as interpreted by the poet Feng Meng-lung (1574–1646).
Here the position of the snake woman is more ambiguous, as Ting
explains.

> The lamia allegedly loves both lust and human flesh, and her magic
> often gets her man into difficulties; but she also loves him dearly and

has not harmed any person. However she forbids him from asso-
ciating with . . . monks. . . . The holy man must therefore subdue
her. [Feng's] poem toward the end of the tale evidently contains
the moral:

> Let me advise you not to love beauty
> Or beauty will certainly turn your head . . .
> If I, the old monk, had not interfered,
> The snake would have eaten him up, flesh and bones.

> (173–74)

As in Feng's poem, the plots of lamia stories usually revolve
around the relationship of three protagonists—a husband; a supernatural, shape-shifting wife; and a holy man or philosopher who
discovers the wife's true identity and saves the husband from her.
This can be clearly seen in the story with which Ting's study
begins. It can be found in Philostratus's *Life of Apollonius*, apparently the earliest recorded version. A poor but handsome student,
Menippus the Lycian, is walking along a road when he meets an
attractive woman who claims that she has been secretly in love
with him for a long time. She invites him to her home, and he
goes along. Her home has every luxury. He falls in love and plans
to marry her, but she is a lamia who is fattening him up with
pleasures before devouring his body. Apollonius the philosopher
detects telltale signs that Menippus is "cherishing a serpent," so
he goes to the wedding and demands to see the bride. Apollonius
challenges her and makes every bit of the magical setting disap-
pear. She weeps and implores Apollonius not to expose her, but
he persists. She finally confesses what she really is and what she
has been planning, and Menippus is saved (Ting 158–59). Later
variants on this theme can be found in medieval works such as
the *Gesta Romanorum* and works by Walter Map, Gervase of
Tilbury, and Geraldus Cambrensis (Ting 161).

Some of these later versions show the influence of folktales of the "supernatural bride" type, especially the legend of Melusine. Melusine is a serpent from the waist down one day a week, though she can preserve a proper human shape for the other six days. Her husband, Raymond, is under strict instructions not to spy on her on the seventh day: he does so, of course, and loses her (see Hallissy 99–109). Such stories seem to me to be antilegends, lamia stories told from a woman's perspective, denouncing superstition, fear, and lack of trust. This (re)interpretation is more or less explicit in one of Mandeville's traveler's tales. On the faraway island of Lango, he writes, dwelled the daughter of Hippocrates, turned into a dragon by the goddess Diana. The girl must remain in this form until a knight comes along bold enough to kiss her on the mouth. The first young man fails the test; he runs away when she appears to him in dragon shape. The dragon pursues him and tosses him to his death from the top of a cliff. The next young man fares a little better; he enters a cave and sees a beautiful woman combing her hair and surrounded by treasure. If he wants to be her lover and claim the treasure, she says, he will first have to become a knight and then must have no fear of her whatever shape she assumes. She promises that she will do him no harm however frightful she appears, for underneath the horrifying veneer she will be just as he sees her now. He becomes a knight easily enough but then must decide whether to risk embracing a dragon: "But when he saw her come out of the cave, in the form of a dragon, so hideous and so horrible, he had so great a fear that he fled again to the ship; and she followed him. And when she saw that he turned not again, she began to cry as a thing that had much sorrow, and anon the knight died. And from that time to this might no man see her, but he died anon. But when there shall come a knight bold enough to kiss her, he shall turn the damsel into her right form and natural shape, and he shall be lord of the counties and isles abovesaid" (22).[20]

Perhaps the most famous literary redaction of snake woman legends incorporating a pro-lamia interpretation is John Keats's poem, "Lamia," published in 1820. According to a note Keats added to the poem, he found his version in Robert Burton's *The Anatomy of Melancholy* (1621) (165n). Burton, as quoted by Keats, drops all allusion to the lamia's intention of fattening and eating Menippus, so the philosopher's treatment of the theme is more sympathetic to the supernatural bride. Otherwise, nearly all the elements of the classical legend are there in Burton's and Keats's versions—the protagonist meets an entrancing woman who persuades him to go home with her and keeps him there by offering him all worldly pleasures; he decides to marry her and she provides, by magic, a wondrous feast; her identity is suspected by the philosopher Apollonius, who challenges her at the wedding feast; when named as a serpent, she disappears with a shriek and the magical feast and sumptuous furnishings go up in smoke. Keats follows this schema in plot but not in spirit. For him, the story is a tragedy. The defeat of Lamia does not represent a happy ending. Far from it. The moral of the story has been turned around. In Philostratus's version, the moral is "Listen to the voice of reason and beware the reptilian allurements of women." In Keats's rendering, it is "Keep your joy private and believe in magic lest cynics and rationalists destroy it." For Keats's hero, Lycius, everything starts falling apart when he remembers the world outside his private dream with Lamia; worst of all, he is vain and boastful enough to want to show his prize off in a public marriage ceremony. To that wedding, uninvited, comes his old teacher, the philosopher Apollonius (of course). One should remember here that philosophers were the scientists of the ancient world: Keats's distrust of "philosophers" should be read as a condemnation of science, rationalism, and materialism. A single cold analytical stare from Apollonius, and Lamia starts to change and dissolve; when he calls her a serpent, she disappears with a shriek, "And Lycius's arms were empty of delight/As were his limbs of life, from that same night."

For Keats, Apollonius, not Lamia, is the lie; Apollonius, not Lamia, is the serpent. A strange transformation occurs when the philosopher is killing Lamia with his baleful stare. As the magical feast fades under his cold eye, the guests feel a "horrid presence." Apollonius stares on, while Lycius beseeches the heavens to send down punishment for the philosopher's "impious, proud-hearted sophistries/Unlawful magic and enticing lies," and in a reversal of the snake imagery he calls on the guests to "Mark how, possessed, his lashless eyelids stretch/Around his demon eyes."

The moral of the story has, of course, already been told a few stanzas earlier:

> Do not all charms fly
> At the mere touch of cold philosophy?
> There was an awful rainbow once in Heaven:
> We know her woof, her texture; she is given
> In the dull catalogue of common things.
> Philosophy will clip an Angel's wings,
> Conquer all mysteries by rule and line,
> Empty the haunted air and gnomed mine—
> Unweave a rainbow, as it erstwhile made
> The tender-personed Lamia melt into a shade.

THE POISONOUS BRIDE

What the protagonists in all the male versions of these stories of snake brides have in common is that they fail to "read the label." The tales revolve round the misogynistic proposition that women are inherently a trap: if the woman is beautiful, the man may not escape intact; if she is also sexually generous, he may not even escape with his life.[21] The extravagant gifts the females offer are the "label" that shows they are deadly: honey will surely turn to poison, and the men should have known it. For Menippus, the warning signs were there for all to read—the woman was both beautiful and forward; she had access to magic and illusion; she offered her chosen man pleasure and luxury. The deal is just too good to be true. Unlike the deluded husband, Apollonius reads the label.

Chaucer's "Merchant's Tale" revolves around a similar proposition. The old man, Januarie, should have known better than to trust his young bride, May. She offered too much joy. As Margaret Hallissy says, "Having constructed an Eden, Januarie should have expected a serpent in it" (96). Mandeville's tale, too, is about labels, though the motif is stood on its head. Here, the young man is only too aware of the label and fails to see that it is not an accurate description of the contents of the package being offered. The bewitched girl's serpentine form labels her as evil and dangerous. But the label is misleading: in reality, she can bring beauty, wealth, and status to anyone brave enough and wise enough to ignore the label and believe her promises. Keats works on a similar proposition: though in Philostratus's tale, Apollonius saves the young man from certain death, in Keats's poem, he deprives him of certain joy.

In the next group of stories, the poisonous woman has no obvious label. The external signs offer few or no clues about the danger she poses except that she is a gift and she is beautiful.[22] It is generally agreed that the earliest accounts of the Poisonous Bride (or Poison Damsel or Poison Maiden) may be found in Indian tradition. The Vish-Kanyâ, Vish-Kanyakâ, Vish-may Kanyâ, or Vishanghâna was a familiar character in ancient Indian literature, a beautiful maiden so charged with poison that her look sometimes caused death.[23] Such maidens were supposedly sent as dancing girls to enemy countries to do all the damage possible.[24] There is a teasing reference to a maxim in the biblical work *Ecclesiasticus* (third century B.C. to third century A.D.) that may suggest an even older history: "Use not much the company of her that is a dancer and hearken not to her, lest thou perish by her charms."[25]

In his discussion of this tradition in ancient India and Persia, Jivanji Modi says that a story in the eleventh-century Indian collection *The Ocean of Story* tells how the king of Vatsa was persuaded by his chief minister to invade the territory of the king of Benares. When the king of Vatsa began his incursion, a series of traps were laid in his path. The chief minister of the king of Benares "tainted, by means of poison and other deleterious substances, the trees, flowering creepers, water and grass all along the line of the march. And he sent poison damsels as dancing girls among the enemy's host, and he also dispatched nocturnal assassins into their midst" (Modi 326).[26] Warned by spies, however, the invading army neutralized the poisons "at every step along the line of the march," and no strange women were allowed to enter their camp. Thus, they were saved.

The theme is also raised in a seventh-century A.D. political drama, *The Signet-Ring of Rakshasa*.[27] The story is set in the early 300s B.C. at the time of the formation of the Maurya Empire by Chandragupta, usually regarded as the first paramount sovereign or emperor of India, and relates the strategies employed by Chandragupta's wily and watchful chief minister, Chanakya, to thwart the many attempts on Chandragupta's life by his rival, King Nanda, and his minister, Rakshasa. The assassination attempts have included poisoned draughts, poisoned food, and nocturnal hit men (just like the strategies employed by the chief minister of the king of Benares), but most threatening of all is the gift of a beautiful girl.[28] This girl has been fed on poisons so that she is thoroughly imbued with venom and can kill with a touch. Chanakya discovers the plot, and the girl is passed on to another rival, Parvatarka.

In another early Indian version of the story, Chandragupta and Parvatarka (here called Parvata) seem to be allies and the killing of Parvata is almost accidental:

> Then Chandragupta and Parvata entered Nanda's palace and began to divide his great store of treasures. Now in the castle there lived a maiden who was cared for as if all treasures were combined in her. King Nanda had had her fed on poison from the time of her birth. Parvata was seized with such a passion for her that he locked her in his heart like his guardian deity. Chandragupta's teacher [Chanakya] gave her unto him, and he immediately began to celebrate the ceremony of taking hands. During this, however, poison was transferred to him through her, because their perspiration caused by the heat of the sacrificial fire, was mixed together. The strength of this poison caused Parvata great agony; all his limbs relaxed, and he said to Chandragupta: "I feel as if I had drunk poison; even speaking is well-nigh impossible. Help me, friend. I am surely going to die." Chanakya, however, advises Chandragupta to let him die, as then he will have the entire treasure to himself. Thus the king of the Himalayan mountain died, and Chandragupta became ruler of two mighty kingdoms.[29]

The best-known Poisonous Bride story concerns Alexander the Great and appears in a Latin-language work of the twelfth century, the *Secretum Secretorum*. Norman Penzer traces the history of this work at some length (*Poison* 18–22). All that need be said here is that it purports to be secret communications between the philosopher Aristotle and Alexander the Great but probably isn't; it was very popular and became the most widely read work of the Middle Ages and contributed more to Aristotle's reputation than any of his fully authenticated writings; it was translated into nearly every European language, including Spanish, Italian, Provençal, Dutch, French, and English. The story about Alexander spread so widely throughout Europe principally because it appeared in the *Gesta Romanorum*, a famous and very popular medieval collection of stories gathered together by monks as fireside recreation and used in their sermons.[30]

The stories that interest us come in a part of the *Secretum Secretorum* where Aristotle advises Alexander on matters of health and conduct. In his well-known consideration of the Poison Damsel theme, Penzer quotes two versions from the *Secretum Secretorum*, the first from the Hebrew translation, the second (slightly different) from the Arabic. I use the Hebrew translation here. Aristotle is warning Alexander not to entrust the care of his body to women and to beware in particular of poisons. Like stories of lamiae, these tales of poisonous brides have a three-character plot featuring deceiver, deceived, and undeceiver; only the undeceiver can "read the label": "Remember what happened when the King of India sent thee rich gifts, and among them the beautiful maiden whom they had fed on poison until she was of the nature of a snake, and had I not perceived it because of my fear, for I feared the clever men of those countries and their craft, and I had not found by proof that she would be killing thee by her embrace and by her perspiration, she would surely have killed thee." In the Arabic version, Aristotle says that the woman would have been capable of inflicting a poisonous bite, and in another manuscript he says, "she surely would have killed thee by her touch and by her perspiration" (Penzer, *Poison* 22–23).

Penzer presents a number of later versions of the legend in Spanish, German, French, Latin, and English. The sixteenth-century French version, "Pucelle Venimeuse" (the venomous virgin), from *Le Cuer de Philosophie* by Antoine Vérard, is one of three later redactions of a fourteenth-century work.

A certain king was once informed by a soothsayer that a child, Alexander, had just been born who was destined to be his downfall. On hearing this disconcerting news, the king thought of an ingenious

way in which to get rid of the menace, and gave secret orders for
several infant girls of good family to be nourished on deadly poison.
They all died except one, who grew to be a beautiful maiden and
learnt to play the harp, but she was so poisonous that she polluted
the air with her breath, and all animals which came near her died.

Once the king was besieged by a powerful army, and he sent this
maiden by night into the enemy's camp to play the harp before their
king. She was accompanied by two others, who were, however, not
poisonous. The king, struck by her beauty, invited her to his tent.
As soon as he kissed her he fell dead to the ground, and the same fate
overtook many of his followers who gathered round her on the same
evening. At this juncture the besieged army made a sortie and easily
overcame the enemy, who were demoralized by the death of their
leader.

Delighted with the success of his experiment, the king ordered
the damsel to be even better cared for, and nourished with even
purer poison than hitherto.

Meanwhile Alexander, grown to manhood, had started his campaigns, besieged and conquered Darius, and made his name feared
throughout the world.

Then the king, anxious to put his long-conceived plan into execution, had five maidens beautifully attired, the fifth being the poisoned damsel, more lovely and more richly clad than the rest; these
he sent to Alexander, ostensibly as a mark of his love and obedience,
accompanied by five attendants with fine horses and rare jewels.
When Alexander saw the lovely harpist, he could scarce contain
himself, and immediately rushed to embrace her. But Aristotle, a
wise and learned man of the court, and Socrates, the king's tutor,
recognized the poisonous nature of the maiden and would not let
Alexander touch her. To prove this, Socrates ordered two slaves to
kiss the damsel, and they immediately fell dead. Horses and dogs
which she touched died instantly. Then Alexander had her beheaded
and the body burnt. (Penzer, *Poison* 24–25)

This folktale-like story begins with a typical folklore feature, the soothsayer's warning. Then the now-familiar plot is elaborated by doubling everything up. There is a prequel in which the maiden's power to kill is demonstrated on an enemy other than Alexander. There are two famous philosophers as Alexander's wise protectors, and there are two slaves on which to test their theory. The methods by which the maiden can kill are also doubled up—her breath kills as well as her kiss.

In the Poisonous Bride stories quoted so far, we have seen six ways in which the beautiful girl can kill—by her bite, touch, perspiration, embrace, breath, and kiss. Penzer's long and learned discussion includes three more ways the poison is transferred from bride to victim—the poisonous glance, intercourse, and venereal disease (*Poison* 28–71). Modi summarizes the nature of the poison damsel as represented in Indian and Iranian tradition as follows:

1. In the "ordinary sense of the word," the term can apply to any young woman who deceitfully harms somebody else.
2. She is born under "an inauspicious configuration or conjugation of planets. So she does harm to anyone who marries her."
3. She is in some way so poisoned or infected with disease that anyone who comes into close contact with her will die. "A woman infected with venereal disease is a poison-damsel of this kind."
4. Her body has been saturated with gradual doses of a poison that can convey itself to another person's body by contact with her.
5. She is "a damsel who treacherously captivates the heart of a person, and then actively gives him some poison, in food or drink" (328).

This is a personal reading of the traditions and to some extent is influenced by Modi's desire to include Iranian traditions about "Susan the Songstress" in the Poison Damsel story type. (Susan was a beautiful and fatal mass poisoner who single-handedly decimated the followers and descendants of famous Persian leader, Rustum.)

However, because of its generality and inclusiveness, Modi's list highlights the misogynistic fears that underlie stories of poisoned damsels. Women, it seems, can be capable of killing men accidentally, on purpose, or as the agents of a third person. The victim can be a husband, a lover, a stranger, or a chance contact, and death may be accomplished by disease or poison or astrology. No one is safe. It is not just poisoned sex men need fear; it is the poisonous sex.

THE POISONOUS SEX

Traditions of sexual poison are fed by a deep current of misogyny derived from epics, classics, the Judeo-Christian scriptures, the works of the Christian fathers, and European medieval monkish culture.[31] In this twisted thought-world, women are not only the root of all evil but the evil itself. Their representatives are Eve, who brought sorrow into the world by eating the apple of knowledge; Pandora, who loosed evil, sickness, and death on the world by opening a casket that should have been kept closed; Harmonia, whose poisoned robe infected mankind with crime and impiety;[32] and "Frau Welt" (Mrs. World), represented as a woman with a lovely face but a putrefied back.[33]

According to the Talmud, even God could not make women sinless:

When God was on the point of making Eve, He said: "I will not make her from the head of man, lest she carry her head high in arrogant pride; not from the eye, lest she be wanton-eyed; not from the ear lest she be an eavesdropper; not from the neck lest she be insolent; not from the mouth lest she be a tattler; not from the heart lest she be inclined to envy; not from the hand lest she be a meddler; not from the foot lest she be a gadabout. I will form her from a chaste portion of the body." And to every limb and organ as he formed it, God said: "Be chaste! Be chaste!" Nevertheless, in spite of the great caution used, woman has all the faults God tried to obviate. . . .

It is told that when Adam awakened from the profound sleep into which he had been plunged and saw Eve before him in all her surprising beauty and grace, he exclaimed, "This is she who caused my heart to throb many a night!" Yet he discerned at once what the nature of woman was. (quoted in Lederer 75)

Many thinkers have been only too ready to say what that nature truly is. Gilgamesh, the great hero of Sumerian and Babylonian epic poetry, was certainly not deceived. When Ishtar tried to seduce him, he replied,

Lady, you speak of giving me riches, but you would demand far more in return. The food and clothing you would need would be such as befits a goddess; the house would have to be fit for a queen, and your robes of the finest weave. And why should I give you all this? You are but a draughty door, a palace tottering to its ruin, a turban which fails to cover the head, pitch that defiles the hand, a bottle that leaks, a shoe that pinches. Have you ever kept faith with a lover? Have you ever been true to your troth? . . . He who comes to you preened like a jaybird ends with broken wings! Him who comes to you like a lion, perfect in strength, you ensnare in pits sevenfold! Him who comes on a charger, glorious in battle, you drive for miles with spur and lash, and then give him muddied water to drink! Him who comes like a shepherd tending his flock you turn into a ravening wolf, scourged by his own companions and bitten by his own dogs! (quoted in Lederer 75–76)

Christian fathers and sixteenth-century reformers also "knew" the true nature of women. Tertullian (A.D. 155–222), whose theological works are the earliest important Christian writings in Latin, wrote in his *De Cultu Feminarum*, "[D]o you not know that you are Eve? God's sentence still hangs over all your sex and this punishment weighs down upon you. You are the devil's gateway, you are she who first violated the forbidden tree and broke the law of God" (quoted in Du Bois 43). The imagery of rape here is remarkable: Eve "violated" the forbidden tree, she is the devil's gateway, the means by which the devil can force himself into men.

Tertullian's opinion was approvingly quoted by Scottish Protestant reformer John Knox (1505–72) in *First Blast of the Trumpet against the Monstrous Regiment of Women*, his bitter polemic against female monarchs, written in 1557 when he was in exile, and printed in 1558. To his version of Tertullian's words, Knox adds the accusation that Eve "diddest persuade and easely deceive" Adam, "whom the devil durst not assault," and that it was thus her fault that "it behoved the son of God to suffre the death" (19). In passing, Knox throws out the opinion that women have "naturall weaknes and inordinat appetites" and have on occasion "murthered the children of their owne sonnes. Yea, and some have killed with crueltie their owne husbandes and children" (14).

All this is part and parcel of a focused attack on women and sex by Christian clerics in Europe in the Middle Ages and the sixteenth century.[34] Medieval preachers seemed to have hated pretty much everything that brings pleasure and ease—sex, the adornment of the body, domestic comfort.[35] For example, Robert Rypon believed that men and women who dress to please each other are, in the eyes of God, "more shameful and foul than the foulest corpses or dunghills," and John Bromyard stated that beds where lovers retire to make love are "the devil's bolster" and "his couch that he resteth him on." In sermons, women are called "an insatiable beast, a continuous anxiety, and incessant warfare, a house of tempest, and hindrance to devotion"; the "snares and traps" that the devil uses to destroy men; "a sow that rolls in the dirt"; "the devil's pack horses"; the devil's "gins and fowling nets"; "weapons of the devil with which the souls of men are slain"; and "the painted tombstone that conceals a rotting corpse" (Owst 378, 386, 393, 395, 402, 392, 396). Perhaps the most ingenious metaphor, however, is the one in which women are compared to decorated chimney stacks: "They ornament their heads like a chimney-top with garlands, crowns and gems set therein; nevertheless, nothing comes forth but foul smoke and temptation to lechery" (Owst 392) Most interesting of all is John Bromyard's polemic against women, who, he contends, dress in finery and go out on the town, thereby inflaming the passions of twenty men (!) and damning the men's souls to hell: "*for this very purpose* the devil thus adorns these females, *sending them forth* through the town" (Owst 395; emphasis added). It seems to me that there are shades of deadly dancing girls and poison damsels here.

Almost universally it is women's love of dress that most provokes these dour puritans and paranoiacs. As so often in the stories we have been looking at, clothing is part of the sin, an inducement to or metaphor for the sexual act: says Tertullian, "If our faith here below were on the scale of the wages awaiting it in heaven, not one of you, my dear sisters, once she had come to know God and her own condition—I am speaking of her condition as a woman—would be hot after pleasure and finery. Rather would she wear rags and mourning, weep and show an Eve plunged in penance. . . . All this baggage, encumbering a woman already dead and sentenced, adds up to hardly more than the trappings of her funeral procession" (quoted in Du Bois 43).

Of course, not only men of religion suffered from this frightening (and frightened?) misogyny. Medical men also "knew" what women really were. For example, in a celebrated treatise, medieval physician Arnold of Villanova (1235–1312) announced, "In this book I propose, with God's help, to consider diseases of women; since women are poisonous creatures, I shall then treat of the bites of venomous beasts" (quoted in Guthrie 113).

English poet Algernon Swinburne (1837–1909) shared this view if his long poem "Dolores" is anything to go by (1:154–68). It is striking how vividly and constantly Swinburne's outpourings evoke (for the folklorist at least) legends of snake women and poisonous brides. The poem begins,

> Cold eyelids that hide like a jewel
>> Hard eyes that grow soft for an hour
> The heavy white limbs, and the cruel
>> Red mouth like a venomous flower;
> When these are gone by with their glories,
>> What shall rest of thee then, what remain,
> O mystic and sombre Dolores,
>> Our Lady of Pain!

For fifty-four stanzas, Swinburne develops the theme hinted at in the last line of the first verse, "Our Lady of Pain." Dolores ("daughter of pain and Priapus") is depicted as monstrously lustful, heartless, destructive, devouring, and promiscuous. Any man who kisses her will "in a trice" exchange "the lilies and languors of virtue/For the raptures and roses of vice." The poem is puzzling: it is hard to tell whether the piece is addressed to a real woman or to women as a whole or whether it is about the sexual act. Furthermore, the poem's subtitle, "Notre Dame des Sept Douleurs" (which, when translated as "Our Lady of Seven Sorrows" rather than "Seven Pains," could refer to the Virgin Mary), perhaps indicates that the work may also be some sort of an indictment of religion or the Church. Be that as it may, the imagery and the underlying hatred of sex and women is unmistakable—images of monstrosity, death, and poison proliferate, as do images of feeding, stinging, and biting and snake allusions.

> O lips full of lust and of laughter
>> Curled snakes that are fed from my breast (stanza 4)

> There have been and there yet shall be sorrows
>> That smite not and bite not in play (stanza 5)

> *As our kisses relax and redouble*
>   *From the lips and the foam and the fangs (stanza 12)*
>
> *The pleasure that winces and stings (stanza 14)*
>
> *The foam of the serpentine tongue*
>   *The froth of the serpents of pleasure (stanza 17)*
>
> *I could hurt thee, but pain would delight thee*
>   *Or caress thee—but love would repel*
>
> *And the lovers whose lips would excite thee*
>   *Are serpents in hell (stanza 49)*

And what about stanza 8? All the familiar scared and scary imagery of death and devouring, pain and poison, is here:

> *Fruits fail and love dies and time ranges*
>   *Thou art fed with perpetual breath*
> *And alive after infinite changes*
>   *And fresh from the kisses of death*
> *Of langours rekindled and rallied*
>   *Of barren delights and unclean*
> *Things monstrous and fruitless, a pallid*
>   *And poisonous queen.*

The key to such fear and misogyny may lie in the traditional division of labor between the sexes, which leaves men powerless in vital areas of their lives. In many cultures, past and present, men do exactly what Aristotle warned Alexander not to do—they entrust the care of their bodies to women. By leaving domestic affairs to women while they get on with war and politics they make themselves dependent on women for food, clothing, and lodging. Women's role as food provider has always allowed the possibility of deliberate or accidental poisoning. In the past, women's role as clothing provider allowed another way for poison to be administered to the unwitting. If sex, too, can be poisoned, then men are helpless before women—bed, board, and clothing may all be potentially lethal. These dangers are explored in the stories we have looked at because the facts of domestic life made them possible. To adapt a commonplace, just as the mountaineer replied to the question "Why climb Everest?" with the rejoinder, "Because it's there," so anyone who asks a poet or storyteller why he tells tales of women poisoning men might answer, "Because they can."

CONCLUSION

By tracking these various manifestations of the poison theme, I am not suggesting that they are related to each other in the narrow sense of a continuous transmission chain or historical succession. Rather, continuity of theme links them. To use a metaphor from the title of the Indian tale collection I have mentioned, *The Ocean of Story* (or, more literally and for our purposes more revealingly, *The Ocean of Streams of Story*), it is like the sea. The sea constantly gives rise to and nourishes a variety of life forms; it is deep and always moving, ever changing yet always the same, lapping on the shores of many lands peopled by men and women of varied cultures and experiences. The processes that sustain(ed) these varied stories can be thought of as such an ocean, itself fed by Indo-European cultural traditions.

The stories in this chapter are identifiable by their concern with skin-to-skin contact. This contact may be direct or indirect. Direct contact is via sex, indirect via beautiful clothing (so often the symbol of sex). The first gives us the more blatant stories about poisonous sex, poisonous brides, and snake women. The second gives us the less direct Indian and classical stories about poisoned garments where the contact is between the protagonist's bare skin and an offered "second skin," the costly robe. Indirect contact also gives modern poisoned dress stories, where the contact is between the victim's skin and a previous victim's second skin, the secondhand dress. In all cases, the engine of the plot, that which turns promise into disaster and transmutes beauty into burning, is the gift. The Indian *khilats* are enforced gifts, and the modern poisoned dresses are gifts from the dead, since the beautiful gown could not have been acquired without the death of the first wearer. The Indian snake women offer limitless sex, and the lamiae's gifts to their lovers are sex, beauty, comfort, and wealth. It is the gift that has the power to seduce, and the gift that has the power to betray those who accept it trustingly. Because it may be contaminated by lust or greed or hate or revenge, the gift may transform sex into suffering and life into death.

This skin → gift → death (sex → gift → suffering) transmutation theme might be imagined as the core of a circle of motifs (heat, poison, perspiration, flammability, disease) and related thematic elements (treachery, betrayal, infidelity, revenge, pollution, vice, and power). In any one story, the transmutation core may connect to any of the surrounding motifs and elements, and all of these may also be interconnected. So a typical modern story will link the transmutation theme to flammability and poison, with hints at treachery on the part of a clothing store or funeral director. The story of Nessus's shirt links the same core to treachery, infidelity, revenge, and flammability. The story of the queen of Ganore links this core to pollution, betrayal, and flammability; stories about poisonous brides link it to treachery and power. In all of these tales, the nature of the sought-after skin-to-skin contact is transformed because mediated by an ambiguous gift. Good is turned into ill, honey is turned into poison, and someone has to die.

NOTES

1. See, for example, Kapferer, "Consommation"; Kapferer, "Mass"; Langlois; Fine and Johnson (and discussions of this essay by Mechling and Langlois 160–61).

2. See, for example, Kapferer, "Persuasiveness"; Campion-Vincent and Renard 195–205. A full-scale inquiry into a French scare about drug-laced tattoos was undertaken by students at a French *lycée*; a report of their work was published by their professor (Hadjian). The English scare was followed in the folklore magazine *Dear Mr Thoms . . .* in 1990–91. See also a series of items in *FOAFtale News* from 1989 following the "Blue Star Acid" scare and the "Mickey Mouse LSD" scare; see esp. Schmidt; Ellis; see also "More on Mickey Mouse LSD"; "Re. Mickey Mouse LSD Rumour."

3. See Klintberg, "Modern"; Bregenhøj. See also Horgan, which suggests that the "mysterious disease that has taken at least 16 lives in the Four Corners region of the Southwest since this past May" may be related to the U.S. biological warfare program. See also Loewenberg; Nkpa.

4. See Mayor, "Nessus"; P. Turner. See also Philps, which reported that the wife of Palestinian leader Yasser Arafat had "used the opportunity of Hillary Clinton's visit to Ramallah on November 11 [1999] to accuse Israel of using poison gas against Palestinian women and children, contaminating the water supply and causing a host of birth defects."

5. "Poisoned Dress" 1945; reprinted in Brunvand, *Choking* 112–13.

6. Two more versions with the "white satin dress" motif appear in Botkin, *Sidewalks*, 524; Schwartz 65–66.

7. This links the legend to rumors of "smallpox blankets," as Mayor notes ("Nessus").

8. See also motif D1402.5, "Magic Shirt Burns Wearer Up."

9. In "The Nessus Shirt," Mayor links the legend to stories about "smallpox blankets"; in "Fiery Finery," she attempts to discover the nature of the poison that burns but cannot be quenched with water (naphtha, sulfur, and lime are the favorites). Maskiell and Mayor, "Killer Khilats," pts. 1 and 2, looks at Indian legends of poisoned "robes of honor."

10. A similar motif may be found in Arthurian legend, when Arthur's wicked half-sister, Morgan le Fay, sends him a mantle intended to burn him alive.

11. The principal source for the discussion that follows is Maskiell and Mayor, "Killer Khilats" pts. 1 and 2. A brief treatment of these stories may also be found in Penzer, *Poison* 9–10.

12. Maskiell and Mayor, "Killer Khilats," pt. 1, 32; Maskiell and Mayor, "Killer Khilats," pt. 2, 170.

13. Maskiell and Mayor, "Killer Khilats," pt. 1, 35; Maskiell and Mayor, "Killer Khilats," pt. 2, 173–74.

14. And see the following item from the Snopes Web page dealing with the poisoned dress (www.Snopes.com/horrors/poison/dress.htm): "Sightings: In 1998 's *Elizabeth*, a poisoned dress meant for Queen Elizabeth 1 kills one of her ladies in waiting instead; Fox's "Beyond Belief' TV program (30 June

2000) claimed this tale was true (based on 'published reports'); and an
episode of *The Drew Carey Show* ('The Joining of Two Unlikely Elements
Is a Mixture,' aired 27 September 1995) featured an embalming fluid–soaked
wedding dress."

15. See, for example, Hallissy 111–16; Lederer esp. 44–52; Du Bois 45, 47.

16. Gershon Legman, the doyen of erotic folklore, devotes twenty-eight pages of
his classic text, *The Horn Book*, to jokes and legends about biting vaginas, and
further references may also be found in Legman's sequels, *No Laughing Matter*
and *The Rationale of the Dirty Joke*. In this chapter I will not be dealing with
folklore and legends about castration, of which there are a huge number.
Again, the best sources for this folklore include Legman, *Horn Book*; Legman,
No Laughing; Legman, *Rationale*. See also Glazer; Gulzow and Mitchell.

17. The "transformation" of the woman's sexual organs worries me: can this be
a reference to clitoridectomy?

18. Lederer 49 quoting Beckwith 29.

19. Lederer 47–48 quoting Penzer quoting Mandeville. This story appears in the
1839 edition of Mandeville's *Travels* but is absent from the 1895 and
1905 editions. It also appears in Hallissy 98.

20. A very slightly different version may be found in Hallissy 97.

21. Indeed, in some cultures there are or have been legends about women who
can kill merely through their insatiable sexual appetite. Famed anthropologist
Bronislaw Malinowski has recorded one such legend from the Trobriand
Islands. Here the story is that on one island all the women are very beautiful
and go about naked. When sailors get shipwrecked there, the women line up en
masse on the beach, ready to throw themselves on the men: "the women do
violence to the men. . . . They never leave them alone. . . . When one has fin-
ished, another comes along. When they cannot have intercourse, they use the
man's nose, his ears, his fingers, his toes—the man dies" (quoted in Lederer 55).

22. The classic study of this motif is Penzer, *Poison*. Other considerations can
be found in works devoted to literary redactions of poison and plague
legends; see especially Barbara Fass Leavy's discussion of Nathaniel
Hawthorne's short story "Rappaccini's Daughter," Margaret Hallissy's discussion of the same story, and her consideration of Oliver Wendell Holmes's
short story "Elsie Venner." Briefer discussions appear in Elwin and Lederer.
A useful discussion of the plague metaphor can be found in Sontag.

23. Elwin 447; Modi 327.

24. Elwin 447; Penzer, *Poison* 12–16.

25. Quoted by medieval Dominican preacher John Bromyard in a sermon; see
Owst 395.

26. Modi is quoting from C. H. Tawney's translation, originally published in
1880. In 1924, Penzer published a ten-volume edition from Tawney's

translation, and this story appears in the appendix to volume 2 (Penzer, *Ocean*). See also Sattar.

27. The translations come from Dhruva 5. The play can now most easily be found in Coulson.

28. Vishâkhadatta's *The Signet-Ring of Rakshasa* (Mudrâ Râkshasa) was a Sanskrit drama in seven acts. The text may be found in Dhruva 5, with the translation on 6.

29. Penzer, *Poison* 16–17, quoting from Johannes Hertel's *Ausgewählte Erzählungen aus Hemacandras Parisistaparvan* (Leipzig 1909).

30. The Poisonous Bride story is no. 11 in Wright. Here it is simply related that the "Queen of the North" nourished her daughter on poison and sent her to Alexander as a gift. This simple outline has a Christian moral imposed on it in which the envenomed beauty symbolizes a soul poisoned by gluttony and luxury. See also Penzer, *Poison* 27.

31. Owst gives a chilling account of medieval preachers' criticism of women and sexually active people of either sex (chap. 7).

32. Brewer 528; see also Mayor, "Fiery."

33. A portrayal of Frau Welt may be found in cathedral carvings at Worms and Nuremburg in Germany. From the front, "Mrs. World" seems to be smiling, clean, comely, and attractively dressed; at the back her clothing is stripped off to show her body crawling with toads and snakes.

34. Du Bois's exploration of the imagery of women's bodies in Spenser's "Faerie Queen" (1590) has a useful section on clerical misogyny, a theme that is also treated in Prusak. See also Lawless.

35. See Owst, chap. 7. The principal preachers Owst studies are the Dominican John Bromyard, Friar Waldeby of Yorkshire, and Robert Rypon of Durham, a contemporary of Geoffrey Chaucer. Incidentally, Chaucer (c. 1340–1400) put together his famous *Canterbury Tales* in c. 1387, and it is interesting to note that in the first printed edition (1476) somebody has scribbled in the margin next to "The Wife of Bath's Tale," "A woman is less pitiful [that is, less given to pity] than a man, more envious than a serpent and more malicious than tyrant, more deceitful than the devil" (Ezard).

KEY TEXTS

Elwin, Verrier. "The Vagina Dentata Legend." *British Journal of Medical Psychology* 19 (1943): 439–53.

Hallissy, Margaret. *Venomous Woman: Fear of the Female in Literature.* New York: Greenwood, 1987.

Hartikka, H. D. "Tales Collected from Indiana University Students." *Hoosier Folklore* 5 (1946): 71–82.

Himelick, Raymond. "Classical Versions of 'The Poisoned Garment.' " *Hoosier Folklore* 5 (1946): 83–84.

Hochsinger, Gloria. "More about the Poisoned Dress." *Hoosier Folklore Bulletin* 4 (1945): 32–34.

Lederer, Wolfgang. *The Fear of Women.* New York: Grune and Stratton, 1968.

Maskiell, Michelle, and Adrienne Mayor. "Killer Khilats, Part 1: Legends of Poisoned 'Robes of Honour' in India." *Folklore* 112 (2001): 23–46.

Mayor, Adrienne. "Fiery Finery." *Archaeology,* March–April 1997, 55–58.

Penzer, N. M. *Poison-Damsels and Other Essays in Folklore and Anthropology.* London: Sawyer, 1952.

"The Poisoned Dress." *Hoosier Folklore Bulletin* 4 (1945): 19–20.

Ting, Nai-tung. "The Holy Man and the Snake Woman: A Study of a Lamia Story in Asian and European Literature." *Fabula* 8 (1966): 148–91.

REFERENCES CITED

Baker, Ronald L. *Hoosier Folk Legends.* Bloomington: Indiana University Press, 1982.

Botkin, B. A., ed. *Sidewalks of America: Folklore, Legends, Sagas, Traditions, Customs, Songs, Stories, and Sayings of City Folk.* Indianapolis: Bobbs-Merrill, 1954.

Bregenhøj, Carsten. "Terrorism, Oranges, and Folklegends." *Tradisjon* 8 (1978): 65–78.

Brewer, E. Cobham. *Dictionary of Phrase and Fable.* 1870; Ware, Hertfordshire: Wordsworth Editions, 1993.

Brunvand, Jan Harold. *The Choking Doberman and Other "New" Urban Legends.* New York and London: Norton, 1984.

———. *The Mexican Pet.* New York: Norton, 1986.

Campion-Vincent, Véronique, and Jean-Bruno Renard. *Légendes Urbaines: Rumeurs d'Aujourd'hui.* Paris: Payot, 1992.

Cerf, Bennett. *Try and Stop Me: A Collection of Anecdotes and Stories, Mostly Humorous.* New York: Simon and Schuster, 1944.

Coulson, Michael. *Three Sanskrit Plays.* Harmondsworth: Penguin Classica, 1981.

Dhruva, K. H., ed. and trans. *Mudrâ Râkshasa; or, The Signet Ring: A Sanskrit Drama in Seven Acts by Vishâkhadatta.* 2d ed. Poona: Oriental Book-Supplying Agency, 1923.

Du Bois, Page Ann. " 'The Devil's Gateway': Women's Bodies and the Earthly Paradise." *Women's Studies* 7 (1980): 43–58.

Ellis, Bill. "Mickey Mouse LSD Tattoos: A Study in Emergence." *FOAFtale News* 14 (June 1989): 3–4.

Elwin, Verrier. "The Vagina Dentata Legend." *British Journal of Medical Psychology* 19 (1943): 439–53.

Ezard, John. "Chaucer's Tales Go Online Complete with Old Graffiti." *The Guardian* (London and Manchester), 25 October 2003, 7.

Fine, Gary Alan, and Bruce Noel Johnson. "The Promiscuous Cheerleader: An Adolescent Male Belief Legend." *Western Folklore* 39 (1980): 120–29.

Glazer, Mark. "The Superglue Revenge: A Psychocultural Analysis." In *Monsters with Iron Teeth*, ed. Gillian Bennett and Paul Smith, 139–46. Perspectives on Contemporary Legend 3. Sheffield: Sheffield Academic Press, 1988.

Gulzow, Monte, and Carol Mitchell. " 'Vagina Dentata' and 'Incurable Venereal Disease': Legends of the Viet Nam War." *Western Folklore* 39 (1980): 306–16.

Guthrie, Douglas. *A History of Medicine*. London: Nelson, 1945.

Hadjian, Joseph. "Le Syndrome de la Rumeur: Des Lycéens de Pierrelatte Enquêtent." *Documents pour l'Enseignement Économique et Social* 78–79 (December 1989–March 1990): 165–67.

Hallissy, Margaret. *Venomous Woman: Fear of the Female in Literature*. New York: Greenwood, 1987.

Hartikka, H. D. "Tales Collected from Indiana University Students." *Hoosier Folklore* 5 (1946): 71–82.

Himelick, Raymond. "Classical Versions of 'The Poisoned Garment.' " *Hoosier Folklore* 5 (1946): 83–84.

Hochsinger, Gloria. "More about the Poisoned Dress." *Hoosier Folklore Bulletin* 4 (1945): 32–34.

Horgan, John. "Were Four Corners Victims Biowar Casualties?" *Scientific American* 269 (November 1993): 16.

Hyde, Douglas. *Beside the Fire: A Collection of Irish Gaelic Folk Stories*. London: David Nutt for the Folk-Lore Society, 1890.

Kapferer, Jean-Noël. "Consommation: Le Cas de la Rumeur de Villejuif." *Revue Français de Gestion* (March–April–May 1985): 87–93.

———. "A Mass Poisoning Rumor in Europe." *Public Opinion Quarterly* 53 (1989): 467–81.

———. "The Persuasiveness of an Urban Legend: The Case of 'Mickey Mouse Acid.' " *Contemporary Legend* 3 (1993): 85–102.

Keats, John. *Poems*. Ed. Gerald Bullet. Intro. Robert Gittings. London: Dent (Everyman), 1974.

Klintberg, Bengt af. "Modern Migratory Legends in Oral Tradition and Daily Papers." *ARV* 37 (1981): 153–60.

Knox, John. *The First Blast of the Trumpet against the Monstrous Regiment of Women. 1558.* Ed. Edward Arber. English Scholar's Library of Old and Modern Works 2. London: n.p., 1878.

Langlois, Janet. " 'Hold the Mayo': Purity and Danger in an AIDS Legend." *Contemporary Legend* 1 (1991): 153–72.

Lawless, Elaine. "Women as Abject: Resisting Cultural and Religious Myths That Condone Violence against Women." *Western Folklore* 62 (Fall 2003): 237–69.

Leavy, Barbara Fass. *To Blight with Plague: Studies in a Literary Theme.* New York: New York University Press, 1992.

Lederer, Wolfgang. *The Fear of Women.* New York: Grune and Stratton, 1968.

Legman, Gershon. *The Horn Book: Studies in Erotic Folklore and Bibliography.* New York: University Books/Cape, 1964.

———. *No Laughing Matter: Rationale of the Dirty Joke, Second Series.* New York: Breaking Point, 1975.

———. *Rationale of the Dirty Joke: An Analysis of Sexual Humor.* New York: Grove, 1968.

Leinweber, David Walter. "Witchcraft and Lamiae in 'The Golden Ass.' " *Folklore* 105 (1994): 77–82.

Loewenberg, Richard D. "Rumors of Mass Poisoning in Times of Crisis." *Journal of Criminal Psychopathology* 5 (1943): 131–42.

Maskiell, Michelle, and Adrienne Mayor. "Killer Khilats, Part 1 : Legends of Poisoned 'Robes of Honour' in India." *Folklore* 112 (2001): 23–46.

———. "Killer Khilats, Part 2 : Imperial Collecting of Poison Dress Legends in India." *Folklore* 112 (2001): 163–82.

Maundeville, Sir John. *Voyages and Travels of Sir John Maundeville, Kt.* Intro. Henry Morley. London: Cassell, 1905.

Mayor, Adrienne. "Fiery Finery." *Archaeology,* March–April 1997, 55–58.

———. "The Nessus Shirt in the New World." *Journal of American Folklore* 108 (1995): 54–77.

Mechling, Jay. "Children's Folklore." In *Folk Groups and Folk Genres,* ed. Elliott Oring, 91–120. Logan: Utah State University Press, 1986.

Modi, Jivanji Jamshedji. "The Vish-Kanyâ or Poison Damsels of Ancient India, Illustrated by the Story of Susan Râmashgar in the Persian Burzo-Nâmeh." *Folk-Lore* 28 (1927): 324–37.

"More on Mickey Mouse LSD." *FOAFtale News* 15 (September 1989): 6.

Nkpa, Nwokocha K. U. "Rumors of Mass Poisoning in Biafra." *Public Opinion Quarterly* 41 (1977): 332–46.

Owst, G. R. *Literature and Pulpit in Medieval England.* Rev. ed. Oxford: Blackwell, 1961.

Penzer, N. M., ed. *The Ocean of Story: Being C. H. Tawney's Translation of Somadeva's Kathâ Sarit Sâgara. Now Edited, with an Introduction, Fresh*

Explanatory Notes, and Terminal Essay, by N. M. Penzer. 10 vols. London: Sawyer, 1924–28.

———. *Poison-Damsels and Other Essays in Folklore and Anthropology.* London: Sawyer, 1952.

Philps, Alan. "Arafat Rebukes Wife for Hurting Hillary Election." *Daily Telegraph* (London), 25 November 1999, 3.

"The Poisoned Dress." *Hoosier Folklore Bulletin* 4 (1945): 19–20.

Prusak, Bernard P. "Woman: Seductive Siren and Source of Sin? Pseudepigraphical Myth and Christian Origins." In *Religion and Sexism: Images of Women in the Jewish and Christian Traditions,* ed. Rosemary Radford, 89–116. New York: Simon and Schuster, 1974.

Reaver, J. Russell. " 'Embalmed Alive': A Developing Urban Ghost Tale." *New York Folklore Quarterly* 8 (1952): 217–20.

"Re Mickey Mouse LSD Rumour." *FOAFtale News* 13 (March 1989): 5.

Sattar, Arshia, trans. and intro. *Tales from the Kathâsaritsâgara.* London: Penguin, 1996.

Schmidt, Sigrid. "*Bild* and the Mickey Mouse LSD Rumour." *FOAFtale News* 16 (December 1989): 1–4.

Schwartz, Alvin. *Scary Stories to Tell in the Dark Collected from American Folklore.* New York: Lippincott, 1981.

Smith, Paul. *The Book of Nastier Legends.* London: Routledge and Kegan Paul, 1986.

Sontag, Susan. *AIDS and Its Metaphors.* New York: Farrar, Straus, and Giroux, 1989.

Swinburne, Algernon Charles. *Collected Works.* 2 vols. London: Heineman, 1927–35.

Thompson, C. J. S. *Poison Mysteries in History, Romance, and Crime.* London: Scientific Press, 1923.

Ting, Nai-tung. "The Holy Man and the Snake Woman: A Study of a Lamia Story in Asian and European Literature." *Fabula* 8 (1966): 148–91.

Turner, Patricia A. "Church's Fried Chicken and the Klan: A Rhetorical Analysis of Rumor in the Black Community." *Western Folklore* 46 (1987): 294–306.

Wright, Thomas, ed. *Gesta Romanorum.* Trans. Charles Swan. 2 vols. New York: Boulton, 1871.

AIDS AGGRESSORS

MIRRORS, CASKETS, AND NEEDLES

We have no natural or acquired immunity against panic.

ROY PORTER, "PLAGUE AND PANIC"

Swinburne's Dolores was accused of eating him alive but not of infecting him with syphilis, typhoid, cholera, plague, or AIDS. Yet infection with disease, either accidentally or deliberately, has been one way tradition has decreed that women can kill men (or more rarely, men kill women). Michelle Maskiell and Adrienne Mayor, for example, suggested that the Indian contaminated garments they studied worked in three ways, through disease as well as poison and fire. They quote a poisoned robe story that closely resembles one of the legends we shall look at in this chapter: "A grim story is told of Safdar Jang, Nawab of Oudh [Awadh] between 1739 and 1754, who, when he was building the town of Faizabad, received a robe of honour from the Emperor of Delhi. When he opened the box he found an image of Mari Bhavani (the godling of cholera or plague), and became so alarmed that he abandoned the site" (36).

In her solo articles "Fiery Finery" and "The Nessus Shirt in the New World," Mayor links poisoned garments to biological warfare via smallpox-impregnated blankets, and in Norman Penzer's and Jivanji Modi's discussions of the Poison Damsel, venereal disease is listed as one of the ways she kills. In this chapter I shall look at a complex of rumors and legends that tell how strangers may attack one and pass on a potent biological poison in the shape of a feared disease, the scourge of the late twentieth and early twenty-first centuries. I think of this complex as the "AIDS Aggressor" legend.

In the form in which the AIDS Aggressor legend was first reported, it was current in the gay community of San Francisco in June 1982, only a year after the condition had first been identified. In his celebrated documentation of the AIDS epidemic in 1980s America, *And the Band Played On* (1987), Randy Shilts reports that "it was around this time that rumors began on Castro Street about a strange guy at the Eighth and Howard bath house, a blond with a French accent. He would have sex with you, turn up the lights in the cubicle, and point out his Kaposi's sarcoma lesions. 'I've got gay cancer,' he'd say. 'I'm going to die and so are you'" (165).

By 1986–87, rumors and stories were circulating on both sides of the Atlantic about HIV-infected gays who were deliberately spreading (or threatening to spread) the virus among the straight as well as gay population. For example, the following article was published in a British tabloid, *The Daily Star*, on 2 September 1986:

Putting the Bite of Fear on You

A young man of our acquaintance has suffered the most nightmarish of attacks outside a seamy Edinburgh nightclub known to be frequented by all manner of persons of a homosexual inclination. Our chum's superficial wounds, one fears, could yet turn out to be of a quite fatal nature.

As our friend walked past the establishment, a bearded and extremely agitated drunk came tottering out of the premises and grabbed him by the hand.

"Have you got AIDS, dearie?" he asked.

"No, no, I haven't," replied our startled acquaintance.

His attacker seized his arm and sank his teeth into it.

"Well—you have now!" he said. And ran off. (Smith, "Rumour" 100)

Similar rumors became affixed to known people, stars such as Rock Hudson. In addition to jokes such as "Question: Where do you get AIDS? Answer: Up the Hudson," there were articles in newspapers such as this one from the 2 August 1987 issue of the British Sunday tabloid *News of the World*:

Cold-hearted Rock Hudson deliberately French-kissed Dynasty beauty Linda Evans when he knew he was dying of AIDS.

The evil star even had open sores on his mouth when the steamy actress was being filmed. And he bragged afterwards; "Great! I gave her a big wet one."

Hudson's callous trick has been revealed by his former lover, Marc Christian, 29, in an interview with an American magazine. (quoted in Smith, " 'AIDS' " 118)

In Sheffield, United Kingdom, Paul Smith received a call from a local journalist working on a story about "male homosexual prostitutes who had deliberately given AIDS to their procurers and clients." Soon after, in 1986, a member of the Police Committee of the Lothian region of Scotland was reported as having said, "I've heard of rent boys who can infect a hundred or more people in a year. It's a lethal weapon they're carrying in their bodies and it's being allowed to run free" (Smith, "Rumour" 101).

By 1987, however, a narrative with a stronger, more legendlike structure and a number of traditional motifs had begun to circulate.

This one featured a woman as the AIDS aggressor and a hetero-sexual male as her victim. According to Jan Brunvand, this story had begun "sweeping the [United States] in 1986 and was dubbed 'AIDS Mary' that year by Dan Sheridan writing in the *Chicago Sun Times*" (*Encyclopedia* 6–7). The same story had also been reported in *USA Today* on 22 October 1986: "Novelist Jackie Collins . . . shared what she said was a true story on Joan Rivers' show. A married Hollywood husband picked up a beautiful woman at a bar. They enjoyed a night of passion at a good hotel; in the morning he rolled over to find a sweet thank you note. Class, he thought, real class. Then he walked into the bathroom and found, scrawled on the mirror in lipstick, "Welcome to the wonderful world of AIDS." Not knowing if the woman had been kidding or not, he didn't dare have sex with his wife, and it could be a long time before he'd know whether he had become an AIDS victim" (quoted in Bird 46). A similar story appeared in the *San Francisco Examiner* in January 1987. This time, the incident was said to have happened to a French businessman who spent a weekend with a Jamaican woman (Brunvand, *Curses* 196).

By early 1987, the story was well known throughout Western Europe and North America. Smith reported that he heard it first in February 1987 from the same local journalist, who called to say that the tale was being told all over Sheffield. The following week, a sensational tabloid newspaper reported that "A British industrialist visiting Miami hired a lady of the streets to keep him company for the night on his stop-over. The following morning when he woke, his companion had gone. On entering the bathroom—so the legend goes—he found the following horrific message scrawled in lipstick on his mirror: 'Welcome to the AIDS club.' "[1] The story was featured in Jan Brunvand's syndicated urban legend column in March, August, and September 1987. It popped up in the Ann Landers column; it was quoted by evangelist Billy Graham on television; it was "the hottest story going in

Toronto"; it was heard in a Welsh hospital and reported in newspapers from many American states as well as from Austria and Sweden. It even appeared in *Playboy* in July of that year.[2] In April an article in the magazine *The Face* spoke about "AIDS terrorists" and warned that "our cosy Western ideas about the disease itself must also change as we face the virus." Story summaries followed: "A city whizz-kid meets a beautiful woman and spends the night with her. A few days later, a bunch of flowers arrives with this message: 'WELCOME TO THE AIDS-TEAM.' Or: A friend of a friend picks a woman up. In the morning she's gone, but a message in lipstick on the bathroom mirror tells him, 'WELCOME TO THE WORLD OF AIDS.' Has it happened to a friend of yours yet?" (Smith, "'AIDS'" 114). The story was rife in Poland too. Dionizjusz Czubala reported in *FOAFtale News* in 1992 that he had recorded the following dialogue from two students at the University of Silesia. The first student says, "I have a couple of friends in those circles, so I heard that a lot of them are sick. They all got the virus from a girl that had come from Warsaw. She slept around with a few guys from Katowice. And she got paid with dope. When she was leaving, she told them jokingly about her disease. Quite possible she did this on purpose." This is plainly a rumor: it's vague and unspecific, there are several people involved, and instead of a punch line there is speculation about motives. Interestingly, the second student responds immediately by "legendizing" her friend's account, supplying the summary of a recognizable legend and so updating and "correcting" the first account: "I heard a similar story. A girl slept with a guy and did not ask for money: instead she left a farewell message on the mirror. When the boy woke up, he read 'Welcome to the AIDS club'" (3).

In time, this version of the legend began to fade from public consciousness and to evolve into another form. Brunvand dubbed the new version "AIDS Harry" because it features a male perpetrator. But I prefer to name the two versions according to the way the final message is delivered, so I think of the earlier story as the mirror version and the later one as the casket version. The casket version seems to have been first spotted in 1989. In Canada, Diane Goldstein reported that in April of that year she saw an article in the *Newfoundland Evening Telegram* headed "Bizarre AIDS story likely a concocted tale." The *Telegram* item was very brief, but Goldstein quotes a fuller and more typical version from about the same time:

> This girl needed a break and decided to go to Florida for a month or two holiday, I think. While she was there she met a man, who seemed to be . . . the man of her dreams. He had money, he treated her like gold and he gave her everything she wanted. She fell in love with him and . . . during her last night there they slept together. The next day he brought her to the airport for her return to St John's. He gave her a small giftwrapped box and told her not to open it until she got home. They . . . said goodbye and she left hoping that someday they would be married and the gift would be an [engagement] ring. The suspense was killing her and . . . she decided to open the gift on the plane. It was a small coffin with a piece of paper saying "Welcome To The World of AIDS." ("Welcome" 24)

This version flourished for another five years or so. The casket was sometimes said to contain just the note or sometimes a toy skeleton; sometimes the "casket" was a miniature coffin, or in some versions—thanks to the "telephone game" effect of oral tradition—a coffeemaker or coffee mug. In a sense, these versions are more "traditional" than the mirror versions, evoking as they do older stories such as Pandora's box. They also recall "poisoned robe" legends from the classics—the Nessus shirt, for example, was kept in an "airtight container," and the robe with which Medea poisoned Glauke was kept in a "sealed casket."

As far as I know, the casket version last appeared in 1990, when *FOAFtale News*, the newsletter of the Society for Contemporary

Legend Research, reported that "A British AIDS counselor warned that infected playboys at Spanish resorts had formed a cult devoted to giving the disease to vacationing girls. He said that in two cases British girls, after a holiday affair in Spain, were given little farewell gifts to carry with them on the plane home. The packages contained a small wooden coffin inscribed with 'Welcome to the death club. Now you've got AIDS.' The two girls are said to be undergoing three months of testing to see if they have in fact caught the disease."[3]

It is interesting to see how, typically of contemporary legends, the locale and some of the details have been updated in this version. The scene is now set in Spain, which for British people is the equivalent of Florida in terms of somewhere to go for relief from the climate; in a reference to other concerns of the time, the Spanish "playboys" are said to have formed a "cult"; and the message has been made more dramatic by the addition of some very inaccurate misinformation.

Both mirror and casket versions of AIDS Aggressor legends recently have been largely replaced by narratives that revert to a simpler, vaguer, more rumorlike form. These stories had begun to circulate in a limited way as early as the end of the 1980s but really took off ten years later. Since the early 1980s, the rumor mill in the United States had been busy with stories about HIV-positive cooks masturbating into fast food and so infecting their customers.[4] In Poland, where AIDS paranoia was rife, Czubala reported that people were supposedly being deliberately infected through food and drink. A high school student recorded in October 1989 told Czubala that "There was a drug addict who learned he had AIDS, so he threw a party for his friends and treated them to some soup in which he had mixed some of his blood. In this way he infected 30 people out of sheer revenge for being ill himself" (2). Tales also circulated about rapelike attacks on young girls by disgruntled carriers: "Among teenagers, stories circulate about carriers who hang out in discos to assault unsuspecting victims in secluded spots. Two of them hold a girl's hands, while the third kisses her on the mouth and passes on the virus with his saliva. Rumor has it that hundreds of 14-year-olds have been infected in this way" (2).

In true rumor-panic style, the Polish stories often focused on "madmen" and threats to children. In May 1990 a student at the University of Silesia told Czubala that a colleague from Bielsko had said that "There is a huge concentration of infected people there. They are terribly aggressive. . . . [I]t is like a vacationland that attracts infected visitors, and the city becomes really dangerous. Last year they supposedly became so aggressive that they were going after people with their needles, especially children." In the same month another student from the same university told Czubala, "I was also told that in Sosnowiec, there is a madman infected with HIV. Everybody is afraid of him because he gets on the tramway and gives the needle to girls, especially the very young ones. Supposedly he's infected dozens so far. Mothers are afraid to let their children play in the street because the madman could come by" (4).

A considerable media frenzy and public panic was initiated in Britain and Ireland in September 1995 when an Irish priest claimed in a sermon that a "promiscuous, tattooed, HIV positive blonde" had been "marauding through Dungarvan near Cork, liberally spreading sexual favours among the village's young men and knowingly infecting up to 80 of them. The girl, 25, who had recently arrived in the village from London, is reported to be 'demented' by her condition."[5] The priest should have read the signs that this was a legend—80 sexual partners in six months? "demented"? "promiscuous, tattooed," and "blonde"? recently arrived from London?—surely not! But he *had* taken it seriously, and for this misjudgment he suffered a week of mockery and media attention and was reprimanded by his bishop. Days later, however, the priest was still insisting that he was "110% sure" the story was true.[6]

An earlier well-known case that also proved to be an illusion was the hoax perpetrated on the magazine *Ebony* and a Dallas talk show in September 1991. A fifteen-year-old girl from Dallas, Texas, calling herself "C.J." wrote to *Ebony* claiming that, after contracting AIDS, she had become obsessed with picking men up in nightclubs in order to pass the HIV virus on. Her letter concluded, "I feel if I have to die of a horrible disease, I won't go alone." A woman who identified herself as C.J. later appeared on a local talk show and reaffirmed that she had been haunting nightclubs in the Dallas–Fort Worth area picking men up and having unprotected sex with them. She showed no remorse, saying, "I blame it on men, period. Not just one. I'm doing it to all the men because it was a man that gave it to me."[7] The whole episode was later found to be a fraud: both the "C.J." who wrote to *Ebony* and the woman who claimed to be "C.J." on the talk show were hoaxers.[8] Though both C.J.s were exposed as frauds, the Dallas deputy police chief was not reassured: "Our attitude is that there is no C.J. as purported to be. However, there are lots of C.J.s out there, either knowingly or unintentionally spreading HIV."[9]

And some sick, malicious, or misguided people indeed acted out the legends in their own lives. Among several cases brought to court was one that Brunvand spotted in 1990 in the *Cincinnati Post*:

"AIDS Mary" Murder

When Jeffrey Hengehold came up for trial in Cincinnati, Ohio, for murdering Linda Hoberg on 25 August 1990, his attorney asked that the charges be reduced. Hengehold had picked up Ms. Hoberg at a bar, had sex with her, then as they parted, the woman had allegedly said to him "Welcome to the world of AIDS." "I felt dead," the sobbing

Hengebold testified. "I didn't understand how a person could do that to somebody else. I lost all self-control. I started hitting her." . . .

Prosecutors countered that the defendant was either making up the story, or that the woman had made the remark as a joke. The presiding judge found him guilty, and he was given 17 years to life.[10]

In Britain, a similar sort of accusation in the summer of 1992 failed to come to court because of legal difficulties.[11] In July 1996 a fifteen-year-old in Edinburgh was stabbed in the face with a blood-filled syringe by a man who claimed to be HIV positive (Baldwin and Hardy), and in March 1997 a heroin addict who was said to have "threatened a baby with AIDS" was jailed for five years ("Five Years"). In 1997 a court in Cyprus jailed a man for transmitting the HIV virus to his partner (Baldwin and Hardy). In 1998 a British newspaper, *The Guardian*, reported that "Mass AIDS tests are being carried out on soldiers at Catterick Garrison in North Yorkshire following fears that two women have been infecting soldiers with the HIV virus" ("Yorkshire AIDS Marys"). In a landmark case, a Somali man living in Surrey in the United Kingdom was found guilty in October 2003 of causing "biological" grievous bodily harm after infecting two women with HIV; a little less than a year later, another man was successfully prosecuted for the same offense.[12] Even more shocking, in 2003 an Illinois man was convicted of injecting his son with HIV-tainted blood, hoping that the child would die and he would thus avoid paying child support (Kettle). In May 2004 British newspapers reported that six foreign health workers had been executed in Libya for supposedly infecting four hundred children with AIDS. Forty-three children died (Popham).

The legend was making its way into film and television, too. It featured, for example, in an episode of the popular British police drama *The Bill* on 12 August 1999. The plot line centered on a man who wrote "Join the Club" on prostitutes' backs and, after using their services, told them, "I have AIDS and now you do too." In this way it echoes the story told by Randy Shilts, but the action is transferred from the gay scene in San Francisco to the underworld of London. One of the interesting things about this episode of *The Bill* was the way it used its legend-based plot to explore legal issues such as the difficulty of proving intention to transmit disease and problems in identifying whether the attacker actually has the disease or is maliciously using the legend to provoke anxiety.

Throughout this period, notices circulated on the Internet warning people against contaminated needles left by drug users in public telephones. A typical notice read, in part, "Drug users are now taking their used needles and putting them into the coin return slots in public telephones. People are putting their fingers in to recover coins . . . are getting stuck with these needles and infected with hepatitis, HIV and other diseases." Oral stories and e-mail messages began to proliferate, warning of infected needles in cinema seats and soda machine coin slots and on the underside of the handles of gas pumps. In the cinema seat form, in 1999 the rumor was reported from Canada, the United States, Germany, Finland, the United Kingdom, Australia, India, Hawaii, Mexico, and Costa Rica.[13]

In their latest book, *De Source Sûre* (2002), Véronique Campion-Vincent and Jean-Bruno Renard describe a rumor-panic outbreak in France about HIV-infected needles in cinemas (234–39). The story was rampant from the end of February to the end of March 2001. A message circulating on the Internet and by e-mail warned people to be extremely careful and to undertake a "minute visual inspection" of seats in public places. The rumor originally circulated in French-speaking Canada; when it reached Paris, it jammed the Ministry of Culture's telecom network for forty-eight hours. A similar panic had broken out in Estonia at the end of 2000 and beginning of 2001. Here it was not just cinema seats which were to be feared. Stories proliferated about deliberately contaminated doorknobs, light switches, and sandboxes on play-grounds. "People were terrified of getting infected at the mani-curist, at the dentist, at the tattoo salon etc," a correspondent to *FOAFtale News* wrote. "At the peak of this mass hysteria stories about all kinds of unusual ways of getting the infection (kissing, staying in the same room, swimming in the same pool with an HIV-positive person, getting bitten by a mosquito etc.) began to circulate. A story about a maniac who deliberately walked round infecting people in Narva spread all round Estonia" (Kalmre).[14] Then, in November 2002, it was reported that the cinema form of the needle legend had resurfaced in Delhi, India, and Melbourne, Australia, after lying dormant for four years. The denouement of the Indian story featured a rather idiosyncratic message: "Welcome to the world of HIV and family" (Sircar). *yikes! (wonder what that was & where?*

Coin slots, gas pumps, and cinemas were not the only places redefined as sites of danger. Stories circulated about people hav-ing infected stickers put on their arms while dancing (recalling earlier scares about drug-laced "tattoos") or being attacked with infected needles while in nightclubs.[15] The earliest appearance of this nightclub motif, as far as I am aware, occurred during February 1987, at the height of AIDS panic in Britain. A freelance journalist told Paul Smith that "a group of friends in a disco in Germany were attacked by a gang of youths who stabbed them with hypodermic needles containing contaminated blood" (Smith, "Rumour" 102). A full eleven years later, stories of night-club attacks were still circulating. In February 1998, for example, a nightclub version was reported from Worthing, a town on the south coast of England predominantly populated by retired people but with a small (and resented) nightclub scene. In this version the clubbers were said to have been pricked with needles while dancing, and telltale notes were left in their purses or coats in the cloakroom.[16] Next door to Worthing is the spa town of Brighton, which has a large student population. An e-mail warning focusing

on fears of needle attacks in Brighton's streets and clubs also circulated that year:

> This could be life or death for somebody. There are these gangs
> running round Britain sticking HIV-infected needles into people then
> handing them a card reading "Welcome to the world of HIV." This is
> not a joke or an urban myth, it's actually happened to somebody Fi
> (the woman whose email I'm using) knows. They've been seen in
> Brighton and Crawley, and last night they were active in The
> Gallery. So you can see why I'm more than a little anxious about
> this. Any of us could have been in The Gallery last night, and most
> of us were planning to go. The idea of this happening to anybody I
> know gives me the shits, hence the warning. . . . These people don't
> just operate in clubs, they operate on the street, while you're
> shopping, anywhere, so being paranoid probably isn't the answer.
> But please, take care. This IS happening and I couldn't take it if it
> happened to you. (Emery)

Nightclub versions were also reported from the coastal town of
Plymouth in southwest England, where the denouement was
"a voice" shouting, "Welcome to the AIDS Club!"[17]

And so it goes on.

SOME PRECURSORS AND PARALLELS

All this rumor and legend activity—and, indeed, the themes and
motifs themselves—are not new. Legends seldom are "new" in any
strict sense of the word, however contemporary they seem: most
often they are reworkings of older themes, motifs, and plots, reactivated by being dressed in modern clothing, adapted to new contexts, and combined in new ways. These stories are no exception.
Even though the first legend we recognize as the AIDS Aggressor
type can be accurately dated to the early 1980s, a little research

shows that very similar stories had been circulating in earlier epidemics and/or about other frightening diseases (syphilis, plague,
typhoid, cholera, and leprosy).[18] I don't propose to dwell on these
analogues and precursors, but I mention them briefly before passing on to discuss the ways collectors, reporters, and scholars have
interpreted the AIDS Aggressor group of legends and rumors.

Probably the earliest similar legend is a story from the medieval
story compilation *Gesta Romanorum*.[19] It is a very complicated tale
about two neighbors who have no respect for the Tenth Command-
ment: one covets his neighbor's land, the other covets his neighbor's
wife. So two men reach an agreement where the wife is given for sex
in exchange for the land. Out of spitefulness, because his own wife
is ugly and he cannot bear that another man should have a beautiful
wife, the neighbor infects the woman with leprosy and sends her
home to her husband. To cure the leprosy, the wife is advised to pass
it on in the same way she acquired it: she has to stand on the street
corner and offer sex to any willing passer-by.[20] So there she stands—
a literal mantrap—and shortly attracts and infects the king's son.
The denouement of this complex story tells how the king's son is
cured and is a typical Bosom Serpent story. So it is full of interest for
folklorists, linking backward to Poisonous Bride stories and forward
to AIDS Aggressors, taking in Bosom Serpent stories and the folklore of cure by transference on the way.

This medieval story is similar in theme but lacks the plot
structure and punch line of the modern AIDS Aggressor tale. But
a later story that has all the characteristics of the modern story
appears in Daniel Defoe's *Journal of the Plague Year*, written in
1722 but purporting to be an eyewitness account of the 1665 plague
of London. Defoe tells how a plague-ridden man assaulted a woman
in the street, saying that "he had the plague and why should she
not have it as well as he?" (181).[21] I think we can take it that this
was a legend current in the plague of London, since Defoe's
supposedly eyewitness account was patched together from hearsay

and reminiscence almost fifty years after the events and has all the hallmarks of oral tradition. (Defoe was probably only five years old when the plague devastated London.) A virtually identical story also appears in Albert Camus's *The Plague* (1947): "a man with all the symptoms [of plague] and running a high fever . . . dashed out into the street, flung himself on the first woman he met, and embraced her, yelling that he'd 'got it.'" Camus may have read this story in Defoe's *Journal* when he was researching for his own novel, but he may have perhaps come across it independently in another source. He certainly is aware of its nature as legend; the man who repeats this story to the narrator is said to be "a mine of stories of this kind, true or false, about the epidemic" (68). There is a later analogue in the work of another French writer, Guy de Maupassant (1850–93). Jan Brunvand, who has pointed out the resemblance of this story to AIDS Aggressor legends, remarks that "it is possible that [Maupassant] based the plot on a legend of his time." The story, "Bed 29," is set during the Franco-Prussian War and tells how the beautiful mistress of a French officer contracts syphilis but lets her condition go unreported and untreated so that she can spread the disease to as many Prussian officers as possible. "On her deathbed," says Brunvand, "she rebukes her disapproving French lover, saying, 'I have killed more than you'" (*Curses* 198).

Lacking the punch line but in other respects similar are further examples from seventeenth-century Europe. It would seem, for example, that there were rumors about people deliberately spreading infection during the devastating outbreak of plague in the Duchy of Milan in 1630. In his great novel *I Promessi Sposi* (The Betrothed) published in 1827, Alessandro Manzoni has a long episode in which his hero is caught in Milan at this terrible time. In this part of the novel, which Manzoni based on historical accounts, much is made of violent and persistent fears about "anointers," people who supposedly went about smearing the doorknobs of houses with a potion that caused plague. Similarly, English diarist Samuel Pepys (1633–1703) recounts how during the plague of London, "bold people"—presumably sick as well as bold—went to burials and deliberately breathed in the faces of healthy passers-by (quoted in Smith, "Rumour" 116).

Nearer our own time, stories about people who deliberately infect others with disease have turned up as comic tales, jokes, and photocopy lore. Paul Smith has found such a story in J. Mortimer Hall's *Anecdota Americana* (1927). Here, a man goes to a brothel and demands a girl with venereal disease. After various discussions, one of the girls calls the madam and says, "Tell him I've got clap. . . . Why shouldn't I make the money?" So this is done. The punch line is just as one would suspect: the girl simpers and says "I fooled you, mister, I ain't got any clap," and the man replies "Oh yes, you have."[22] A similar but much wittier and more convoluted tale appears in Vance Randolph's posthumously published collection of erotic stories, *Pissing in the Snow*. A visitor to town makes straight for the brothel and asks to be infected with the clap. The long unrolling of the denouement consists of a list of people whom he hopes will be infected in turn, ending with the preacher who expelled him from Sunday school.[23] Smith quotes this story in both of his 1990 essays on AIDS folklore: he also quotes from a February 1987 joke sheet put together by high school students in Doncaster in the United Kingdom. The traditional ballad of Robin Hood is subverted so that Maid Marian sleeps with each of the Merry Men. Maid Marian then announces that all the Merry Men now have the pox, to which they retort that now she has AIDS (Smith, "Rumour" 114). A final comparison should perhaps also be drawn to GIs' stories about deliberate infection with incurable venereal disease circulated among U.S. forces during the Vietnam War (Gulzow and Mitchell; Ivey).

Needle legends also have earlier analogues, as Diane Goldstein points out in her analysis of these stories ("Banishing"). A very early analogue comes from second-century Rome and relates to "persons who made a business of smearing needles with poison and then pricking whomsoever they would." Two mid-twentieth-century examples come from a 1938 rumor-panic in Halifax in the United Kingdom, during which anonymous assailants were believed to be randomly cutting women with razors, and from 1940s Louisiana, where it was believed that "needle men" were walking the streets injecting people to take them to the Charity Hospital for medical experiments (cited in Goldstein, "Banishing").

AIDS AGGRESSORS: APPROACHES AND INTERPRETATIONS

Some Theories

Interpretations of this legend-and-rumor complex have naturally varied according to which version has been current. Only one overarching approach can be made to suit all variants—that is, the standard "legend as warning" interpretation. Thus, both mirror and casket variants are often seen as a warning against carelessness in sexual encounters and needle variants as advising caution in practically everything. I have never been convinced by the "cautionary tale" approach. I find it just too slick. It can be—and usually is—applied to more or less any contemporary legend regardless of teller and context, and though, like so many overarching explanations, it can be made to fit almost anything, it fails to recognize the diversity of real-life storytelling and storytellers' individual motivations for telling stories.

Of course, I will not deny that sometimes it *is* framed as a cautionary tale. When the editor of *Ebony* decided to print the letter from "C.J.," he did it "as a warning to readers" (Bird 45), and, of course, the majority of e-mail versions such as the one circulating in Brighton and those on Internet Web sites have been circulated or presented quite explicitly as cautionary tales. However, I would argue that this is often no more than a convention of the medium. Warnings are a really popular form of on-line communication; journalists, too, love a story with a moral as well as a shock. It is thus no surprise to find that contemporary legends in the mass media are often framed as warnings. But to apply this interpretive framework to every telling as if a legend was a unitary and static entity will not do. As Linda Dégh once pointed out, a legend is the sum of numerous individual legend tellings ("Belief"); it follows that tellers will have their own interpretations of its meaning and will have different motivations for passing it on.

A similar but subtler approach is to see the legends as punitive embodiments of conservative attitudes toward sex, especially promiscuous sex and above all homosexual sex. (Congressman William Dannemeyer was supposed to have said during an October 1985 debate on homosexual rights, "God's plan for man was for Adam and Eve not Adam and Steve" [quoted in Treichler 47].) There is no doubt that AIDS has been perceived as God's or Nature's revenge against sex outside of monogamous heterosexual relationships. Similar beliefs were current during outbreaks of plague. Boccaccio's introduction to the *Decameron* (stories told by people who fled Florence to escape the Italian plague of 1348) asserts as much: "Some say that [the plague] is descended upon the human race through the influence of the heavenly bodies, others that it was punishment signifying God's righteous anger at our iniquitous way of life." Daniel Defoe had similar thoughts about the plague of London in 1665: "Doubtless the visitation itself is a stroke from Heaven upon a city, or country, or nation where it falls, a messenger of [God's] vengeance, and a loud call to that nation or country or city to humiliation [that is, humility] and repentance" (Smith, " 'AIDS' " 133–34).

Sexually transmitted diseases (STDs) in particular have been seen as the weapon of God's vengeance. Referring to Allan Brandt's social history of venereal disease, Sander Gilman observes that since the nineteenth century, venereal disease has been seen as "an affliction of those who wilfully violated the moral code . . . a punishment for sexual irresponsibility" (91). Sexual contact is of course one of the ways of contracting HIV, and conservatives often focus on this aspect of the condition.

From this perspective, AIDS legends can easily be seen as "Heaven-sent folklore" (to quote the title of an article by Michael Goss). "It comes as a shock," says Goss, "to realize that the integral relationship between moral and physical corruption, between spiritual sickness and the material kind, is believed in just as strongly today" as in times past. Yet this is what AIDS legends seem to demonstrate. They seem "to promote a strangely archaic vision where divinely-inflicted disease is dealt out as a punishment for human laxity. . . . The gods are just and of our pleasant vices make instruments to plague us; we've had that message before and often" (6–7). He ironically adds, "AIDS lore supports the status quo; the old, secure moral order which applied before free-thinkers came along and complicated everything" (10).

Most contemporary legend researchers regard mirror and casket forms of AIDS Aggressor legends as embodiments of this sort of attitude. Commenting on mirror versions, Elizabeth Bird, for example, says, "In legend the man she infects is usually married, or at least seeking illicit sex (in earlier variants the woman is often a prostitute). She is, then, the embodiment of the just reward—like many legends she demonstrates that immoral behavior will be punished horribly and disproportionately" (50). Similarly, Gary Fine says that the legend "warns against the dangers of impersonal sexual activity, behavior once taken for granted but now seen as threatening" (6). Developing this hypothesis, Fine later suggests that the story also embodies women's revenge against men's sexual crimes: it is "the crime of rape turned on its head. . . . It is about sexual promiscuity but it is *also* about sexual violence in the urban village" (6).

This sort of approach is more interesting but remains pretty predictable. In my opinion, the best work on AIDS legends is both more specific and more imaginative. Among this work I should mention Paul Smith's two 1990 essays, which situate legends in the "cultural complex" to which they belong. Thus he presents not only legends and folktales but also jokes and graffiti, child lore, popular fallacies, conspiracy theories on the origins of AIDS, political comment, rumor, and literary parallels. A similar inclusive look at AIDS legends appears in Dionizjusz Czubala's study of "Polish legends about HIV-infected people." It likewise examines a whole complex of legend, belief, and behavior: stories about the isolation of AIDS sufferers; stories about conspiracies, special hospitals, or hospital wards; stories about businesses or medical practices closed down because of HIV-infected workers; stories about prostitutes and students and children and foreigners and friends-of-a-friend and drug addicts and "madmen"; reports on public reaction to the crisis; and general misinformation about and hostility toward people suspected of having AIDS.

A second insightful approach has involved examining legends within a given community and linking legend transmission to culture, behavior, and social norms. Diane Goldstein does this in her essay "Welcome to the Mainland: Welcome to the World of AIDS." In this essay, she seeks to account for what seems a puzzling thing— why mirror versions of AIDS Aggressor legends failed to interest Newfoundlanders but casket versions spread like wildfire. She reports that in 1988, very few Newfoundlanders knew the mirror version; by 1989, however, she was able to collect more than five hundred versions, with casket versions outnumbering mirror versions by about three to one. By 1991, only three of her students had heard the mirror version but seventy-two knew the casket version.

In the rest of the essay, Goldstein contextualizes the casket version in Newfoundland culture and geography to analyze why the mirror version doesn't work for Newfoundlanders but the casket version does. Her answers include: mirror versions demand an anonymous attacker, but nobody is anonymous in a lightly populated island such as Newfoundland; shifting the action to Florida works because it is a location beyond the protective barrier of the sea; a version with a girl victim—an innocent and otherwise virginal girl at that—works better in light of Newfoundland girls' sexual norms than versions where the woman is a sexually active predator. She concludes that the casket story is "as much about the dangers of the world outside the island, as it is about AIDS" ("Welcome" 28).

A third way of looking at these stories may be seen in a fascinating conference paper given at the 1992 annual conference of the International Communication Association that examined just one term used in AIDS lore. Using concepts drawn from Turner 1984 and Payne and Risch 1968, Ivan Emke argues that disease is a (sociopolitical) language and deconstructs the concept of the "carrier." The notion of carriers relies on a concept of disease as an entity that can be harbored and passed on, he says. Carriers are thought of as having access to a repository of infection: they are "a euphemism for 'guilty.'" In this way, HIV in physical bodies serves as a metaphor for PWAs [people with AIDS] in the social body.

Finally, the work of one commentator on the AIDS crisis has sections that can be read as a detective story uncovering the identity of a character usually considered purely legendary. One of the earliest examples of AIDS Aggressor legends is that quoted by Randy Shilts in *And the Band Played On*. It is the story of "a strange guy . . . a blond with a French accent [who] would have sex with you, [then] point out his Kaposi's sarcoma lesions. 'I've got gay cancer,' he'd say. 'I'm going to die and so are you.'" This story was obviously spreading as a rumor throughout New York in June 1982. Throughout the book's more than six hundred pages, Shilts increasingly identifies this figure with a star of the gay scene, an employee of Air Canada, Gaetan Dugas. Shilts plainly thinks he has found the "strange guy with the French accent."[24] His case is made up in part from what sounds like anecdotal evidence and in part from official documents and media statements.

Dugas had been involved in the gay scene since the early 1970s and, according to Shilts, was estimated "easily" to have had "2,500 sexual partners." In 1980 Dugas was diagnosed with Kaposi's sarcoma, a very rare form of skin cancer that was later seen as symptomatic of AIDS. Researchers at the U.S. Centers for Disease Control (CDC) began suspecting that he was the "missing link" that connected cases in an outbreak of GRID (gay-related immune deficiency, as it was then called). "At the center of the cluster diagram [of GRID cases]," Shilts wrote, "was Gaetan Dugas, marked on the chart as Patient Zero of the epidemic." He died of AIDS in March 1984, four years after his skin cancer was first diagnosed. During that time, according to Shilts, Dugas remained sexually active. Shilts reports that Dugas insisted that all that was wrong with him was the cancer and that when he was advised to give up sex for the sake of the health of others, he replied, "Of course, I'm going to have sex. . . . Nobody's proved to me that you can spread cancer." Contradictorily, though, he believed that "somebody gave this thing to me." Of course, we don't know how Shilts was so sure these were Dugas's words, but as Shilts develops his story of the growth of the American AIDS epidemic, he persistently returns to Dugas and more and more closely associates him not only with "Patient Zero" but with the rumor of the "strange guy" in the bathhouse, attributing to Dugas statements that increasingly reflect the "strange guy's" words. One of Shilts's entries for November 1982, for example, reads, "Back in the bathhouse, when the moaning stopped, the young man rolled over on his back for a cigarette. Gaetan Dugas reached up for the lights. . . . [H]e then made a point of eyeing the purple lesions on his chest. 'Gay cancer,' he said, almost as if he was talking to himself, 'Maybe you'll get it too.' " At around the same time, Shilts writes,

> Gaetan Dugas's eyes flashed, but without their usual charm, when [a woman from the CDC] bluntly told him he must stop going to the bath houses. The hotline at the Kaposi's Sarcoma Foundation was receiving repeated calls from people complaining of a man with a French accent who was having sex with people at various sex parlours and then calmly telling them he had gay cancer. . . .
>
> "It's none of your goddam business," said Gaetan, "It's my right to do what I want to do with my own body."
>
> "It's not your right to go out and give other people disease," [she] replied. . . .
>
> "It's their duty to protect themselves," said the airline steward, "They know what's going on out there. They've heard about this disease."
>
> [She] tried to reason further but got nowhere.
>
> "I've got it," Gaetan said angrily. "They can get it too."

Shilts's discussion of Dugas ends with these reflections: "Whether Gaetan Dugas actually was the person who brought AIDS to North America remains a question of debate and is ultimately unanswerable. . . . In any event, there's no doubt that Gaetan played a key role in spreading the new virus from one end of the United States to the other. . . . At one time, Gaetan had been what every man wanted from gay life; by the time he died, he had become what every man feared" (439).

It seems plain to me that Shilts thinks he has uncovered the origin of a legend. Shilts sees Dugas as the original AIDS Aggressor.

A Personal Approach

I was at first inclined to consider stories about AIDS Aggressors as part of the "Poison and Honey" group, agreeing with Gary Fine that these stories played on the collective paranoia of men about women. Later reflection, however, has led me to think that AIDS Aggressor legends are more than that—and in very interesting ways. I believe that the anxiety in these legends—paranoia, if you will—is more about sex than women and is more about disease than sex. There are two aspects of this anxiety that seem to lead to this conclusion: first, the way the legends reflect AIDS information/misinformation; second, the way the legends use this "information." In 1987, Michael Goss prophesied that "We could be seeing only the start of AIDS-lore. Each emerging phase will match (if in distorted form) fears arising from the latest information-cum-speculation" (26). I think this is exactly what has happened.

Yet, oddly enough, I do not think AIDS Aggressor legends can be regarded primarily or simply as medical legends. A comparison with Bosom Serpent stories shows that whereas tellers of Bosom Serpent stories are concerned with physiological processes, tellers of AIDS Aggressor legends are not. One moment the victims are healthy, the next they are doomed, dying, or dead. And that's it. The emphasis is not on the disease but on the means by which the death sentence has been delivered. To my mind, that makes them stories about disease as a social phenomenon not as a medical one.

As I now see it, the development of AIDS Aggressor stories reflects AIDS awareness in the general public and is best understood in the context of public information and public information campaigns. In the following paragraphs I outline the development of AIDS awareness and try to link it to the development of the legends. As AIDS information changes, the stories also change.

As Diane Goldstein puts it, "the shape and nature of risk" are "retheorized" through the legends ("Banishing" 51). Initially, in the mirror type and its precursors, the connection between honey and poison is quite as evident as it is in stories of poisonous brides, but the connection is progressively weakened. Casket versions loosen or reinterpret the relationship between sex and death; needle legends dispense with it altogether, locating the site of danger not in the privacy of the bedroom but in public places.

The AIDS story begins in 1979, when a physician at the New York Medical Center identified a group of patients as suffering from a rare skin cancer, Kaposi's sarcoma. Although the disease is not normally fatal, these young men were surviving only a few months, two years at most. By June 1981, twenty-six such cases had been reported. Simultaneously, five cases of *Pneumocystis carinii*, an illness suffered only by people with depressed immune systems, had also been reported; by June, two of the patients had died, and ten new cases had arisen (Gilman 89). In the same year, another medical doctor in New York had seen a Dominican woman with "an inexplicable illness" (Altman 31). Medical officials began to recognize that some new disease was emerging. Owing to the fact that all the reported early cases clearly fitting the emerging pattern had occurred among young homosexual men, this disease was initially defined as "gay-related immune deficiency" (GRID). By April 1982, 248 cases had been reported in New York and San Francisco, and by November the figure had risen to 788 cases in thirty-three U.S. states. During this time, casualties had quadrupled: nearly 300 people had died (Shilts 200–1, 209). Those studying the disease now recognized that it was not confined to young homosexual men and that it expressed itself in a number of ways, so the more general term AIDS (acquired immune deficiency syndrome) began to be used.

At a December 1982 press conference, the CDC suggested that the reported occurrence of the disease "among homosexual men, intravenous drug-users, and persons with hemophilia suggest it may be caused by an infectious agent transmitted sexually or through exposure to blood or blood products" (Shilts 206–7). Haitians were later added to this list to arrive at the "4 Hs" thought to be at risk. But there was no mention of heterosexuals, another word beginning with the letter *H*. In her excellent essay, "AIDS, Homophobia and Biomedical Discourse," Paula A. Treichler says that in fact researchers had recognized as early as 1984 that HIV could be transmitted to heterosexuals, but the CDC only "somewhat reluctantly" expanded its list to include them in 1986 (44). By the time President Ronald Reagan delivered his much-criticized May 1987 speech on the AIDS crisis, 36,058 Americans had been diagnosed with the disease, and 20,849 had died (Shilts 596). In the mid-1980s, figures showed the number of reported cases of AIDS doubling every ten months (Clarke 25). In October 2003 it was reported that as many as 50,000 people in the United Kingdom (a small country) were thought to be living with HIV, although only half had been diagnosed ("So Now You Know"). Worldwide, in 2002 alone, it was estimated that 40 million people (by some estimates 46 million) were infected and that 3 million had died (Boseley).

Two aspects of the way that HIV/AIDS was classified and presented in the early days have special resonance for the emergence of AIDS Aggressor legends—its implicit classification as a sexually transmitted disease and the fact that researchers sought sociological rather than biomedical explanations for the emergence of disease.

Sander Gilman draws out the significance of the STD classification in "AIDS and Syphilis: The Iconography of Disease": "This label structured the understanding of AIDS in such a marked manner that PWAs were not only stigmatized as carriers of an infectious disease, but also placed within a very specific category . . . as a disease from which homosexuals suffered as a direct result of their sexual practices and related 'life-style.' . . . The idea of the person afflicted with an STD, one of the most potent in the repertory of images of the stigmatized patient, became the paradigm through which people with AIDS were understood and categorized" (90).

This leaves AIDS and those who suffer from it vulnerable to all the "free-floating iconography" (88) of older scourges such as syphilis, especially the image of the polluted patient responsible for his/her own problems and punished for his/her own sins. The relevance to AIDS Aggressor legends is plain. First, as Gilman observes, such conceptions restrict disease "to a specific set of images, thereby forming a visual boundary . . . The creation of the image of AIDS must be understood as part of [an] ongoing attempt to isolate and control disease" (88). Furthermore, "The more heterosexual transmission of AIDS becomes a media 'fact,' the greater the need for heterosexuals to retain the image of AIDS as a disease of a socially marginal group" (105). Two unchallenged assumptions in AIDS Aggressor legends are that HIV/AIDS is indeed an STD and that infection can be avoided by not belonging to or consorting with "marginal groups." Gilman is adamant that HIV/AIDS "is thought to be caused by a retro-virus . . . spread by direct contact with infected body fluids. . . . Sexual contact is not necessary to contract the virus" (90). It is not, therefore, a disease like syphilis; it is more like hepatitis B. The question, then, surely becomes, if AIDS had first been classified with hepatitis B, would AIDS Aggressor legends have arisen in the form they did—or at all?

Second, what would have happened if, instead of seeking sociological explanations for the emergence of disease, researchers had looked for biomedical ones? Treichler writes that "in the service of" the sociological explanation, "both homophobia and sexism are folded imperturbably into the language of the scientific text" (49). "The original list"—that is, the 4 Hs—"has structured evidence collection in the intervening years and contributed to a view that the major risk factor in acquiring AIDS is being a particular kind of person rather than doing particular things" (44). Together, these two important (mis)conceptions of HIV/AIDS structure both legends and—perhaps more surprisingly—public health campaigns.

As an illustration of these processes and their effects, I shall briefly look at the U.K. government's 1986–87 public health campaign. The high-profile, £20 million campaign aimed to reduce the incidence of AIDS by advocating "safe sex" and safe drug use. The measures being promoted included such things as not sharing needles or sexual partners, using condoms, and avoiding casual sexual encounters or encounters with people with unknown sexual histories. Television and billboard advertisements appeared depicting a giant iceberg raising just its tip above a murky ocean, with the slogan "AIDS: Don't Die of Ignorance." As the slogan shows clearly, the purpose of the campaign was educational, but the images that carried this message evoked either ridicule or fear and, although the campaign included some instruction about how (not) to behave, it offered little or no information about the disease itself. Simply, the campaign was not educational enough. The U.K. government had sought to portray everyone as potentially at risk through risky behavior, but the message was understood as being about risk groups. People responded not by altering their own behavior but by getting tested if they suspected the person they had been with came from one of these risk groups. In other words, the risk was always posed by *someone else's* behavior. Diane Goldstein makes a similar point in relationship to American and Canadian public health education campaigns: "Findings from health interview surveys . . . indicate that roughly 96 percent of adults know that HIV can be transmitted through sexual intercourse, from pregnant women to their babies perinatally, and by sharing needles with an infected person. Nevertheless . . . only 13 percent of Canadians report they have changed their behavior because of AIDS. Even people who are aware of their own risk conclude that the behavior of others is more risky than their own" ("Banishing" 59).

One of the consequences of the (unintended) focus on unsafe people was the addition of prostitutes—already stigmatized and, in terms of sex, "Other"—to the list of risk groups. Another was the rise of the concept of the "carrier." The media fell back on the old metaphor of disease as invader. Following the logic of the metaphor, HIV positive people were co-opted into the role of Trojan horse. A line was drawn between the healthy and the sick, "them" and "us," and victims of disease became polluted aggressors lying in wait to infect the general public. (For a detailed consideration of the term *carrier*, see Emke.)

Conversely, by trying to change behavior through fear and moral prescriptiveness, the AIDS awareness campaign failed to educate the public about the condition. People were left unsure about how easily the HIV virus could be transferred from one person to another. They had been told that it could be passed via body fluids but were left with the fear that a single contact of any body fluid on any part of the body might be enough to kill. We know now that the connection between body fluids and death is far from this direct. AIDS is a syndrome, not a single disease: it cannot be transmitted directly; the diseases from which sufferers die occur because the immune system has been compromised; the immune system is believed to be compromised by a retrovirus that is thought to be passed from one person to another via body fluids; to be HIV positive indicates only the presence of an antibody in the blood, it doesn't indicate an infection. But all of this passed people by. The rumors and legends taught that AIDS was a disease that could be directly, quickly, and easily transmitted from person to person and that to be HIV positive was a synonym for having AIDS. To be infected was not only an immediate and inevitable death sentence but also to pose an obvious danger to others. No amount of public education attempts could counteract popular understandings. In all legendary cases, just one encounter with an HIV-positive person is enough to welcome someone to the AIDS club and to certain death. These stories reveal quite frightening levels of fear and prejudice and ignorance, which seem to me to be the direct result of a public health information failure on a large scale.

But what is perhaps most interesting to a folklorist is the way that although the legends form public opinion, they also follow public understandings. First, the legends assume that HIV/AIDS is a disease acquired through contact with an "infected" person's body fluids. The earliest rumors and legends assume that homosexuals and homosexual sex are the culprits, but reassuringly the danger is located beyond the pale of "regular" people and "regular" behavior. Initially, the legends contain the threat within the gay community and the places where they meet for sex. Then, as it becomes clear that heterosexuals ("regular people," "people like us") can also contract HIV, the legends tell how "we" may be at risk through gays; the victims now are random heterosexual persons assaulted by homosexuals who dash out onto the street to bite or kiss or spit on passers-by. By 1986–87, mirror versions of the legends started to appear. This was the time when AIDS hysteria was at its peak, the British government was launching its "Don't Die of Ignorance" campaign, and it was generally understood that not only gay men were vulnerable to the infection, mirror versions of the legends started to appear. It was now assumed that semen rather than other body fluids carried the virus and that HIV/AIDS was a sexually transmitted disease. Again, though looked at one way, the legends are threatening, in another light they are quite reassuring: heterosexuals are at risk, but only under certain circumstances. The danger comes from strange women— possibly prostitutes, certainly "easy" and therefore obviously members of a risk group—and is liable to strike when men engage in sexual misbehavior away from home. Homophobia is no longer folded into these particular texts, but sexism certainly is: a willing female is always implicitly a dangerous and polluted one, just as in poison and honey stories. Thus, once again, the stories contain the risk, defining it as contact with recognizable, polluted, and stigmatized Others in unusual circumstances far from home.

But with the appearance of the casket versions in 1989–90, the poison and honey connection starts to weaken, as does the notion of risk groups. Sociological explanations of disease are still reflected in these legends, but they show a growing awareness that it's easier to be at risk than at first thought. What changes the perspective is that casket stories are told from the female point of view: first, the female is now the victim, the male now the aggressor; second, "love" enters the equation. The girl victim is not just sleeping around or cheating on her partner, as practically all the victims in mirror versions are; she is an innocent who is "really in love" (Goldstein, "Welcome"). Whereas mirror versions feature two guilty parties, in casket versions only one person has loose morals. The other person involved is just an innocent duped by an evil foreigner. The danger is thus much less easy to avoid. Whereas mirror versions set a cozy boundary between being safe and being sorry and—looked at one way—offered reassurances that avoiding casual sex in foreign places would keep you safe, these stories sow the seeds of doubt. They begin to recognize that there is such a thing as risky behavior, not just risky people.

Finally, what of needle legends? These pretty much dispense altogether with the sex-death connection. The site of danger is now located not in the bedroom but in public places. All the victims are now "innocent"; their sexual activity, like their sexual persuasion, is irrelevant. Death can visit anyone, anywhere, at any time. The aggressors may be the modern outsiders ("queers" or "hookers" or "druggies"), but they may also be a variety of old bogeymen ("maniacs" and "madmen").

In her detailed consideration of these legends, "Banishing All Spindles from the Kingdom," Diane Goldstein lucidly argues,

"Though contemporary scholarship has always seen legend in some sense as a critique of culture . . . that critique . . . is rarely understood as potentially critical of . . . authoritative constructions of truth." This has caused an "under-reading of the resistant voice" in the case of some legends and specifically in stories about sickness and health. She goes on to explore needle narratives as "a disguised critique of medical authority and resistance to what is seen as the inappropriate extent of bio-medicine's reach into the domain of intimate experience."[25] Needle narratives, Goldstein suggests, "externalize the risk, cast it out of the bedroom (where we don't want it) and back into the outer world (where we will take our chances)." Thus, the stories resist the imputation of medical authority that "oneself and one's partner are sites of danger." The tales are a way of reclaiming the home and "re-theorizing the shape and nature of risk" (148–51).

I have a lot of sympathy with the view that many legends are invitations to resist medical orthodoxy. (I think that's what is happening in many nineteenth-century Bosom Serpent legends).[26] However, I wonder whether this reading of needle legends is a little optimistic. I am not confident that it is the voice of resistance that is heard in needle stories. I would like to think it is so, but I wonder whether what is heard is really the voice of panic. These stories could easily be read as the narratives of people who no longer know where the danger lies and imagine it is everywhere, people whose sense of likelihood and proportion have been swept away by a typically modern combination of ignorance and information overload.

As represented by the content of the legends, "sites of danger" initially were imagined as safely tucked away in the gay community. Then they came nearer as HIV-positive homosexuals erupted on the streets and even nearer as infected heterosexual women threatened careless heterosexual men in bars and bedrooms and bathrooms. The danger crept still closer—now, according to legend, a careful and virginal young woman might be at risk simply for falling in love with the wrong man. At each stage, however, one could do something to protect oneself (though the remedy becomes ever more desperate—first one could avoid frequenting "gay" areas, then one could resist the temptation to sin with wild women during one-night stands, then one could be careful not to fall in love on vacation). But, needle legends come with no remedy attached. There is nothing one can do to protect oneself from the randomness of attack and disease. There is no such a thing as "risky behavior," because it's life itself that's risky.

NOTES

1. *Daily Star*, 25 February 1987, quoted in Smith, "Rumour" 98.
2. Brunvand, *Encyclopedia* 6–7; Smith, " 'AIDS' " 114.
3. "Legends"; from item in the *Sun* (London), 6 March 1990.
4. Janet Langlois carried out an exemplary study of this legend among her students; see also Brunvand, *Encyclopedia* 252.
5. Braid and MacKinnon; see also Jury and Murdoch; Sharrock and O'Kane.
6. O'Kane; Sharrock and O'Kane; see also "AIDS Mary in Ireland."
7. The letter and a transcript of the talk show can be found in Elizabeth Bird's insightful treatment of this episode.
8. Bird; see also "AIDS Mary on Dallas Radio Talk Show."
9. *New York Times* quoted in Bird 54.
10. *Cincinnati Post*, 30 January 1991, reported in " 'AIDS Mary' Murder," courtesy of Jan Brunvand.
11. Baldwin and Hardy; see also "AIDS Ray?"
12. Chrisafis; Laddin.
13. Goldstein, "Banishing," quoting reports on alt.folklore.urban; see also "Needles"; Hiscock; Brunvand, *Encyclopedia* 285–87.
14. Readers familiar with contemporary legendary motifs will recognize some of the unusual ways of contracting the HIV virus from legends about bizarre ways of getting pregnant.
15. Goldstein, "Banishing," offers an exemplary treatment of "needles" legends. See also Brunvand, *Encyclopedia* 285–87; for an example with racist overtones, see Ellis, "Needling."
16. *Worthing Herald*, 5 February 1998, quoted in Simpson.

17. Granville; for an Australian version and see Braunstein.
18. Sontag perceptively points out that the diseases we most fear are those which degrade and disfigure while leaving the mind intact. Her list of such diseases includes all these plus cancer (44–45).
19. Hooper 226–30; see also Ellis, " 'Haec' " 77. My thanks to Véronique Campion-Vincent for a copy of this story.
20. There is a huge folklore of cure by transference that deserves a chapter to itself in any history of medical folklore; see, for example, Froome, McConnell, and Sircar. Hortense Calisher's short story, "Heartburn," also utilizes this motif. The tale combines the idea that disease may be cured by transferring it to another person (in this case an unbeliever) with the Bosom Serpent motif. I thank Paul Smith for this reference and text.
21. Paul Smith was the first person to find this story and point out its similarity to AIDS Aggressor legends; See his " 'AIDS' " 129–30; "Rumour" 115.
22. Hall, tale 182 quoted in Smith, " 'AIDS' " 129.
23. Randolph 61–62 quoted in Smith, " 'AIDS' " 129.
24. See Shilts, esp. 21–23, 78–79, 83–84, 130–31, 137–38, 146–47, 156–57, 196–98, 200, 208, 247, 251, 348, 438–39.
25. In "Organ Theft Narratives as Medical," Campion-Vincent also considers legends as medical and social critique.
26. I have also argued something similar in the case of "vermin in boils." See Bennett, "Vermin."

KEY TEXTS

Crimp, Douglas, ed. *AIDS: Cultural Analysis, Cultural Activism.* Cambridge: MIT Press, 1996.

Czubala, Dionizjusz. "AIDS and Aggression: Polish Legends about HIV-Infected People." *FOAFtale News* 23 (September 1991): 1–5.

Goldstein, Diane E. "Banishing All Spindles from the Kingdom," Chapter 7 of *Once Upon a Virus: AIDS Legends and Vernacular Risk Perception.* Logan: Utah State University Press, 2004.

———, ed. *Talking AIDS: Interdisciplinary Perspectives on Acquired Immune Deficiency Syndrome.* St John's: Memorial University of Newfoundland, [1990].

———. "Welcome to the Mainland, Welcome to the World of AIDS: Cultural Viability, Localization, and Contemporary Legend." *Contemporary Legend* 2 (1992): 23–40.

Smith, Paul. " 'AIDS: Don't Die of Ignorance': Exploring the Cultural Complex." In *A Nest of Vipers,* ed. Gillian Bennett and Paul Smith, 113–41. Perspectives on Contemporary Legend 5. Sheffield: Sheffield Academic Press for the International Society for Contemporary Legend Research in association with CECTAL, 1990.

————. "Rumour, Gossip, and Hearsay: The Folklore of a Pandemic." In *Talking AIDS: Interdisciplinary Perspectives on Acquired Immunity Deficiency Syndrome*, ed. Diane E. Goldstein, 95–121. ISER Research and Policy Papers 12. St John's: Memorial University of Newfoundland, [1990].

REFERENCES CITED

"AIDS Mary in Ireland." *FOAFtale News* 38 (December 1995): 8.

"AIDS Mary Murder." *FOAFtale News* 22 (June 1991): 9.

"AIDS Mary on Dallas Radio Talk Show." *FOAFtale News* 25 (March 1992): 11.

"AIDS Ray?" *Dear Mr Thoms . . .* 27 (September 1992): 15–16.

Altman, Dennis. *AIDS and the New Puritanism*. London: Pluto, 1986.

Baldwin, Tom, and James Hardy. "Life for Those Spreading AIDS Deliberately." *Daily Telegraph* (London), 8 February 1998, 5.

Bennett, Gillian. "Vermin in Boils: What If It Were True?" *Southern Folklore* 54 (1998): 185–95.

Bird, Elizabeth. "CJ's Revenge: Media, Folklore, and the Cultural Construction of AIDS." *Critical Studies in Mass Communication* 13 (1996): 44–58.

Boseley, Sarah. "Government U-Turn on AIDS Crisis." *Guardian* (London and Manchester), 26 November 2003, 17.

Braid, Mary, and Ian MacKinnon. "Myth of the AIDS Avenger." *Independent* (London), 13 September 1995, 4.

Braunstein, Albert. "Australian HIV Legend." *FOAFtale News* 50 (November 2001): 10.

Brunvand, Jan Harold. *Curses! Broiled Again!* New York and London: Norton, 1989.

————. *Encyclopedia of Urban Legends*. New York and London: Norton, 2001.

Calisher, Hortense. "Heartburn." In *In the Absence of Angels*, 63–78. Boston: Little, Brown, 1948.

Campion-Vincent, Véronique. "Organ Theft Narratives as Medical and Social Critique." *Journal of Folklore Research* 39 (January–April 2002): 33–50.

Campion-Vincent, Véronique, and Jean-Bruno Renard. *De Source Sûre: Nouvelles Rumeurs d'Aujourd'hui*. Paris: Payot, 2002.

Camus, Albert. *La Peste*. 1947. Translated by Stuart Gilbert as *The Plague*. Harmondsworth: Penguin, 1965.

Chrisafis, Angelique. "Man Guilty of Infecting Two Women with HIV." *Guardian* (London and Manchester), 15 October 2003, 2.

Clarke, David. "HIV/AIDS Research: Contribution from a Sociological Perspective." In *Talking AIDS: Interdisciplinary Perspectives on Acquired Immune Deficiency Syndrome*, ed. Diane Goldstein, 23–37. ISER Research and Policy Papers 12. St John's: Memorial University of Newfoundland, [1990].

Czubala, Dionizjusz. "AIDS and Aggression: Polish Legends about HIV-Infected People." *FOAFtale News* 23 (September 1991): 1–5.

Defoe, Daniel. *The Journal of the Plague Year*. 1722; London: Dent (Everyman), 1948.

Dégh, Linda. "The 'Belief Legend' in Modern Society: Form, Function, and Relationship to Other Genres." In *American Folk Legend: A Symposium*, ed. Wayland D. Hand, 55–68. Berkeley: University of California Press, 1971.

Ellis, Bill. " 'Haec in Sua Parochia Accidisse Dixit': The Rhetoric of Fifteenth-Century Contemporary Legends." *Contemporary Legend*, n.s., 4 (2001): 74–92.

———. "Needling Whitey." *FOAFtale News* 16 (December 1989): 5–6.

Emery, David. *Welcome to the World of AIDS*. 1998. http//urbanlegends.about.com/library/weekly/aa052198.htm?once=truc&.

Emke, Ivan. "Excising the Body Politic: The AIDS Carrier Panic in Canada." Paper presented at the Forty-second Annual Conference of the International Communication Association, Miami, May 1992.

Fine, Gary Alan. "The City as a Folklore Generator: Legends in the Metropolis." *Urban Resources* 4 (1987): 3–6, 61.

"Five Years for Addict Who Made AIDS Threat." *Daily Telegraph* (London), 4 March 1997, 11.

Froome, Derek, Brian McConnell, and Sanjay Sircar. "A Folk Cure for VD." *FLS News* 40 (June 2003): 9–10.

Gilman, Sander L. "AIDS and Syphilis: The Iconography of Disease." In *AIDS: Cultural Analysis, Cultural Activism*, ed. Douglas Crimp, 87–108. Cambridge: MIT Press, 1996.

Goldstein, Diane E. "Banishing All Spindles from the Kingdom," Chapter 7 of *Once Upon a Virus: AIDS Legends and Vernacular Risk Perception*. Logan: Utah State University Press, 2004.

———. "Welcome to the Mainland, Welcome to the World of AIDS: Cultural Viability, Localization, and Contemporary Legend." *Contemporary Legend* 2 (1992): 23–40.

Goss, Michael. "AIDS: Heaven-Sent Folklore." *Folklore Frontiers* 5 (1987): 5–10, 23–27.

Granville, Liza. "AIDS Infection Legend." *FLS News* 29 (June 1998): 15.

Gulzow, Monte, and Carol Mitchell. " 'Vagina Dentata' and 'Incurable Venereal Disease': Legends of the Viet Nam War." *Western Folklore* 39 (1980): 306–16.

Hiscock, Philip. "More Needles." *FOAFtale News* 45 (November 1999): 5.

Hooper, Wynnard, ed. *Gesta Romanorum; or, Entertaining Moral Stories.* Trans. Charles Swan. 2 vols. 1894; New York: AMS, 1970.

Ivey, Saundra K. "Query." *Folklore Forum* 3 (1970): 69.

Jury, Louise, and Alan Murdoch. "Town Shocked by a Priest's Revelations." *Independent* (London), 13 September 1995, 3.

Kalmre, Eda. "AIDS Narratives in Estonia: Some Considerations." *FOAFtale News* 49 (June 2001): 1–2.

Kettle, Martin. "Man Injected Son with HIV to Save Cash." *Guardian* (London and Manchester), 7 December 1998, 2.

Laddin, Matt. "HIV Bigamist Jailed for Infecting Woman." *Independent* (London), 13 January 2004, 17.

Langlois, Janet. "'Hold the Mayo': Purity and Danger in an AIDS Legend." *Contemporary Legend* 1 (1991): 153–72.

Leavy, Barbara Fass. *To Blight with Plague: Studies in a Literary Theme.* New York: New York University Press, 1992.

"Legends in the Tabloids." *FOAFtale News* 18 (June 1990): 10.

Maskiell, Michelle, and Adrienne Mayor. "Killer Khilats, Part 1: Legends of Poisoned 'Robes of Honour' in India." *Folklore* 112 (2001): 23–46.

"Needles in Vending Machines and Pay Phones." *FOAFtale News* 44 (May 1999): 10.

O'Kane, Maggie. "The Priest, the Angel of Death, and the Whispered Distress of a Small Irish Town." *Guardian* (London and Manchester), 14 September 1995, 1, 6.

Payne, Kenneth W., and Stephen J. Risch. "The Politics of AIDS." *Science for the People*, September 1984, 17–24.

Popham, Peter. "Libyan Court Orders Six Medics to Be Executed by Firing Squad." *Independent* (London), 7 May 2004, 24.

Porter, Roy. "Plague and Panic." *New Society*, 12 December 1986, 11.

Randolph, Vance. *Pissing in the Snow and Other Ozark Folktales.* Ed. Rayna Green. Annot. Frank A. Hoffman. Urbana: University of Illinois Press, 1986.

Sharrock, David, and Maggie O'Kane. "'AIDS Revenge' Shocks Ireland." *Guardian* (London and Manchester), 13 September 1995, 2.

Shilts, Randy. *And the Band Played On: Politics, People, and the AIDS Epidemic.* New York: St. Martin's, 1987; London: Penguin, 1988.

Simpson, Jacqueline. "AIDS Legend." *FLS News* 27 (June 1998): 12.

Sircar, Sanjay. "AIDS-Needle Legend, 2001." *FLS News* 38 (November 2002): 13.

Smith, Paul. "'AIDS: Don't Die of Ignorance': Exploring the Cultural Complex." In *A Nest of Vipers*, ed. Gillian Bennett and Paul Smith, 113–41. Perspectives on Contemporary Legend 5. Sheffield: Sheffield Academic Press for the International Society for Contemporary Legend Research in association with CECTAL, 1990.

————. "Rumour, Gossip, and Hearsay: The Folklore of a Pandemic." In *Talking AIDS: Interdisciplinary Perspectives on Acquired Immunity Deficiency Syndrome*, ed. Diane E. Goldstein, 95–121. ISER Research and Policy Papers 12. St John's: Memorial University of Newfoundland, [1990].

"So Now You Know: Things We Learnt Last Week." *Observer* (London), 19 October 2003, 29.

Sontag, Susan. *AIDS and Its Metaphors*. New York: Farrar, Straus, and Giroux, 1989.

Treichler, Paula A. "AIDS, Homophobia, and Biomedical Discourse: An Epidemic of Signification." In *AIDS: Cultural Analysis, Cultural Activism*, ed. Douglas Crimp, 31–70. Cambridge: MIT Press, 1996.

Turner, Brian. *The Body and Society: Explorations in Social Theory*. London: Blackwell, 1984.

"Yorkshire AIDS Marys." *FOAFtale News* 43 (February 1989): 16.

KILLING THE PRODIGAL SON

"Just help yoreself," Big Billie said;
Then set the hatchet in his head

—ROBERT PENN WARREN, "THE BALLAD OF BILLIE POTTS"

A broadside sold in the streets of London in Charles Dickens's and Queen Victoria's day reported,

The Liverpool Tragedy

Showing How a Father and Mother Barbarously Murdered Their Own Son.

A few days ago a sea faring man, who had just returned to England after an absence of thirty years in the East Indies, called at a lodging house in Liverpool, for sailors, and asked for supper and a bed; the landlord and landlady were elderly people, and apparently poor. The young man entered into conversation with them, and invited them to partake of his cheer, asked many questions about themselves and their family, and particularly of a son who had gone to sea when a boy, and whom they had long given over as dead. At night the land-lady showed him to his room, and when she was leaving him he put a large purse of gold into her hand, and desired her to take care of it till the morning, pressed her affectionately by the hand, and bade her goodnight. She returned to her husband and showed him the accursed gold; for its sake they mutually agreed to murder the trav-eller in his sleep.

In the dead of night, when all was still, the old couple silently creeped into the bed-room of their sleeping guest, all was quiet; the landlady approached the bedside, and then cut his throat, severed the head from the body, the old man, upwards of seventy years of age, holding the candle. They put a washing tub under the bed to catch his blood. And then ransacking the boxes of the murdered man they found more gold, and many handsome and costly articles, the pro-duce of the East Indies, together, with what proved afterwards to be a marriage certificate.

In the morning, early, comes a handsome and elegantly dressed lady and asked, in a joyous tone, for the traveller who had arrived the night before. The old people seemed greatly confused, but said he had risen early and gone away. "Impossible!" said the lady, and bid them go to his bed room and seek him, adding, "you will be sure to know him as he has a mole on his left arm in the shape of a straw-berry. Besides, 'tis your long lost son who has just returned from the East Indies, and I am his wife, and the daughter of a rich planter long settled and very wealthy. Your son has come to make you both happy in the evening of your days, and he resolved to lodge with you one night as a stranger, that he might see you unknown and judge of your conduct to wayfaring mariners."

The old couple went up stairs to examine the corpse, and they found the strawberry mark on its arm, and they then knew that they had murdered their own son; they were seized with horror, and each taking a loaded pistol blew out each other's brains.[1]

This story, more commonly called the Murdered Son, the Tragic Homecoming, or the Tragic Mistake, is number N321 in Thompson's motif index ("Son returning home after a long absence unwittingly killed by parents"). It is also listed as type 939A in Aarne-Thompson's type index. As described by Maria Kosko (*Fils*), who is the only person to have undertaken a full-length monograph on this story, it has three basic plot elements: the incognito return of the hero; the murder of the "stranger" by greedy hosts who intend to rob him of his fortune; and the recognition of the victim as the murderers' son.[2]

The "Liverpool Tragedy" (c. 1860) plainly demonstrates this classic pattern, as does a story printed in *Western Folklore* in 1949, almost a hundred years later, and told to Richard Dorson as one of his "Polish Tales from Joe Woods":

Father and mother killed their own son, Alexander, for money. Mr. Alexander Bock had eighteen year old son, little farm—mortgaged. Ten years after, son come home, want to get surprise for his parents. They sent him to America to make money to pay off the mortgage. He comes back with money as a surprise. He comes to the inn and meets old friends, his godfather, mayor of the village, Csanok. Godfather didn't recognize him, now 28, with mustache, whiskers. But when boy tell him, he was awful glad; they drink together. Then Mr. Bock invite him to see his parents in the morning, have a big party.

Alexander calls on them, asks for room. They don't recognize him. He asks if his money will be safe. "Oh, yes." That night mother and father can't sleep, thinking of all that money. They get up, cut his throat, bury him in the manure pile. But shepherd boy behind store see everything.

Next morning the godfather comes over, "Where's Alexander?"

"Haven't seen him."

"Why he went to see you last night. I had wine with him at the inn. He was bringing money to surprise you."

Mother faints. Father says, "No, we didn't see anybody."

Chief of police comes around to investigate. He offers shepherd boy an apple. "Did you see anything?" He tells.

In most senses, this is a classic contemporary legend. Until recently, it was extremely widely diffused. Kosko collected 120 versions, and subsequent researchers have added to this list. In the region of 150 versions were available for this chapter though, according to Tom Cheesman, there may be "thousands of versions in print and oral tradition" (89).[3] The earliest known versions come from chapbooks and broadsides sold in the streets of London and Paris in 1618, but the story is almost certainly much older—maybe by as much as a century (Barbeau and Sapir 47). It is known to have spread widely throughout Europe until the end of the nineteenth century both in print and by word of mouth.

Another feature that makes it a classic contemporary legend is that it has been found in a multiplicity of media. According to Kosko, "This tragic theme was legend in the countryside, a song at fairs, *fait divers* in newspapers, historical event in chronicles, *exemplum* in sermons, drama in the theatre" (*Fils* 10). Other scholars describe it as "in a state of mutation never finalized" (Fabre and Lacroix 94). It is known to have been told as a "shocking ballad" in Germany from the 1740s to the 1860s (Cheesman); it was current as a local legend in the last years of the nineteenth century in Kentucky and Missouri (Rothert; Penn Warren; Randolph). It was popular as a dismal ballad in French-speaking Canada in the 1920s (Barbeau and Sapir); it was refashioned into a novel in Norway in 1928 (Kosko, *Fils* 159–60); it was told as news in New York in 1931 and identified as an "old chestnut" by columnist Alexander Woollcott, who had a sharp eye for a contemporary legend; and it was published as part of a ghost story in England in 1934 (Briggs and Tongue).

Many versions are structured, too (as the "Liverpool Tragedy" and Dorson's Polish story are), in a way very typical of contemporary legend telling. In an early essay, Daniel Barnes drew attention to the elliptical nature of contemporary legends. There is, he said, always a missing element in the story, and that missing element is "much of the plot itself": "Unlike *Märchen* plots . . . urban legend plots conceal functions, and for much the same reason that mystery plots do; it is a necessary requirement of the genre that this be the case. In both urban legends and detective stories, what is to be discovered (uncovered) is the 'real plot'" (70). Hence, either the denouement or the coda always spring a shocking or humorous surprise. As so often, there is a clincher to support the final discovery and revelation—in this case, the old standby of a birthmark. The coda at the end, too, is very typical of contemporary legend in its insistence on adding yet another layer of horror, however improbable. Scholars have pointed out how often contemporary legends end in death, madness, or hair turning white.[4] In the "Liverpool Tragedy" we have the unlikely but shocking ending of two elderly people taking a brace of pistols and shooting each other.

As is also commonplace in contemporary legends, the narrators neglect to explain some of the more unlikely elements of the plot (how, for example, would almost-destitute old folks have come by a brace of pistols?) but seem acutely aware of other problem places. In AT 939A it is essential for the plot that the son lodges incognito with the parents. The first difficulty—that of a stranger turning up and demanding lodging from an old couple—is nearly always disposed of by saying that the parents are innkeepers. Dorson's Polish version suffers from lacking this feature. As we shall see later, the second difficulty—the son's being incognito—is much harder to deal with. What plausible reason can there be for him not to tell his parents who he is? Most narrators spend some time trying to solve this problem. (A summary can often be distinguished from a performed version by the presence or absence of this feature.) In a unique moralistic twist, the writer of the "Liverpool Tragedy" solves the problem by having the son deliberately conceal his identity so he can assess whether his parents are worthy of his generosity, but most storytellers explain it by the son's misjudged sense of humor or his desire to increase the surprise of his return. Then follows the discovery, which in the "Liverpool Tragedy" is effected by the arrival of a wife but is more often achieved rather elaborately by having the returning son first visit the home of his sister or brother or some other connection and reveal his identity, as in Dorson's story.

So far then, in the way it is told, in its longevity and geographical spread, and in its circulation via a multiplicity of media, it is a typical contemporary legend. However, there is one discordant factor. As far as I know, only one version of the story has been recorded since Dorson's Polish story of 1949, despite the fact that social and political conditions in the world since then should have constituted an ideal breeding ground for the tale. This story appears in German folklorist Helmut Fischer's 1991 legend collection *Der Rattenhund* (The Rat Dog), and it shows the way a modern story might be told in times of war and social disruption. Story 94 is titled "Die Mordeltern" ("The Murdering Parents," the usual title for German variants of AT 939A).[5] In this story, told by a man of seventy, after the Second World War, when Germany was devastated in defeat, undesirables as well as innocent victims of war roamed the land, and nobody could trust anybody. A returning soldier came back to his native place and found no one at home to greet him. Neighbors told him that his parents were indeed at home but were hiding. They advised him to go there as a traveler and "make yourself known tomorrow." This he did, but his mother didn't trust this "stranger" because she saw a rifle in his bag. So, when he had gone to bed, the old couple killed the visitor. The next morning, the neighbor called at the house and said, "So, your Will is back again?" Then they knew they had murdered their own son. The story, according to Fischer's inform- ant, had been told many times. It shares two and possibly all three of the plot elements Kosko identifies as central to the 120 ver- sions she studied, though here the second element of this classic pattern has been transformed by making the (unjustly suspected) robber the son rather than the parents and by giving fear rather than greed as the motive for the murder.

It is perhaps because so few modern versions apparently exist that folklorists and students of popular literature have neglected this legend. Apart from Kosko's monograph, I can think of only a handful of essays—a passage in Véronique Campion-Vincent's "Les Histoires Exemplaires" and her "The Tragic Mistake," a chapter in Cheesman's *The Shocking Ballad Picture Show* (1994) (which deals with German street literature), and a study of popu- lar narratives by French semioticians Daniel Fabre and Jacques Lacroix. Also, a few students of European literature have studied it in the context of Albert Camus's *Le Malentendu* (discussed later in the chapter) or as part of a search for the origins of sensational eighteenth-century "Destiny" plays.[6] Nevertheless, I believe the story will surface one day soon and that it will again spread like wildfire through oral and visual channels and the printed word, as classic contemporary legends do.

A BRIEF HISTORY OF AT 939A

In determining the boundaries (and therefore the history) of the story, much depends on what one takes to be the engine driving the plot. The two principal approaches focus on either the "mis- take" or the "homecoming," as the two most common names for the story ("The Tragic Mistake" and "The Tragic Homecoming") attest.

The difference of emphasis in the two approaches is slight but significant. Concentrating on the "mistake" element of the murder and playing down the "homecoming" has allowed researchers to extend the history of AT 939A into recent times. This is, for instance, what Ray B. Browne does in his compilation of stories from the U.S. South, *"A Night with the Hants" and Other Alabama Folk Experiences* (1976). He has a story he calls "The Evil Son" in which a son puts on blackface to disguise himself and breaks into his parents' house, where he is killed by a stranger who has taken refuge there for the night. The "robber's" identity is discovered when the old couple lay him out for burial. Browne (132–33) links his story to motif N338.3, "Son killed because mistaken for somebody else," and to the dominant motif of the Murdered Son story, N321, "Son returning home after long absence unwittingly killed by parents." In her 1998 study of the legend Campion-Vincent includes Browne's story as an example of AT 939A and uses it as a link to modern narratives about people who unwittingly kill neighbors and relatives (not solely sons). These are then treated as transformations of the older legend. Contemporary reshapings of the legend, she argues, change the focus of the legend to the justifiable murder of a would-be attacker and substitute the fear motive as found in Fischer's story for the greed motive as identified by Kosko (Campion-Vincent, "Tragic Mistake" 70–75). This type of story was quite commonplace during the 1970s and 1980s, so if we accept Campion-Vincent's argument that these stories are transformations of the Murdered Son type, the history of the legend could be extended by at least three decades. This gives it a life span of at least four centuries.

The attractions of this classification are obvious, but I do not find it entirely convincing. There is a crucial difference between motifs N338.3 and N321—that is, the presence or omission of the phrase "after long absence." Browne is obviously right to link his tale to motif N338.3 but not, in my opinion, to see it as an example of N321, because there is no indication that the son in Browne's story has returned home after a long absence. Trivial as this may seem at first glance, I think it is crucial to the story. I am inclined to see the long absence as the engine that drives the plot. It adds irony and poignancy to the tragedy and rationalizes the misidentification of the traveler as "stranger" instead of "son" (this son really *is* a stranger). It also links the story to traditional themes such as the perils of travel and homecoming, absence and return. Another reason I cannot accept Browne's story of "The Evil Son" (or Campion-Vincent's legends of evil neighbors) as examples of AT 939A is that, in all the texts I have studied, the son is not evil at the point at which he returns; indeed, all the irony and much of the tragedy of the story depend on his being virtuous at the time of his return, whatever he may have been in the past.

In the discussion that follows, I shall be looking at AT 939A in relationship to the homecoming theme as epitomized by perhaps the most famous homecoming story of all, the Christian parable of the Prodigal Son. I shall suggest that many versions of this story are mirror images of the parable, with the roles and characters reversed to bring about a horrific tragedy. I shall also be looking at the perils-of-travel theme (which is another element—though a subsidiary one—of the parable of the Prodigal Son). In particular, I shall discuss this theme as epitomized by travelers' tales of a Bloody Inn and look at the ironical interplay of these two themes when it is to the rapacious keeper of the Bloody Inn that the unfortunate traveler returns home after his long absence. From this point on, therefore, following Cheesman's example, I shall generally refer to this story as "Killing the Prodigal Son."

SEVENTEENTH-CENTURY TEXTS

The consensus among scholars is that the earliest known version of this story is a chapbook printed in London in 1618. Copies are

available in Oxford in the Bodleian Library and in London in
the British Library, and the text is reproduced as an appendix to
A. W. Ward's Introduction to George Lillo's eighteenth-century play
Fatal Curiosity, which I shall discuss later in the chapter. Entitled *Newes from Perin in Cornwall*, the 1618 text is subtitled,
"A Most Bloody and Un-Exampled Murther Very Lately Committed by a Father on His Owne Sonne (Who Was Lately Returned
from the Indyes) at the Instigation of a Mercilesse Step-Mother.
Together with Their Severall Most Wretched Endes, Being All
Performed in the Month of September Last. Anno 1618." [7] The
story features a father of "honest life and ample possessions"
cursed with a "wilde and misgoverned" son. "So wilde and rancke
grew the weeds of disobedient stubbornness in him" that he went
to sea and became a pirate. The story then goes on to narrate his
adventures at sea. Attacked by Turks, he leaps into the ocean
wearing a belt stuffed with booty. Once safe on shore, he takes
a steady look at his past life, where he finds "much matter of
grief . . . viz theft, piracy, murder, drunkenness, swearing, lust,
blasphemy and the like." Fearing the Last Judgment, he resolves
to repent and reform and to become a respectable tradesman.
Unfortunately, he tries to make this new start by selling one of
his jewels, which turns out to have been stolen, and he is sent to
the galleys. The narrator spends some time describing the man's
sufferings as a slave: "His dinner and his supper [were] course
[coarse?] bran and water, his morning breakfast and afternoon
bever [beverage?] the Buls pizle [penis][8] and the Bastinado. . . .
Now he began to call to minde his disobedience to his parents;
and to thinke what a quiet life and full of pleasure it had beene for
him, to have sit in his furd [furred?] gowne at his study in the university, or warme and dry at some honest Tradesman's shop in the
Citty; to have had warm dyet [diet?] twice a day and welcome,
and not have begged course bran and water, and have gone without it." When the galley calls at a port, he escapes and files off his

chains and then makes his way to England. However, calling to mind "his stubborn carriage, and wilful disobedience," he is "ashamed to be known" as his parents' son, apprentices himself to a ship's surgeon, and sets off on another journey. He goes to the Indies and makes a fortune before eventually returning home. He is again shipwrecked, again secures some of his fortune in a belt, and again swims ashore. This time, he arrives on the coast of Cornwall and makes his way to "Perin" (modern-day Penryn). The story then goes on as one would expect, with the young man identifying himself to his sister, going incognito to his father's house (his mother has died and his father has remarried while he has been away), mistakenly showing his wealth to his stepmother and being murdered for his money. The sister arrives in the morning and discloses the identity of the stranger; the father and stepmother kill themselves; the sister is distraught; the murder "made all the standers by with a general voyce cry out; It was the Bloodiest and most Inhuman murther, the Countrey was ever guilty of."

Two things are of note in this story. The first is the resemblance of the first part of it to the parable of the Prodigal Son. The second is that only a month later, in October 1618, a broadside was published in Paris recording the "histoire admirable et prodigeuse d'un Père et d'une Mère qui ont assassiné leur propre fils sans le cognoistre [strange and prodigious story of a father and mother who murdered their own son without recognizing him]." These events supposedly happened in Nîmes in October 1618 (Seguin 187–88). The French version is not a copy of the English version; each appears to be completely independent of the other. For example, in nearly half of its sixteen pages, *Newes from Perin* plays on "the perils of travel" theme, telling of the son's fantastic misadventures at sea and in foreign parts. This element is missing from the French broadside: using only a few sentences, it tells how the son joins the Swedish army, covers himself with glory, and accrues considerable wealth. The "Prodigal Son" element is also treated differently. The father-son relationship in the English version starts off closer to the parable in that it features an honest and wealthy father and a scapegrace son. (These contrasts are later reversed: the father turns rapacious under the evil influences of poverty and a bad woman, while the son becomes honest and generous under the benign influence of suffering and enforced time for reflection.) In the French version, right from the start, the father is impoverished and wicked and the son noble and (eventually) wealthy. Given the relative slowness of early seventeenth-century communications, for two such different versions of the same tale to have turned up in two different countries within such a short space of time is a fair indication that it had been circulating in oral form (and maybe in written form too) for some time previously. Kosko (controversially) argues that there was probably what she terms a "pure" version of the legend circulating before 1618. She also mentions that Johannes Bolte argued that a Germanic tradition had been contemporaneous with or had even predated the 1618 French and English chapbooks. As evidence, he assembled a number of previously unknown texts and argued that an inn, the Sign of the Golden Sieve, where some versions of the story were located, had genuinely existed in the early seventeenth century (*Fils* 28).

But to return to the Prodigal Son—. This is surely one of the best-known New Testament narratives. Throughout sixteenth- and seventeenth-century Europe the story was retold in countless Latin and vernacular dramas, songs, novellas, paintings and engravings, and of course sermons. It was a popular theme in cloth paintings and frescoes decorating the walls of private homes and inns in Elizabethan and Stuart England. In continental Europe, too, Protestants and Catholics alike, rich and poor, city people and country people all found it appealing (Cheesman 87).

Let us remind ourselves of the events. Here the story is told in the resonant language of the Authorized Version (Luke 15:11–32),

A certain man had two sons; and the younger of them said to his father, "Father, give me the portion of goods that falleth to me." And he divided unto them his living. And not many days after, the young man gathered all together, and took his journey, into a far country, and there wasted his substance with riotous living. And when he had spent all, there arose a mighty famine in that land; and he began to be in want. And he went and joined himself to a citizen of that country; and he sent him into the field to feed swine. And he would fain have filled his belly with the husks that the swine did eat; and no man gave unto him.

The son reflects that his father treats his servants better than this and resolves to return home, confess his faults, and ask his father to take him back, not as a son but as a servant.

Let us see how this theme is treated in *Newes from Perin*. This story also features a rich and virtuous father and a wild and graceless son. The Cornish son, like the biblical son, leaves home under inauspicious circumstances and comes to grief in foreign parts through sheer recklessness. The way the son's sufferings are described in *Newes from Perin* strongly recalls the words of the biblical parable. The son in the parable "would fain have filled his belly with the husks that the swine did eat; and no man gave unto him." The son in *Newes from Perin* was also near starvation and began to think how good it would be "to have had warm dyet twice a day and welcome, and not have begged course bran and water, and have gone without it." Both sons repent and resolve to return home but feel themselves unworthy of a son's place in the family.

But let's see how the stories go on. In the parable, the father recognizes the returning son "while he was yet a great way off" and runs to greet him, calling on the servants to "Bring forth the best robe, and put it on him; and put a ring on his hand, and shoes on his feet. And bring hither the fatted calf, and kill it; and let us eat and be merry; For this my son was dead, and is alive again; he was lost and is found." The biblical story ends so well because although the son is greedy and eventually poor, the father is rich and generous, and because although the son has been absent for a long time and has suffered various misadventures, the father loves his child so much that he is able to recognize him even while he is still "a great way off." But what if the roles were reversed and, at the point of return, the father was poor and greedy and the son rich and generous? What if it was the son in whose power it was to alleviate the suffering of the father (not vice versa)? And what if the father did not recognize the son at all? The homecoming could be very different. And so it is in *Newes from Perin*. While the son has been on his travels, the character and situation of both father and son have been reversed. The father has impoverished himself by giving his daughters generous dowries; he has also lost his wife and married a hard and grasping woman. Meanwhile, the son has reformed and become extremely rich. He has also been so changed by his adventures that his father, blinded by greed, takes him for a complete stranger. So, instead of all being gainers from the son's return, as in the parable, all are losers: instead of the fatted calf being killed, it is the son who is killed; and instead of joy and feasting, there is horror and suicide. This plot, which inverts the biblical parable through a series of reversals and transformations, is common to very many stories of the AT 939A type. However, the situation and characters of the central players always stay in binary opposition to each other, whatever the reversals. The stories revolve through four sets of contrasts—stranger and son, avarice and generosity, penury and wealth, evil and good—which are played out at the homecoming.

Stories of Killing the Prodigal Son remained popular throughout the seventeenth century. Kosko has collected three further versions that claim to relate events occurring in 1618: a German version from 1634 warning of the sin of avarice; a 1651 version from a

Belgian Jesuit, Antoine de Balinghem, purporting to tell of events happening in Poland and warning of the punishments that follow acts of inhospitality; and a 1704 story from the sermons of Abraham Santa Clara (*Fils* 79–81, 90–91). Kosko also cites a 1621 novella, "Acte Abominable d'un Père Avare et Desnaturé" (An Abominable Act of an Avaricious and Unnatural Father), by Abbé Jean Baudoin (*Fils* 65–79). Literary scholar A. W. Ward refers to a version in Gottfried Schultz's *Chronica* of 1656 (here said to have happened in Bohemia in 1649) and notes that similar tales were circulating about or in other German towns (Lillo 219). Another seventeenth-century English account that follows the text of *Newes from Perin* appears in Sir William Sanderson's *A Compleat History of the Lives and Reigns of Mary Queen of Scotland . . . and Her Son James*, published in 1655–56 (James VI of Scotland became James I of England in 1603 and reigned until 1625). This was later reprinted in Frankland's *Annals of the Reign of King James and King Charles the First* (1681).[9] It tells of "a calamity of wondrous note" that happened at "Perinin" in Cornwall and follows immediately after an account of the death of Queen Elizabeth's favorite, adventurer Sir Walter Raleigh, in 1618.

EIGHTEENTH-CENTURY TEXTS

The story continued to be told throughout the eighteenth century. In addition to those Kosko assembled, Fabre and Lacroix have discovered another newspaper version from 1796, and Cheesman says that fifteen German ballad versions remain extant, "including chapbooks dating from the 1740s to the 1960s and two very widely sung vernacular ballads" (90–91), although unfortunately he does not present texts of any of the eighteenth-century versions or say how many are from this period. This may not seem an impressive haul, but three hundred years is a long time for such ephemeral material to be preserved, and this handful of extant written texts must represent the mere tip of the iceberg. In Cheesman's opinion, this was "the single most often recomposed story in German shocking ballads between the mid eighteenth century and the mid nineteenth" (85).

The four texts Kosko presents in full (*Fils* 104–23) include a story from a 1727 German newspaper reporting events that supposedly happened in Corbeil, France, in July of that year; a longer story from an Italian broadside about a murder purportedly committed in Marseille in June 1732; an even longer and well-developed 1760–61 text, usually called "The Visitor" or "The Normandy Inn," from the *Public Ledger*, an English magazine; and an Italian novella by Vincenzo Rota published posthumously in 1794. Rota's work relies on two seventeenth-century versions, *Newes from Perin* and Abbé Baudoin's 1621 novella, though Rota says that his tale was inspired by rumors of a "well-known case" [*caso notissimo*].

The Italian broadside, in the manner of such literature, has a typically lengthy title that summarizes the plot: "The terrible and lamentable case which happened in the town of Marseille, in which one sees how a perfidious and villainous innkeeper called Saverio Polinder, together with his wife, Anna Salusti, dealt death to a guest who lodged at their inn in order to acquire a large sum of money and how, after his death, they learned that he was their own son. They were arrested by the judiciary and condemned to be ignominiously broken on the wheel, after which the inn was set alight and burnt to the ground." The inverted Prodigal Son theme is quite well developed in this story. When he is only ten years old, the son runs away from home to see the world, going to Spain and enlisting in the army. He serves with distinction and becomes indispensable to his captain, who dies and leaves the boy a fortune. A short time later, he decides to return home to bring comfort to all his kin. He arrives at the inn without being recognized and seeks out his godfather, reveals his identity, and reiterates his intention of bringing joy and comfort to his family by his presence and his fortune. The inevitable murder, discovery, and retribution follow. Finally, the inn is set alight and burned down "to serve as an example to those who do not sufficiently fear Divine Justice."

"The Normandy Inn" is also interesting. It was originally published in the London review the *Public Ledger* in a column written by the Reverend William Dodd under the pen name "The Visitor." Three years after the tale's initial publication, Dodd brought together several of his columns in a two-volume anthology, *The Visitor* (1764). "The Normandy Inn" is introduced by a three-page preamble reflecting on the mixture of good and evil found in humankind and offering the story as an illustration of this general observation. Highly literary, the story is notable for its take on the Prodigal Son motif and for its double-revelation denouement. A widowed innkeeper has eight children, all of whom leave home to pursue independent lives except the eldest and the youngest, who are devoted to their father. When the youngest is only sixteen, war breaks out between France and Britain, and he is conscripted into the army. At this point we know nothing of the character of the father or of the sons. The younger son constantly writes home demanding money and complaining of suffering and starvation, but the father cannot help him. The story then moves straight on to the arrival at the inn of an impressive-looking army officer whose identity is revealed neither to the father nor to the reader. He gives a purse of gold to the innkeeper for safekeeping, instructs him to look after his horse and prepare a grand dinner for several guests on the following day. Then he leaves, saying he has other calls to make in the area. We hear nothing more until the next day, when the innkeeper's brother, a priest, arrives and asks for the young officer. The innkeeper denies all knowledge of the young man and a debate ensues between the innkeeper and the priest. The priest eventually asks the innkeeper whether it had not occurred to him that the young man looked very like his long-lost son. The innkeeper faints. The priest tells how the son had acquitted himself well and had been promoted to lieutenant and returned with a hundred louis d'or. He had been amused to find that his father did not recognize him and had been determined to keep the secret until the following day, when he could invite all the relatives to a celebration dinner. He had left the purse of gold to cover present and future expenses.

And thus to the double revelation—the young officer is obviously the son. But where is he now? Murdered and hidden under the bed. Now for the motive: the father has killed the stranger so that he can send money to ease the sufferings of his much-loved younger son. "It is thus," the story concludes, "that the wounded heart . . . succumbed to the disordered transports of paternal affection." Here is another twist in the inversion of the biblical theme. This father loves the son too much and is prepared to go to any lengths, including the murder of a wealthy guest, to relieve him of his sufferings. But the cruel irony is that the wealthy guest *is* the (no longer) suffering son.

Perhaps the best known eighteenth-century redaction is George Lillo's play *Fatal Curiosity*, first performed at the Little Haymarket Theatre in London in May 1736 under the title *Guilt Its Own Punishment; or, Fatal Curiosity* but published in 1737 as *Fatal Curiosity: A True Tragedy*. It was very popular: the British Library holds eighteen texts (fifteen in English, three in German) dating from 1737 to 1791, and it was revived several times with various alterations. The most enduring altered version was prepared in 1782 by London dramatist George Colman (1732–94), manager of the Haymarket Theatre, where the play was performed, between 1777 and 1789. Perhaps the most famous revival was that of 1796 at Drury Lane Theatre. This performance had a distinguished cast dominated by the famous Kemble family. John Philip Kemble

(1757–1823), possibly the most famous actor of his day who had become manager at Drury Lane in 1788, played the father; his sister, the equally famous actress Mrs. Sarah Siddons (1755–1831), played opposite him as the mother. The final revival was in Bath in 1813 under the title *The Cornish Shipwreck; or, Fatal Curiosity*.

It is worth dwelling a little on Lillo's play because it was very influential in spreading the story throughout eighteenth-century Europe and also because much of what we now know about the story comes from scholars interested in Lillo and the European playwrights he influenced. *Fatal Curiosity* claims to be based on a real event and leads straight back to *Newes from Perin*, which it follows very closely. It is generally assumed that Lillo found the story in Frankland's *Annals*. This seems particularly likely in view of the fact that, in the *Annals*, the Penryn story follows immediately after an account of the death of Sir Walter Raleigh, and in the opening lines of *Fatal Curiosity*, Old Wilmot describes Raleigh's arrival in Plymouth and his subsequent arrest and execution.

The situation is quickly set up in the first scene. Old Wilmot and his wife, Agnes, have fallen from prosperity to penury in the fifteen years since their son left home; Charlot, the girl Young Wilmot left behind, is wearied with waiting for him but remains faithful to him and still dutiful toward his parents. Through conversation with a faithful retainer, Randal, we discover that Old Wilmot's former nobility of character has been replaced by cynicism and rapacity. We first see Young Wilmot, accompanied by his friend, Eustace, in scene 3, which is set on the coast of Cornwall. Young Wilmot makes it plain that he is "flying to relieve" his parents of sadness and want. The reasons why the son might not be recognized are also spelled out early on: not only has the son been absent for fifteen years, but he has returned from India sunburned and wearing Indian attire.

This drama shows the inverted Prodigal Son theme in one of its strongest aspects. All the elements of the biblical parable are here but have been changed to their binary opposites. The father, once noble and generous, is at the point of the son's return completely transformed. His loyal retainer comments on this very early in the play so the audience can make no mistake about it:

> *O Fatal Change! O, horrid transformation.*
> *So majestic a temple, sunk to ruin*
> *Becomes the shelter and abode*
> *Of lurking serpents, toads, and beasts of prey.*
> *And scaly dragons hiss and lions roar*
> *Where wisdom taught and music charmed before.*
>
> *(act 1, scene 3)*

The comfortable and gracious home and the happy occupants have likewise been transformed because of the profligacy of Old Wilmot. The author apparently does not notice the inconsistency of this situation with the earlier portrayal of the man as wholly noble, but it fits very well with the reversals of the characters and roles of the biblical parable. In the New Testament story it is, of course, the son who is prodigal, but according to Agnes's account at the end of the play it is the father who has wasted his substance here:

> *Barbarous man!*
> *Whose wasteful riots ruin'd our estate*
> *And drove our son, ere the first down had spread*
> *His rosy cheeks, spite of my sad presages*
> *Earnest entreaties, agonies, and tears*
> *To seek his bread 'mongst strangers, and to perish*
> *In some remote, inhospitable land—*
>
> *(act 3, scene 1)*

When Young Wilmot arrives, he is shocked by what he sees in his former home:

> *What wild neglect, the token of despair*
> *What indigence, what misery appears*
> *In each disorder'd, or disfurnished room*
> *Of this once-gorgeous house! What discontent*
> *What anguish and confusion, fill the faces*
> *Of its dejected owners!*
>
> *(act 2, scene 3)*

It is to this home that the son returns, but he has the power to alleviate all the distress:

> *I shall see my parents, kiss the tears*
> *From their pale hollow cheeks, cheer their sad hearts*
> *And drive that gaping phantom, meagre want*
> *For ever from their board; crown all their days*
> *To come with peace, with pleasure and abundance*
> *Receive their fond embraces and their blessings*
> *And be a blessing to them.*
>
> *(act 1, scene 3)*

So the contrast between the rich and noble son and the evil and indigent father is set up and is ready to be played out. The son can supply the robes and the rings and the fatted calf that the biblical father gave the long-lost son, but the happy release from suffering and the promise of a joyful homecoming are thwarted by the greed of man and the harshness of fate.

The success of Lillo's play in London inspired continental imitations, which are documented by A. W. Ward in his introduction to the 1906 edition of the play. In 1781, Karl Philipp Moritz produced *Blunt oder der Gast,* and there were also two editions of a translation by W. H. Brömel, *Stolz und Verzweiflung* (Pride and Despair), were printed in 1785 and 1791. The most famous and successful German redaction of the Killing the Prodigal Son theme was Zacharias Werner's *Der Vierundzwanzigiste Februar* (24 February) of 1812. This play is supposed to have been inspired by hearing a "well-known anecdote" read at Goethe's house in 1809; in a footnote to this passage, Ward adds that the story was circulating in Geneva in 1808, and in June 1880 the *Neue Freie Presse* of Vienna published a similar story. A frankly derivative play, *29 February*, was written by Adolf Müller, trying to outdo Werner for sensation. Müller later adapted the play and, giving it a happy ending, called it *The Illusion*.

These were not the only plays based on our theme. Kosko lists roughly twenty theatrical adaptations from the eighteenth to the twentieth century and considers six twentieth-century versions—*The Return*, by Gertrude Robbins, performed in Dublin in 1913; *Lithuania*, by Robert Brooke, played on the Greek front in 1913 and in Chicago in 1915; *Pauvre Matelot*, an opera with words by Jean Cocteau performed in Paris in 1927; *A Knocking in the Night*, by George Gravely, performed in London in 1928; *Nispodianka*, by Rostworowski, played in Poland in 1929; and *Le Malentendu*, by Albert Camus, played in Paris in 1944.[10] M. Frauenrath, who has also studied the story in some detail, found thirteen plays on the theme and analyzed three of them in some detail: Lillo's *Fatal Curiosity*; Werner's *Der 24 Februar*; and Camus' *Le Malentendu*.

NINETEENTH-CENTURY TEXTS

The discussion has so far concentrated on the ways the story twists the homecoming theme in the parable of the Prodigal Son, but now I will turn to the other theme I see as important. In 1865, English folklore collector Robert Hunt published his famous story compilation, *Popular Romances of the West of England*. On page 442 of the third edition (1923) our story can be found under the heading "The Penryn Tragedy." Hunt seems to have taken it from a history of Cornwall published in 1838, which, in turn, was borrowed from an earlier, unacknowledged source, possibly from the seventeenth century. The story begins with a phrase strongly reminiscent of the opening lines of *Newes from Perin*: The father "had been blessed with ample possession and fruitful issue, unhappy only in a younger son" (Hunt 442). However, rather than following the *Newes from Perin* text, Hunt's version goes more or less straight into an account of the son's misadventures. "Taking liberty of his father's bounty," we are told, "he went roving to sea" and became a pirate. There follows an encounter with a Turkish warship, an accident with gunpowder that scuttles the ship, a long swim to the island of Rhodes, an attempt to sell a stolen jewel punished by being sent to the galleys, a mutiny and the murder of the officers, a second shipwreck and second feat of swimming, and a fortuitous landing in Cornwall. These adventures resemble but are not identical to the adventures recounted in *Newes from Perin*, reading like a misremembered summary of it. But, though the playing out of the tragedy follows the usual pattern, the Prodigal Son theme is absent except in a brief phrase at the start of the narrative: the errant son took "liberty of his father's bounty." So what interest there is in this story lies as much with the perils the son encounters on his travels as with those of his homecoming.

During the nineteenth century, the perils-of-travel motif became the focus of many (though not all) versions of this story, especially those printed in chapbooks and broadsides. To introduce this literature, let us return for a moment to the *Liverpool Tragedy*. The broadside version that opened this chapter was printed by James Catnatch, a prolific London chapbook and broadside seller working out of Seven Dials, London, between 1813 and his death in 1841. We know that the *Liverpool Tragedy* was being sold on the

streets of London in the middle of the 1800s because we have an
account from that time of a "running-patterer" (a seller of street
ballads and broadsides), who described it as one of his best-sellers
(Canning 96–100). But it is clear that the Catnatch version was
not the only one circulating. I have a copy of a second contemporaneous version, a chapbook printed by J. Evans and Sons, with
the same title but a more moralistic and explicit subtitle, "A
Warning to Disobedient Children and Covetous Parents. In Five
Parts." The two versions have quite different emphases. As we
have seen, the Catnatch broadside starts with "a seafaring man"
returning home and concentrates on his murder by the lodging
house keepers, who turn out to be his parents. Very little is said
about why he left home, why he had been absent for thirty years,
or what had happened to him during that time. In contrast, three
of the five parts of the Evans version describe the son's adventures
at sea. He sets off for Brazil, is shipwrecked, is cast up on a rock,
is tempted by the devil, repents of his disobedience to his father,
is rescued, and goes to India, where he marries a wife and makes
a fortune of "ten hundred pounds in gold." Not until part 5 does
the narrator reach the disastrous homecoming. The murder is just
the last and most gruesome of the perils of travel that are the
main focus of this long story.

According to Jean-Pierre Seguin, the author of a lively account
of nineteenth-century French street literature, the perils of the
route and the return were major themes in chapbooks of the day.
These hazards might include encounters with highwaymen and
footpads, traveling acrobats, or wandering peddlers on the look-
out for benighted peasants. He cites the instance of a lurid broadside printed in Avignon in 1867 relating the violent sexual assault
of a young girl by twenty-nine individuals in the Var départe-
ment. According to this story, the girl was a target simply because
she was a stranger and traveling on foot. Among the chief perils of
travel, however, is the danger of spending the night at a wayside

inn run by a rascally and murderous innkeeper. In a large number of these tales, a veteran returning from war or army service is falsely accused of some crime. These men come back gallant but broke and fall victim to a crooked innkeeper's accusations of theft or arson; they are exonerated only at the eleventh hour by a sudden or miraculous turn of events. One of the most popular of these stories tells of a soldier who was wrongly accused of arson. His avaricious host had insured his property for a sum several times its real value and took the opportunity of the veteran's arrival to set fire to the building and blame the guest. Seguin, who gives a text of this broadside, remarks, "this story was well known, in more or less related versions, and had a prodigious success for almost half a century. . . . [I]nfantrymen, sailors, simple soldiers and officers, legionnaires, decorated heroes, survivors of the wars of the First Empire, of Africa, Italy, the Crimea and the Army of the Rhine succeeded each other as alike as brothers" (186–87). Similarly, Louis Chevalier deals with the ubiquity of the themes of disguise and dangerous return journeys in chapter 3 of *Splendeurs et Misères du Fait Divers* (The Splendors and Miseries of Fait Divers[11]), seeing them as a particularly relevant in post-Napoleonic France. He draws attention to two aspects of these stories—in the dangers-of-return category, he includes stories about the fatal return of soldiers to their native lands, and in the category of disguise he includes stories of false accusations of murder and arson and stories about deceptive appearances, people who appear charming and benevolent but who are really thieves and murderers (103 –16).[12]

There are several points of interest to folklorists in this material. First, the stories form a bridge to Helmut Fischer's postwar legend, where the veteran returns and his parents suspect him of robbery and murder and so kill him. Second, in many versions, the broadside writer draws explicit attention to a contemporary moral that may be drawn from the tale. This suggests that the writer knew that he was dealing with material that was traditional to the point of overuse and was either mocking it or trying to make it relevant. Several broadsides devoted to this theme, for example, praise the benefits of fire insurance or warn of the risks run by those who insure their property for more than it is worth. Seguin even suggests that some of these versions were distributed free by peddlers on behalf of insurance companies (187).

Very often stories that tell of the perils of travel converge with another traditional motif, that of the "Bloody Inn" as well as with the homecoming theme. Kosko discusses two such legends where the perilous homecoming is the story within the story about murdering innkeepers, the Jerusalem Inn at Danzig (modern Gdansk, Poland) and the legend of Babylas. The story of the Jerusalem Inn seems to have been first published as a ballad in 1804. It tells how, at the beginning of the nineteenth century, there was a little house on the outskirts of Danzig called Jerusalem. It was isolated and dilapidated and opened its doors only to provide a last drink for men condemned to die on the nearby scaffold. Its history was the terror of the age, according to the ballad. An inn had previously existed on the site, offering good service and delicious wines to princes and counts. The innkeeper's name was Jerusalem. Though he seemed a good man, he was actually a treacherous scoundrel who thirsted for gold and blood. When his son left to study abroad, the innkeeper commanded him not to return unless he came equipped like a prince. Meanwhile, though his reputation remained intact, the innkeeper was secretly committing many crimes. One day, late at night, a carriage drawn by six horses arrived at the door of the inn; bystanders thought the traveler was a viscount. The "viscount" is, of course, killed in his sleep for his money. His bags are searched, and the innkeeper realizes he has murdered his own son, who has returned, as commanded, equipped like a prince. Maddened by grief and remorse, the innkeeper confesses to a long list of horrid crimes. He requests that, when he is led to the scaffold, he should be taken to his inn for a last drink. This is done. Then the inn is destroyed, and a little house is built on the spot. Thereafter, the house is known as Jerusalem, and condemned men on the way to the scaffold are offered a last beverage there in memory of the innkeeper and his terrible deed (Kosko, *Fils* 128–43).

Another legend that uses the wicked innkeeper motif as well as the motif of the injunction to the son to return only when he is a rich man is the story of Babylas, which appeared in Pamphile Lemay's *Contes Vrais* (True Stories), published in Quebec in 1899. The centerpiece of this collection is four stories about an inn haunted by the ghost of an innkeeper who has murdered his own son. The last one is entitled "Sang et Or" (Blood and Gold). (Kosko, *Fils* 233–35 summarizes the text.) The story is a very typical version featuring avaricious parents and a virtuous son sent off to make his fortune. The wife is unfaithful, the innkeeper kills her lover, and the couple have to leave the area. They set up as innkeepers, and the house soon gets an evil reputation so that travelers are afraid to sleep there. The next part of the story unfolds as one would expect, but after the murder the crime is not discovered, and the couple's grief for the man they now know is their own son is soon assuaged by the thought of the money. The wife dies, but the old man lives on. People now avoid his premises as if it were the gateway to hell. One morning he is found dead in front of the hearth. The priest discovers him and says, "Requiescat in pace," at which point, a terrible and mysterious voice replies, "Non est pax impiis" (no rest for the wicked).

Not every version is as melodramatic as these stories. As the century progressed, every melodramatic version probably had a counterversion designed to expose the tale as an "old chestnut (the "I am in the know" factor that Sandy Hobbs distinguishes as one of the features of contemporary legends told as "good stories" ["Social Psychology"]). We have seen that in France by the mid-nineteenth century, the stories of Killing the Prodigal Son had become sufficiently worn out and unconvincing to lead broadside writers to assign contemporary "morals" to it either seriously or in jest. In Germany, ballad versions definitely mock the stories they relate. Cheesman quotes a story titled "An Old, Shocking Ballad with an Entirely New Practical Application" (92–94, appendix 9). It begins in traditional style. The father is a joiner, and the son, Gottlieb, apprentices himself to a tanner and leaves home to work as a journeyman. The parents subsequently fall more and more into debt and take the lease of an inn. Just at the moment when their landlord has become particularly pressing for the rent, the son turns up incognito, and they see his heavy money belt. The parents cut Gottlieb's throat and bury him in the stable. They discover his identity next day when they find and read his diary. They give themselves up to the law and are publicly executed. So far, so ordinary. But the moral of the story is subverted in the continuation:

> *This is a horrible story*
> *But such a thing was able to take place*
> *Because in those days after all*
> *Nobody knew about photography . . .*
>
> *If Gottlieb had sent his photograph*
> *To his parents*
> *They would have recognised him*
> *The moment they saw him . . .*
>
> *So you who are living in foreign lands*
> *Do not spare your money*
> *Send your picture home quickly*
> *To preserve yourselves from harm. (quoted in Cheesman*
>   *94–95)*

An extensive prose advertisement for a photographic establishment follows.

THE TWENTIETH CENTURY

An American take on the Bloody Inn motif goes back to a late-eighteenth-century tradition about a band of Kentucky river pirates and robbers. The James Ford gang were said to hide out in Cave-in-Rock and operate a ferry on the Ohio River until the death of their leader in 1833. One of the roads from the ferry led to a highway tavern, the proprietor of which was a member of the Ford gang, Billy Potts. It was said that more than one traveler had eaten his last meal and spent his last night at that inn. It was also believed that bones turned up by the plow in adjoining fields were those of Potts's victims. The inn is still supposed to be there, now turned into a barn, its walls and floor marked with ineradicable blood stains.

The many legends attributed to this gang include one about Billy Potts and his son. This story was told in 1924 by Otto Rothert in his *The Outlaws of Cave-in-Rock* (284–306) and repeated by B. A. Botkin in his 1955 *A Treasury of Mississippi River Folklore* (209–12). It begins with a traveler on horseback making his way toward Ford's Ferry from the south. After he has crossed the Ohio River, he meets Billy Potts's son, who says that he is going the same way and would welcome the traveler's company. They have not gone far before young Potts takes out a pistol and robs the other man. Two farmers witness the robbery and report young Potts to the authorities, so he is forced to flee. The story then proceeds as one would expect except that at the end young Billy is run through with a sword while taking a drink from a well. More significantly, there is no clincher to convince the parents of the traveler's identity; the son has a birthmark that might have identified him but, as luck would have it, the sword wound has obliterated the evidence. Rothert says that this story is part of the secret history of the Ford gang, one of the few traditions that have found their way into the outside world. He had heard it from an old man who had heard it in his childhood; as far as the old man was aware, it had never been printed. Rothert seems to imply that the story may have a factual basis. Kosko's discussion of the legend takes its historicity for granted. She dates the murder to between 1795 and 1833. It was not until the nineteenth century, however (she argues) that the Billy Potts story was integrated into legends about the brigands of Cave-in-Rock (*Fils* 230).

Another Kentucky version may be found in a poem by America's first poet laureate, Robert Penn Warren (1905–89), "The Ballad of Billie Potts." A headnote to the poem says that he had heard the story in his childhood from an elderly relative. It was not till later, he says, that he came across another version "in a book on the outlaws of the Cave-Inn-Rock, or Cave-in-Rock" (presumably Rothert?). Penn Warren's version is set in a region of Kentucky called "Between the Rivers." The telling of the legend (often humorous and in dialect) is interpolated with a parenthetical elegiac commentary on the tragedy of the land and the human condition. It is a wonderful poem, a fine reworking of the story, that draws on local legend and uses both the Prodigal Son and the Bloody Inn motifs. Initial humor becomes final tragedy, and the poem ends with a moving presentation of grief at the death of a son. Penn Warren's version initially follows Rothert's quite closely. "Big Billie" is a rogue, "sharp at swap and trade," who prospers where other people fail. His wife is a little, sharp-eyed, secretive woman. Big Billie is ostensibly an innkeeper, but his real trade is murder and highway robbery. At midnight Big Billie sends runners to his gang with information about well-heeled travelers staying at the inn. The traveler's doom is sealed; when he sets out the following morning, he is already as good as dead.

One night the runner does not show up, and the couple's adolescent son, Little Billie, is sent as the messenger. Being full of "piss and vinegar," he tries to rob the traveler himself. However, he is not quick enough, the traveler pulls a gun, and Little Billie is wounded. The parents fear that the traveler will report Little Billie to the authorities, so he is sent into exile, and they hear no more of him. He returns—of course he does—and meets an old acquaintance, Joe Drew, who recognizes him only with difficulty. In the dialogue that follows, the poet plays with the notion of luck to which he will return in the final lines. Billie has done well in the West: he tells Joe that his luck has "helt out fer fair," so he has risked returning home to see if his parents are still alive. They are alive, says Joe, but they might as well be dead for it looks as if Little Billie took their luck with him when he went West. "Little Billie laughed and jingled his pockets and said, 'Ain't nuthin wrong with my luck.'"

So Billie arrives at the inn and thinks it will be a good joke to tease his parents by concealing his identity:

> And he joked them and he teased them and he had his fun
> And they never guessed that he was the one
> Had been Mammy's darling and Pappy's joy
> When he was a great big whickering boy
> In the land between the rivers.

Playing his role of wealthy but uncouth traveler to the hilt, Little Billie jingles his money, eats to bursting, and then demands fresh drinking water. The comedy suddenly turns chilling, as the old woman says,

> "Pappy, why don't you take the young gentleman down to the
> spring so he kin get hit good and fresh?"

And the old woman gave the old man a straight look,
She gave him the bucket but it was not empty but it was not
   water.

So Billie's fate is sealed. He turns out not to be so lucky after all, for of course, it is a hatchet that is in the bucket, and when he bends down to drink at the spring, Big Billie strikes him from behind and kills him. The old folks gloat over their astuteness and their own good luck, but then Joe arrives and asks for Little Billie.

The mood of the poem darkens still further as the couple try not to realize they have killed their son. So the poem moves to its somber and poignant ending as the old couple in panic and terror grabble in the earth and uncover the traveler's grave. The stranger cannot possibly be their son, the wife tells the husband, for he was just a boy who "called me Mammy and hugged me tight." She recalls how much they loved him and how she loved to count his toes and kiss him on the birthmark on his breast, a birthmark that was clover-shaped for luck. The end comes suddenly and brutally simply:

The old man said: "Git his shirt open."
The old woman opened the shirt and there was the birthmark
   under the left tit.
Shaped for luck.

The poem ends with an elegiac stanza that provides a succinct summary of the irony of the story. Here, the means of identification is the birthmark that had been the symbol of Billie's luck. It is emblematic, the poet implies, of the tragedy of all homecomings where a child returns under a fatal illusion of filial duty and parental goodness to kneel "At the feet of the old man/Who is evil and ignorant and old." In this respect, the poem not only reflects the fate theme of Lillo's play but also shares the unremitting pessimism of Camus's (in)famous reworking of the story in *Le Malentendu*. It is thus an archetypical as well as particularly fine reworking of the legend.

A not dissimilar story but without the elegiac commentary or philosophical shaping was related to the renowned folklore collector Vance Randolph in 1925. The narrator was Ed. Wall of Pineville, Missouri, who said that he had heard it first sometime in 1890. It was supposedly a true story about some people in Arkansas. Randolph was clearly unaware of the Kentucky story, for his footnote refers readers only to plays by Lillo and Werner and the legend of St. Julian Hospitaller (1 n. 2).[13] The parents run a ferry; they build "a good house," and travelers sometimes stay there. The only son runs away from home when he is ten years old. Equipped with all the appurtenances of wealth, he later returns home and makes himself known to a local storekeeper and says that he is intending to "give his paw and maw a lot of money out of [his] saddlebags." When the storekeeper next sees the old man, he comments on the son's happy return. "The old man did not say anything and pretty soon he went home." The old woman kills herself, and the old man "never amounted to much after that. Sometimes he would just lay under a tree all day." Just before he dies, he tells the storekeeper, "It was my boy come to our place that night . . . but me and Maw didn't know him. There was gold and silver in them saddlebags. So Maw she cut his throat, and we buried him under the chicken house."

Even while Penn Warren was composing "The Ballad of Billie Potts," the story was being debunked as an "old chestnut" in the American press. As far as I am aware, the first such treatment came from the pen of Alexander Woollcott under the heading "Folk-Lore" in his "Shouts and Murmurs" column in the *New Yorker* in 1931. Talking about his correspondence with a reader who was trying to track down the origin of a story "told for true," Woollcott relates that he had discussed these sorts of narratives with an English journalist, Valentine Williams, who, like himself, was an "amateur collector of such yarns":

> Over the breakfast cups one morning . . . Mr. Williams told me that, for the past quarter of a century, he had been maddened by the repeated recurrence in newspapers all over Europe of a story which never varied in essentials, and which might, for purposes of identification, be labeled The Adventure of the Returning Stranger. The date, the proper names, even the language might vary, but always the story concerned a native in some country in the eastern part of Europe returning from America after many years with his pockets full of gold, and seeking shelter for the night with greedy old peasants who promptly killed him for his money and then found evidence among his papers that they had murdered their own son. Doubtless it had been his pretty plan to greet them at breakfast with the Czechoslovakian equivalent of "Surprise! Surprise!"
>
> At intervals of about six months, Mr. Williams said, he would come upon this story in England or France or Germany. Each time it would be published as having happened the night before, and each time apparently in good faith. . . .
>
> I assured Mr Williams that the Adventure of the Returning Stranger was, to my notion, a perfect specimen of folk-lore, but that it seemed to have been confined to European circulation. Only two weeks later, published as hot news on the front page of the New York *Herald Tribune*. . . . [T]here appeared a breathless report with these headlines

PARENTS KILL RICH SON

POSING AS A STRANGER

POLE HOME, AFTER 18 YEARS IN U.S., GOES UNRECOGNIZED

And the story which followed was none other than Mr. Williams's old favorite—as it was in the beginning, is now, and ever shall be, world without end.

In January 1935 a *Time* magazine correspondent discussed this theme and contributed a version in which the events were supposed to have happened in Yugoslavia. In this one, the traveler's mother and sister commit the murder.[14] An Associated Press features writer, Cynthia Lowry, had also come across the legend. Responding to Dorson's story in *Western Folklore*, she observes that "The 'Polish Murder' saga is another traditional bit of rumor—and it pops up from time to time as gospel in some of our most reputable newspapers—and from a number of different countries. That's the one about the boy who left his native land when young, came to America and made a pile of money. Finally he decides to go back to Poland (Italy, France, Spain—any place) to see his aged parents" (174–75).

It was a newspaper account such as this that French novelist and playwright Albert Camus (1913–1960) saw and used as an incident in his famous 1942 novel, *L'Etranger* (usually translated as *The Outsider*). The protagonist is in jail (his ultimate offense is that he did not cry at his mother's funeral): "One day, when inspecting my straw mattress, I found a bit of newspaper stuck to its underside. The paper was yellow with age, almost transparent, but one could still make out the letter print. It was the story of a crime. The first part was missing, but one gathered that the scene was some village in Czechoslovakia." The story resembles the one Woollcott debunked, with the difference that the son returns home from some unspecified foreign country with his wife and child. His mother and sister now keep an inn, where he checks in under an assumed name. They kill him with a hammer and throw his body in the river. The wife turns up and identifies him as the long-lost son, the mother hangs herself, and the sister throws herself into the well. Camus's character concludes, "I must have read that story thousands of times. In one way it sounded most unlikely, in another, it was plausible enough. Anyhow, to my mind, the man was asking for trouble; one shouldn't play fool tricks like that" (*Outsider* 82).

Camus takes up this observation in his full-length treatment of the story, *Le Malentendu* (The Misunderstanding) (1944).[15] The play revolves round two axes drawn from legendary treatments of the theme—the motif of the Bloody Inn and the Killing the Prodigal Son theme. There are five characters: "the mother"; the sister, Martha; Jan, the lost son; Maria, his wife; and the old servant (mostly referred to simply as "le Vieux," the Old Man). The scene is set at a Bloody Inn, where Martha and the mother are in the habit of killing rich guests so they can save up enough to retire to the home by the sea Martha craves. They have almost enough; this will be their last job. Their method—we learn all this in the opening scene—is to serve the victim a cup of drugged tea and then drag him to the river and drown him. As soon as Jan enters in the next scene, we know he is the lost son. The play develops as one would expect, except that it is his passport that reveals his true identity, which is later confirmed by his wife. The mother drowns herself, the sister shuts herself in her room to await death (cf. Goldstein). Camus uses the characters and situation to present a bleak nihilistic picture of a world manipulated by a malevolent God who is a negation of all traditional concepts of deity and all that religion teaches, a God who is his own denial. This non-God or anti-God is represented in the silent but ever-present person of the Old Man, who orchestrates the tragedy by ensuring that the mother does not see the passport in time to save her son but that his identity is revealed just when it can do most harm. As the play ends, Maria beseeches God: "Oh my God! I cannot live in this desert! . . . I put myself in your hands. Have pity on me. Turn your face toward me! Hear me, give me your hand! Have pity, God, on those who love each other but have been separated!" The Old Man appears and says, "You called me?" and Maria answers, "Oh I don't know. But help me, because I need someone's help. Have pity and consent to aid me!" The play closes with the Old Man's one-word reply, "No."

It was not a success. Indeed, many audience members greeted it with roars of laughter, and critics called it a "literary Grand Guignol," a "crazy story," or a "tragic vaudeville." They were particularly impatient, it seems, at the final part of act 2, where Martha and the mother "calmly discuss fate and death at the bedside of the man they have already half killed. The veiled warnings, the hinted menaces, the [final] scene provoked an access of hilarity," and the play finally drew to a close "amid one wave of applause and another of boos" (Kosko, *Fils* 328–31).

Kosko is quite harsh regarding the play. She says that Camus intended to write "a tragedy of the absurd" but failed on both counts. The play cannot be a tragedy, she says, because there is no chance of events turning out differently and because the implacable and unrepentant sister, not the grieving mother, is the chief personage; and it cannot be absurd because the final act demonstrates the traditional view that crime does not pay (it would only have been absurd, she says, if the murderers had gotten away with their crime). I think this is too conventional a view of what constitutes the nature of "tragedy" and a rather mistaken notion of what the "absurd" constitutes in terms of the history of the theater. It is a shame, too, that Kosko fails to approach the play as a redaction of the legend the history of which she is discussing. For me, one of its principal fascinations is the way that Camus returns to and explores the implications of the legend he had briefly used in *L'Etranger*.

In the opening scene, Camus explores the logic of the Bloody Inn motif. In legends, the standard plot needs no more logic than that the inn is bloody, so blood will be spilled. Death is inevitable once one has set foot there. This dynamic is to a degree exploited in the play. Everything Jan says becomes a reason for killing him, every chance of his real identity being discovered is thwarted, every hesitation of the mother is counteracted by the implacable Martha, and every time he thinks about leaving, something changes his mind. Jan is at the Bloody Inn, and the moment he set foot inside the door, his fate was sealed. Yet if these events were not a legend, but "real," as newspaper stories should be, this logic would not do. There must be reasons for the killing, some psychological "explanation" of the murderers' state of mind, so Camus explores the implications of treating "legend" as "fact." The play offers two possible explanations through the banal yet shocking dialogue of Martha and the mother, a surface reason and an underlying reason. The women need money to escape from their unsatisfactory lives; murder is a method that has presented itself, and they have become habituated to it and it consequently doesn't seem so dreadful. The mother says that she didn't bother to look at the traveler; it was enough to know that he had "the face of a victim." Underlying this surface rationale, though, is a view that informs the whole play, again expressed through the women's reflections on their criminal behavior—a despair of life, a view of death as preferable. In their view (and that of the author, it seems), it is life that is cruel, not death. Therefore murder is a form of mercy killing. We are at the Bloody Inn, and its owners' dreary philosophy colors the play and is the informing principle of the denouement.

It is the "Killing the Prodigal Son" motif, however, that is most thoroughly raked over in the play—in this case to expose the lack of any sort of logic in the standard story in newspapers and legends. (Camus obviously knows that it is a legend and is in a sense playing with the genre.) The dialogue between Jan and Maria in act I, scene 3 exposes all the implausibility of the incognito homecoming, an implausibility that all or most other redactions try to disguise. Jan overtly pictures himself as the returning Prodigal. He tells Maria that he had expected his mother to recognize him and run to welcome him. But she barely glanced at him. He had come bringing his fortune and perhaps a little happiness too. He had expected the fatted calf, but all he got was a beer— which he had to pay for. It isn't as easy as one would expect for a stranger to become a son again, he reflects. Maria, the voice of common sense throughout the play, is impatient with him. One must expect to be treated as a stranger if one comes as a stranger, she says. All he had to do was say "It's me," and everything would have fallen into place. Warming to her theme, she asks why he hadn't told his mother he was coming, adding, "sometimes it's important to do what everybody else does." When Jan assures her he will find some means to make himself known, Maria retorts that the means are simple—one just says, "Hey! It's me." Needless to say, this is not what happens.

Scene 4 explores the reasons why a long-lost son might decide to return home after such an extended absence. Duty and responsibility, the need for one's family, the call of one's homeland— these are the reasons Maria and Jan debate. Maria makes it plain that she thinks his obligation to his mother and sister are figments of his imagination, merely "the voice of his solitude." He won't listen but simply starts up another argument: "One cannot be happy in exile or when one is forgotten. One cannot be a stranger for ever. I want to rediscover my homeland and to make those I love happy. I cannot see further than that." Maria tells him that he could have done all this in a simple straightforward way. In addition, audience and readers know that the dream of a homeland is an illusion, too. The land that Jan has left behind is the promised land of blue seas and clear skies of which his sister dreams, and the place he wants to reclaim as a homeland is the dreary country that has driven her to murder.

Scene 5 goes on to explore the inevitable mismatch of Jan's and Martha's expectations about how he should behave. This is the first and perhaps most fundamental "misunderstanding" of the title. In his mind, he is the returning hero who will resume a son's role and status. He thinks Martha and the mother will expect him to show concern for the family; conversely, he expects them to accord him a loving welcome. To Martha, however, he is merely

KILLING THE PRODIGAL SON

a paying guest, as she keeps on insisting. Every attempt to behave like a brother is treated as an inappropriate familiarity and is coldly repulsed. Scene 6 continues this exploration. A conflict now exists between Jan's desire to disclose his identity and a growing desire to conceal it so he can get to know the women and assess their needs (or deserts?—shades of the *Liverpool Tragedy* here). If the mother can be made to confess that she misses her son, the conflict will be resolved, and he can reveal himself. But the mother does not admit to missing her son: "an old woman even unlearns to love her son; the heart wears out." Martha tartly adds, in words ominously capable of two meanings, "A son who came back here would find what any client is assured of finding. . . . Every man we have received has been accommodated." Despite this reproach (or threat), Jan continues to try to assume a son's role without admitting he is the son. The mother gets up to leave, and he immediately jumps up to help her. She says, "Leave me alone, son, I am not an invalid. Look at these hands, they are still strong. They can still support a man's legs." Jan does not respond to the rebuke or wonder what she means by saying her hands are strong enough to support a man's legs (though the audience/reader knows she is referring to the fact that she lifts the victim's legs while Martha lifts his arms as they carry his drugged body to the river). Instead, he snatches at the word *son*: just a figure of speech, says the mother. So act 1 can be thought of as a thorough interrogation of the implications of travelers' tales of Bloody Inns and the logical gaps in the homecoming legend.

The action of act 2 passes to the murder, but Camus still has not exhausted the ironic possibilities of the theme. Martha's arguments with Jan in act 1 have centered on what she sees as his misunderstanding of his position in the household. Whereas he has thought of himself as the Prodigal Son, to them he is just another guest, just another victim. After the murder, the mother spells out this mismatch of expectations. She had tried to stop him drinking the drugged tea, she says, but it was too late. But he had at least learned his lesson: the house was not his home. Martha agrees: the house was not his home, but it wasn't anyone else's home either. Reminding us again that we are at the Bloody Inn, she says, "Nobody will ever find either neglect or warmth here. If he had understood this sooner he would have saved himself and we would have been spared the trouble of teaching him that this room is for sleeping in and this world is for dying in."

In the first scene of the final act, the Old Man brings the women Jan's passport, which, in an earlier scene, the audience had seen him silently remove before they could find and read it. Jan's identity is at once revealed. The mother's response is the standard one: "I knew this day would come. . . . I didn't recognize him and I killed him. I can go now and join him at the bottom of the river." Martha, however, is made of sterner stuff. When her mother accuses her of having recognized him all along, she denies it but adds that even if she had, it would have made no difference. In the second scene, Maria returns to confirm the victim's identity and to spell out the Prodigal Son theme for a final time: "He wanted to make himself known to you again, to find his home again, to bring you happiness, but he couldn't find the words. And while he searched for the words he was killed." And again later, "He wanted to bring you his fortune, and to make you both happy, and this was all he was thinking about alone in his room while you were planning his death." Martha's response is chilling: her dying task will be to convince Maria that everything has now assumed its ordained shape, which is that "no one is ever recognized."

So there it is as far as the Prodigal Son theme is concerned. As the implacable Martha tells the grieving Maria, "He has got what he wanted, he has found what he was searching for. Everything is in order. Understand that neither for him nor for us, neither in life nor in death, is there any homeland or any peace." And so the play draws to its final bleak conclusion: there can be no escape, no hope of comfort or salvation, no God except the malevolent Old Man who thwarts all human aspirations and blights all human hopes and dreams.

Our trail draws to a close with this desolate view of the human condition. After 1944, there are Dorson's Polish story published in 1949, Fischer's postwar German story published in 1991, and several texts or discussions in articles dealing with hoaxes or journalists' culture.[16] However, interest in this story (except as a relic of an older legend tradition) has sharply declined in modern times. Campion-Vincent, for example, says that she has "found no attested occurrence in the press later than 1937, no plays after 1944, and the latest attested ballads have been found in 1952 and 1969" ("Tragic Mistake" 67). That seems to be about right. The only oral account with anything like the traditional structure and motifs, Fischer's German story, is now more than fifty years old. As I said initially, this seems odd in view of the fact that the story seems ideal for times of war and social upheaval, and there have been plenty of those since 1945. It is possible, of course, that similar stories have been told in Bosnia and Kosovo, in Chechnya and Afghanistan, in Iraq and on the West Bank, but local people have been too busy trying to stay alive to record them and folklore collectors have kept well away from such troubled places. Time will tell.

NOTES

1. For a facsimile, see Hindley 1:5. The broadside is also reproduced in "Liverpool Tragedy," *Dear Mr Thoms . . .* 19:21.
2. I make no apologies for drawing heavily on Kosko in the following discussion. It is one a way of bringing her very valuable work to the attention of those who do not read French. However, I have tried wherever possible to consult her sources. I have traced most of the English and French texts but have not tried to find the German ones since I cannot read that language. Translations from the French are my own and are often somewhat "free." I regret any inaccuracies.

3. Additional examples can be found in Fabre and Lacroix; Seguin; Campion-Vincent; Cheesman. In preparing this chapter, I have also come across a handful of versions that, as far as I am aware, have not previously been cited in the literature.

4. Hobbs, "Going Mad"; Goldstein; Hobbs, Cornwell and Chiesa 251–52.

5. Quoted in Campion-Vincent, "Tragic Mistake" 70–71. Kosko (*Fils* 35) mentions a wartime text, a diary that contains the story of a murder committed in Bavaria (parents murder their son, who has just returned from America). The diarist has a commentary in which he links the story to the rise of Nazism and concludes that the horrors of the Nazi regime are caused by a cosmic psychosis, the unleashing of a horde of demons that had previously been held in chains.

6. See Kosko, "A Propos"; Virtanen; Freeman.

7. I thank Paul Smith for finding this text for me; also the version discussed above, p. 165.

8. The penis of a dead bull was used to flog malefactors.

9. Frankland's story appears in the appendix to Lillo ed. Ward.

10. See Kosko, *Fils* 301–31; Campion-Vincent, "Tragic Mistake" 65.

11. The French expression "fait divers" is virtually impossible to translate. It is used to signify little stories of bizarre or comical happenings that are used to fill column inches in newspapers.

12. Chevalier's discussion (113–14) includes a consideration of an 1831 short story by Honoré de Balzac, "L'Auberge Rouge."

13. The legend of St. Julian Hospitaler is a sort of Murdered Son in reverse. Here the parents, dressed as pilgrims, go in search of their long-lost son (Julian) and eventually arrive at his house in his absence. Julian's wife welcomes them and gives them the matrimonial bed for the night. Julian returns and, seeing two people in his bed, rashly assumes that his wife is being unfaithful to him. He kills his parents. (See "Julian the Hospitator" in Metford).

14. "Native's Return." This story was also followed in several issues of the folklore magazine *Dear Mr Thoms* . . . . See "The Liverpool Tragedy."

15. I used Camus, *Caligula suivi de Le Malentendu*. The translations are my own.

16. See, for example, MacDougal 288–89; Hughes 194–97; Darnton 189–92; Stephens 141.

KEY TEXTS

Campion-Vincent, Véronique. "The Tragic Mistake: Transformations of a Traditional Narrative." *ARV: Scandinavian Yearbook of Folklore* 54 (1998): 63–79.

Cheesman, Tom. "Killing the Prodigal Son; or, The Politics of Popular Enlightenment." Chap. 3 of *The Shocking Ballad Picture Show*, 85–118. Oxford: Berg, 1994.

Kosko, Maria. *Le Fils Assassiné (AT 939A): Étude d'un Thème Légendaire.* FF Communications 198. Helsinki: Suomalainen Tiedeakatemia, Academia Scientarum Fennica, 1966.

REFERENCES CITED

Barbeau, Marius, and Edward Sapir. *Folk Songs of French Canada.* New Haven: Yale University Press, 1925.

Barnes, Daniel R. "Interpreting Urban Legends." *ARV* 40 (1986): 67–78.

Botkin, B. A. *A Treasury of Mississippi River Folklore.* New York: Crown, 1955.

Briggs, Katharine M., and Ruth L. Tongue, eds. *Folktales of England.* London: Routledge and Kegan Paul, 1965.

Browne, Ray B., ed. *"A Night with the Hants" and Other Alabama Folk Experiences.* Bowling Green, Ohio: Bowling Green University Popular Press, 1976.

Campion-Vincent, Véronique. "Les Histoires Exemplaires." *Contrepoint* 22–23 (1976): 217–32.

———. "The Tragic Mistake: Transformations of a Traditional Narrative." *ARV* 54 (1998): 64–79.

Camus, Albert. *Caligula suivi de Le Malentendu: Nouvelles Versions.* Paris: Éditions Gallimard, 1958.

———. *The Outsider.* Trans. Stuart Gilbert. Intro. Cyril Connolly. Harmondsworth: Penguin, 1966.

Canning, John, ed. *The Illustrated Mayhew's London.* London: Wiedenfeld and Nicolson, n.d.

Cheesman, Tom. *The Shocking Ballad Picture Show.* Oxford: Berg, 1994.

Chevalier, Louis. *Splendeurs et Misères du Fait Divers.* Paris: Perrin, 2004.

Darnton, Robert. "Writing News and Telling Stories." *Daedalus* 104 (1975): 175–94.

Dorson, Richard M. "Polish Tales from Joe Woods." *Western Folklore* 8 (1949): 131–45.

Fabre, Daniel, and Jacques Lacroix. "Sur la Production du Récit Populaire: À Propos du 'Fils Assassiné.'" *Arts et Traditions Populaires* 18 (1970): 91–140.

Fischer, Helmut. *Der Rattenhund.* Cologne: Beiträge zur rheinischen Volkskunde, 1991.

Freeman, E. *The Theatre of Albert Camus: A Critical Study.* London: Methuen, 1971.

Goldstein, Diane. "Deranged Psychopaths and Victims Who Go Insane: The Depiction of Mental Health and Illness in Contemporary Legend." Paper presented at the Conference on Contemporary Legend, Aberystwyth, July 2004.

Hindley, Charles. *Curiosities of Street Literature.* 2 vols. London: Broadsheet King, 1966.

Hobbs, Sandy. "Going Mad." Paper presented at the Conference on Contemporary Legend, Sheffield, 1990.

———. "The Social Psychology of a 'Good' Story." In *Perspectives on Contemporary Legend,* II ed. Gillian Bennett, Paul Smith, and J. D. A Widdowson, 133–48. Sheffield: Sheffield Academic Press for CECTAL, 1987.

Hobbs, Sandy, David Cornwell, and Mecca Chiesa. "Telling Tales about Behavior Analysis: Textbooks, Scholarship, and Rumor." In *Experimental and Applied Analysis of Human Behavior,* ed. Julian C. Leslie and Derek Blackman, 251–70. Reno, Nev.: Context, 1999.

Hughes, Helen MacGill. *News and the Human Interest Story.* New Brunswick, N.J.: Transaction, 1981.

Hunt, Robert. *Popular Romances of the West of England: or, The Drolls, Traditions, and Superstitions of Old Cornwall.* 3 d ed. 2 vols. 1865; London: Chatto and Windus, 1923.

Kosko, Maria. "A Propos du Malentendu." *Comparative Literature* 10 (1958): 376–77.

———. *Le Fils Assassiné (AT 939A): Étude d'un Thème Légendaire.* FF Communications 198. Helsinki: Suomalainen Tiedeakatemia, Academia Scientarum Fennica, 1966.

Lillo, George. *The London Merchant and Fatal Curiosity.* Ed. A. W. Ward. Boston: Heath, 1906.

"The Liverpool Tragedy." *Dear Mr Thoms . . .* 19 (February 1991): 20–22; 21 (June 1991): 19–20; 23 (October 1991): 30–32; 25 (April 1992): 31.

The Liverpool Tragedy; or, A Warning to Disobedient Children and Covetous Parents. London: Evans, n.d.

Lowry, Cynthia. "Folktales." *Western Folklore* 8 (1949): 174–75.

MacDougal, Curtis D. *Hoaxes.* London: Macmillan, 1940.

Metford, J. C. J. *Dictionary of Christian Lore and Legend.* London: Thames and Hudson, 1983.

"Native's Return." *Time,* 28 January 1935, 49.

Newes from Perin in Cornwall. London: E. A., 1618.

Randolph, Vance. "Bedtime Stories from Missouri." *Western Folklore* 10 (1951): 1–10.

Rothert, Otto. *The Outlaws of Cave-in-Rock: Historical Accounts of Famous Highwaymen and River Pirates Who Operated in Pioneer Days upon the Ohio*

and *Mississippi Rivers and over the Old Natchez Trace*. Cleveland: Clark,
1924.

Seguin, Jean-Pierre. *Nouvelles à Sensation: Canards du XIXe Siècle*. Paris: Colin,
1959.

Stephens, Mitchell. *A History of News: From the Drum to the Satellite*.
Harmondsworth: Penguin, 1988.

Virtanen, Reino. "Camus' *Le Malentendu* and Some Analogues." *Comparative
Literature* 10 (1958): 232–40.

Warren, Robert Penn. *Selected Poems, 1923 –1943*. New York: Harcourt, Brace,
1944.

Woollcott, Alexander. "Folk-Lore," in "Shouts and Murmurs" column.
New Yorker, 12 December 1931, 36.

DISPOSSESSED

THE BODY SNATCHERS

The theft of the body is no crime, for whereas the animal's carcass is property the carcass of a man is not.

HILARY MANTELL, *THE GIANT O'BRIEN* *

This chapter deals with horrors perpetrated, or said to have been perpetrated, because the victim has lost possession of his/her own body, which has become a commodity. These are stories and rumors which the press and media have seized upon and made into local or national causes célèbres. The interaction of the oral and the written word is nowhere more evident than here. It is difficult to know how many of the stories were originally spread along oral conduits and were then taken up by the press or vice versa, or, indeed, if this was a simultaneous process. It hardly matters. Though most of the stories I quote come from the press (for it is easiest to collect and preserve them in this form), there is plentiful evidence of a simultaneous and widespread communication of the same narratives and rumors through informal channels. Moreover, the way the reporters write up their stories—what they choose to highlight and the language they use—indicates where the social and cultural pressures lie and is instructive in its own right.

The stories I deal with in this chapter both concern body parts acquired by somebody else; in one, the body part has obviously been stolen; in the other, the missing organs are *perceived* to have been stolen. In one a rumor becomes more like legend and less like news as it grows; the other shows the opposite process, rumor becoming more like news as more facts come to light. In both cases, the outrage consists of someone claiming ownership or making use of another person's body or body parts.

CANNIBALIZATION

Perhaps the dominant legend of the last decades of the twentieth century was about the cannibalization of the body. Here, I use the term *cannibalization* in an expanded sense to mean the removal of body parts by force or stealth so that someone else may use them for his or her advantage. I am aware that I am extending and perhaps diluting the usual meaning of the term, but using it in this way helps to stress that what is happening is both horrific and taboo. In this extended sense, the focus of the word is not on the ingestion of one person by another (though this has also been claimed) but on the plundering of a body and the use of its constituent parts by someone else for personal gain—specifically, the illicit taking and trading of bodies and their organs for cash, research, or transplant surgery.

Some of the earliest references in the contemporary legend literature refer to events supposed to have happened in Estonia in the 1950s. Mare Kõiva reports many stories of human bloodsuckers. An old lady told Kõiva, "After the war there had been blood takers, blood-suckers in Tartu. They had been dark men, but they had also some Estonians in their company. A blonde girl danced with a young man at a party and started to try how her ring would fit on his finger. And finally she left it there. But later she phoned and asked him to bring her ring back. The boy went but did not come back. His family started to search for him and found him when half of his blood had been removed from his body and he had fainted. But he still survived" (8). Köiva also reported that when she was a schoolgirl, she and her friends were terrified by rumors that people were driving black cars (supposedly Russian Pobedas) round the country, kidnapping people and sucking their blood. The drained bodies were later thrown out and left by the roadside (7). This is an interesting story because it has the potential of connecting modern-day organ-theft legends with older traditions about child abductions, many of which feature the cannibalization of the body, especially blood-taking. In the 1880s, for example, in Tsientsin, China, massacres and riots took place after a rumor spread that children's eyes were being stolen to make developing fluid for photography, a new technology at the time (Campion-Vincent, "Organ Theft Narratives" 26); in Lyons in 1770, it was alleged that surgeons captured a child every night to take its arm and try to sew it on to the body of a one-armed prince; in Paris in 1750, in the midst of a panic about disappearing children, it was said that the supposedly leprous King Louis XV abducted children and used their blood to try to cure himself (Farge and Revel 104–13); and Luise White has studied stories of vampire firemen in colonial Africa who since the end of World War I have been said to capture people to take their blood.

I am wary of making strong claims that all these legends are related to each other or to the modern legend complex, because dating a legend and tracing its history are among the most difficult and most perilous of scholarly activities. The human mind is not particularly inventive, especially when it comes to horrors, and runs always in the same old grooves. However, these rumors and stories are at least suggestive. One nineteenth-century story in particular has motifs and a structure that are very like the legends of the "black Volga" we shall explore later. This tale comes from volume 3 of Benjamin Thorpe's *Northern Mythology*, published in London in 1852, and is entitled "The Bloody Coach at Antwerp."

> This is a wonderfully beautiful carriage with four horses. In it sits a lady richly clad, who carries with her many sweetmeats and dainties, for the purpose of enticing such children as are out playing late in the streets; to whom she also promises that she will give them at her castle her little daughter for a playmate. If her artifice fails, she will drag them into the carriage by force, and stop their mouths, to prevent their crying out. She then conveys the poor little creatures far away to a great castle, where their great toes are cut off and they are suffered to bleed to death. Their blood is used as a bath for a great king, who is suffering from a grievous malady. . . . [T]he children . . . must be under seven years of age. (290)

It was not until the 1970s and '80s, however, when folklorists started to take an interest in the sort of material we now call "modern," "urban," or "contemporary" legends, that stories of cannibalized body parts began to capture the imagination of researchers. As far as we can tell from the scholarly literature, at that time the stories took the form that children were being abducted in cars (often black Volgas) and their organs taken for spare-part surgery for rich foreigners. This legend first drew attention when it surfaced in Poland in the mid-1970s, and it remained current ten years later not only in Poland but also in Russia, Belorussia, the Ukraine, and Mongolia. Between 1977 and 1989, "the distribution was so intense," says Dionizjusz Czubala, "that you could hardly meet a Pole who was not familiar with it. It was a time of panic among children, teachers and parents, intensified by the media" (1). Common elements included children coaxed into black or red

cars or otherwise abducted and their blood drained or their organs
taken for spare-part surgery for rich Arabs or Westerners.

Two of the stories Czubala presents cover most of the main
themes of this group of narratives. The first was told in 1977:

> Do you know what has happened in Bedzin? Staska told us yester-
> day. Near the castle there was a black Volga. Some guests were visit-
> ing the castle, the hill, and maybe the church. There was a nun with
> them. They are building a new road and the place looks ruined. Not
> far from there a group of children were playing. The nun took one of
> them by the hand and went to an empty house. The men followed
> her. They came out without the child. They got into the Volga and
> went away.
>
> When the mother learned about that they started to look for the
> child and found it dead. The blood had been removed and the body
> left behind. "I heard that the blood is taken to West Germany to cure
> leukaemia," said Teresa. "Yes, it is true. It is similar to a story from
> Czeladz. A child was kidnapped and dustmen found it in a garbage
> site somewhere in Katowice."

The second story was told by a woman on a Black Sea beach in
the summer of 1989:

> I remember one of these stories because I was shocked by it. I am
> very sensitive to the macabre, and it was a terrifying story. A couple
> had two children. They were on holiday. A sister and a brother went
> far away from their parents. A couple of nice looking people came
> up. They gave them chocolates, took them by the hand and carried
> them away. The children disappeared. They were found dead in a
> place one hundred km away with their eyes plucked out. A gang of
> hired murderers was at large, who took children to their car and car-
> ried them away into a lonely place. They killed the children, plucked
> out their eyes and took the pupils. I heard it six years ago. In the end

the murderers were caught. It was written up. I thought there would be a big trial but they worked for a well-known oculist and the whole thing was hushed up. Nothing came of it. (1, 2)

Probably the most detailed presentation of the contemporary organ-theft legend is Véronique Campion-Vincent's *La Légende des Vols d'Organes* (1997).[1] Her account begins in Latin America in the 1980s. Here, the rumors took two forms. One resembled the Eastern European stories: a sinister car or ambulance was said to be cruising the streets of the poorer quarters of various cities, abducting children so that their bodies could be plundered. The other reflected growing fears in the region about the adoption trade: orphaned children supposedly destined to be placed with loving families were instead ending up on the operating table, with their organs transplanted into the bodies of sick children from wealthy Western countries. The earliest stories circulating in Latin America involved the plundering of children's bodies; theft of eyes then became the focus, followed by theft of kidneys. Though the three variants interpenetrate, Campion-Vincent believes that it is possible to say that those involving the use of bodies as organ banks focused almost exclusively on children and more or less disappeared in late 1988 after a series of robust denials. Tales involving the theft of eyes followed; those involving kidneys evolved a little later, from about 1990. In 1997 stories of kidney thefts were the most dominant form of the legend in America and Western Europe. These stories more often featured adult males than children, though versions continued to appear featuring children who disappeared at Euro Disney or in central Paris.

Since Campion-Vincent's book was written, very many more stories (rumors, legends, and factual accounts) about illicit organ sales and kidney thefts have begun to appear. The work of Nancy Scheper-Hughes and Lawrence Cohen has demonstrated that fears of eye and kidney thefts were rampant in South America, South

Africa, and India in 1996–98 (Scheper-Hughes, "Global" 192). In 1999 Egypt's general prosecutor was reportedly investigating allegations that an organization north of Cairo charged with caring for homeless children was killing them and selling their body parts for profit (BBC News, "Egyptian"); between July 1999 and August 2000, the *Bangkok Post* printed no fewer than thirty-four articles reporting and discussing an Iraqi organ-theft scandal (Chapman); and, more recently, British newspapers have reported that four Russian doctors have been arrested in Moscow for plotting to kill a man for his kidneys (Walsh). This must be only the tip of the iceberg.

The following paragraphs trace the history of this potent complex from the mid-1980s to the turn of the century.

Baby Parts

This was the name given to the rumors by the U.S. Information Agency when it tried to debunk the story at the beginning of 1987. Anecdotally, according to a BBC correspondent, there had been rumors as early as 1985 about a "death strip" of road between Rio de Janeiro and Sao Paulo, Brazil, where children were mown down so their little bodies could be stripped of organs (Pukas 16). However, a story about hijacked adoptions seems to have really gotten the rumor mill going. An article appeared in an Honduran newspaper alleging that instead of being placed with loving families, children from Guatemala, Honduras, and Costa Rica had been used to supply spare parts for people in Western Europe, Israel, and the United States. The first accusation (January 1987) was that a "fattening house" had been discovered where thirteen handicapped children who had been abducted or bought from impoverished families awaited adoption. But the adoptions never happened because the children were actually sold for ten thousand dollars apiece to be dissected and used in organ transplants. A month later, the story appeared in Guatemala. This time, fourteen children (some of them newborns) had supposedly been found in a fattening house: the fee was now said to be twenty thousand dollars. In April of that year, *Pravda* took up the story, alleging that thousands of Honduran children had been sent to the United States, where their organs had been donated to save the lives of children from rich families. The official Soviet news agency, Tass, took the story up, and it then, as Campion-Vincent puts it, "went on a world tour." In Latin America the rumors received apparent confirmation from official or quasi-official sources. A Guatemalan police officer claimed to have uncovered an illicit adoption network run by two Israelis selling children for seventy-five thousand dollars, and a Paraguayan judge alleged that there was a secret orphanage where Brazilian babies were kept until they could be killed and dissected in U.S. hospitals, where their organs were kept in cold storage for future transplants (Schreiberg 12–13). Despite continued and energetic denials by official organizations in Latin America, Israel, and the United States, such stories continued to be believed and widely disseminated through 1988. The rumor mill went relatively quiet between 1989 and 1992, bursting into life again only in 1990, when it was alleged that three thousand Brazilian children had disappeared on their way to Italy for adoption. (In fact, the figure was simply a computational error.) When the rumors appeared again in roughly 1992, most of them took the form of stories about eye thefts.

Eye Thefts

The baby parts story had been largely media generated, but the story that began to replace it was transmitted mainly by word of mouth through rumors. In Guatemala, where the reports flourished in the early 1990s, they were regarded as a *bola*, a Guatemalan term for a story, rumor, or juicy bit of gossip that gives the inside story of national events. The media did not take up eye theft stories until they resulted in attacks on foreigners.

The tales began to appear in the Andean regions of Latin America, in Central America, and in Brazil by the mid-1980s. Eyes were most often said to have been stolen, but some stories mentioned other organs. The rumors typically told of abductions followed by mutilations: the child reappeared, blinded, scarred, or missing a kidney. In its pocket there was a sum of money (sometimes a substantial amount, sometimes only a derisory sum) and a note saying "Thank you for your eyes" (or kidneys or organs). The abductions were said to have been carried out by strangers dressed in black leather and armed with machine guns who burst out of big black shiny cars or red ambulances.

The rumors spreading in Brazil were usually more somber. In these stories, the child did not survive and the crime was discovered only when the body was unearthed and the eyes, heart, lungs, or liver were found to be missing. Major hospitals in the country were said to be engaged in a vast international organ trade. There were multiple sightings of large blue or yellow vans driven by Japanese or Americans patrolling the poorer districts looking for victims who would not be missed. Delinquents, street children, the poor, and the mentally ill were said to be the principal targets. They were thrown in the back of the vans, and the mutilated corpses were later dumped beside the road, thrown over the walls of the municipal cemetery, or put out with the hospital garbage. Denials only publicized and reinforced the stories. The fear was so acute that children were kept out of school, sent away to relatives in the country, or locked up while their parents went to work.

For about ten days at the end of 1988, Lima, the capital of Peru, was invaded by rumors of eye thefts. It was said that groups of men dressed like doctors but carrying machine guns were driving around the poor districts of the city abducting children. The children were later found wandering around with bandages over their eyes and thank you notes in their pockets. The eyes were allegedly being sold to pay off the national debt. Two attempted lynchings of foreigners followed this panic. In one case, three young French tourists were forcibly removed from the police station, where they had been taken for their protection; in the other, some researchers into infantile diarrhea were denounced as eye thieves and set upon.

Two sensational articles published simultaneously in Britain and France at the end of 1991 told the story of a poor little Argentine boy, one of several from the barrios whose kidneys were stolen and sold on the black market for forty-five thousand dollars to Americans, Brazilians, or rich people from their own country (Radford 36).[2] In Mexico in 1989, David Schreiberg heard a story about a traveling salesman "who boarded a bus with a leaky suitcase. When a suspicious bus driver opened it, he found it full of children's eyes and kidneys, wrapped in plastic and chilled with melting ice."[3] Schreiberg reports that police chiefs said that similar stories had been circulating for at least two years and that newspapers were full of rumors under headlines such as "Undocumented Children, Victims of Those Who Traffic in Organs," "20,000 Kidnapped Each Year in Tijuana and Ciudad Juárez," and "Traffic in Human Organs Probable Cause of Kidnappings." He comments, "Millions of educated and uneducated people—particularly in Latin America—firmly believe that the United States has created, in essence, an international network of child murderers, backed by gruesome teams of medical butchers" (12). Official inquiries launched by the Mexican authorities in 1990 and 1992 in the light of persistent rumors such as these concluded that there was indeed an illegal trade in children, but for adoption or prostitution, not for organ transplants. The rumors continued, however. A 1995 Associated Press story reported the deaths of sixty-one babies at a Mexican hospital and some parents' belief that hospital staffers were running an organ racket ("More Organ Sale Rumours").

In Guatemala, stories of organ thefts led to serious attacks on foreigners in 1994. Sixty people were hospitalized after a riot caused by rumors that an American woman detained for routine questioning was selling babies' organs. The following month, another American woman was almost beaten to death by a mob of angry villagers in western Guatemala after being accused of abducting an eight-year-old boy who was actually at a religious event and who subsequently returned home.[4] John Shonder, an American working in Guatemala City at that time, remembers his secretary telling him that the body of a little child had been found on the roadside with the chest open and the heart and other organs missing. A note (in English) had been left on the child's thoracic cage. It said, "Thank you for the organs." Shonder recalled that in the following weeks the numbers of corpses said to have been left at the roadside multiplied: some reports said five bodies had been found, others said eight. In some rumors, instead of a thank you note, the killers had supposedly left a handful of U.S. dollars. Another story told of a street urchin found dazed and blind. When he was taken to hospital, the doctors found that his corneas had been removed. Again, the child's pockets were full of dollar bills. Everyone Shonder encountered thought that the rumors were true, and graffiti appeared throughout the city alleging "Gringos child stealers." Violent incidents followed in March. Shonder recalls seeing a particularly lurid television report supposedly devoted to uncovering illegal adoptions. The reporter picked up a young child by the legs and asked the attendant, "This one here, how much are his eyes worth? His liver? His kidneys?" This irresponsible broadcast was routinely cited as proof of the rumors, and attacks on foreigners followed. These were serious enough for America to recall Peace Corps volunteers to the capital and advise tourists to leave the country altogether.

In January 1995 a respected British weekly newspaper, *The Observer*, reported, "Strange rumours are circulating in Havana.

Children are being snatched from their mothers by men on motorcycles and their bodies found days later without their internal organs. Tourists are being kidnapped, butchered and sold as pork for New Year celebrations. . . . [T]he stories are widely believed. . . . Some Cubans are saying the children's organs have been stolen for transplants; others fear that believers in Santeria . . . require them for sacrifice" (Dimmick). The heading for this item was "Cuba Sickened by Pork Pies," a double entendre relying on Cockney rhyming slang, in which *pork pies* means "lies." [5]

The rumors later assumed a slightly different form, absorbing elements from the black Volga variants. Now it was alleged that people dressed as clowns and riding in Volvos were abducting children. The rumors spread to Honduras, and sixty clowns publicly burned their costumes as a protest (Campion-Vincent, *Légende* 41).

Kidney Thefts

When stories of organ thefts began appearing in the United States and Western Europe in the early 1990s (see Brunvand 149–54), it was of course citizens of affluent countries who were generally said to be the victims of an illegal trade in organs. The stories initially utilized a very varied set of motifs, some new, some similar to the legends circulating in the poorer countries. A couple from Sweden were said to have gone on vacation to Brazil and been approached by a small boy who asked them to sign a petition against the denuding of the tropical forest. The petition was, in fact, a consent form to donate their kidneys for transplantation. A woman holidaying in Goa contracted appendicitis and had to be operated on. According to rumor, it was discovered that although her appendix was still intact, one of her kidneys was missing. [6] In Italy, rumors circulated that women shopping in boutiques in Bari and Palermo had vanished from changing rooms. They were said to have been taken to a secret basement equipped as an operating room or to a truck, similarly equipped for surgery, parked outside the shop, where their organs were removed. A criminal gang was thought to be carrying out organ thefts to order. In Turin a story circulated about a young man who was waylaid by a beautiful woman and taken to a truck equipped for surgery, where a kidney was taken from him (Stilo and Toselli).

Equally frightening rumors circulated in Europe and the United States among parents and (particularly) children in 1991. Though the threat to children is not explicit (there is no outcome, no closure, to these stories), they have quite a lot in common with legends of the black Volga type, especially those later circulating in Honduras. The stories involve "killer clowns" cruising city streets in cars or ambulances and abducting children.[7] Reports also circulated freely in Britain about bogus social workers who were calling at homes and demanding to see the children, who were then "interfered with."[8] Inflamed by the real-life child abductions carried out by Marc Dutroux,[9] rumors of "phantom photographers" who loitered at school gates began to proliferate in Belgium. Rumors also circulated about a green or white Mercedes that trailed children on their way to school. In Italy, rumors spread about black ambulances touring the streets of Bologna to take children away, of gypsy women trying to catch children and hide them under their skirts, and of women dressed as nurses accompanied by men dressed as carabinieri luring children into ambulances by telling the children that their parents had been injured (Stilo and Tosselli).

In Britain and Ireland, the bogus social worker scare and the killer clowns scare were soon followed by accounts of organ thefts. Folklorists began to report hearing such stories in 1992 in southern England, the English midlands, and Northern Ireland. Similar stories had surfaced in Australia in 1990, in Germany and the United States in 1991, in Ireland in 1992 (discussed later in this chapter); Sweden in 1994; and in Denmark in 1996.[10] Several versions were circulating. The simplest (and perhaps the earliest) tells of a person (usually a man) discovered wandering about with a mysterious scar and later diagnosed as having had a kidney removed. The following example comes from Ireland, courtesy of Irish proverb scholar Fionnuala Williams, who heard the story in a class and passed it on to me: "A married couple go to Rio de Janeiro where they notice there are great extremes of wealth and poverty. Shortly after arriving the man disappears. His wife contacts the police and the embassy in an effort to find him. After a while she flies home as she is short of money. Several weeks later the man is discovered wandering the streets of Rio de Janeiro in a dazed state. He is taken to hospital for a medical check-up where it is discovered that one of his kidneys has been removed" (personal communication, October 2001).

English folklorist Roy Vickery heard a more elaborate version in the tearoom of the Natural History Museum in London in 1992:

> I heard a nasty story at the weekend. There was this woman who lived in Scotland, and her son lived in London—he's just moved down and found somewhere to live—so she was coming down to find out how he was. When she got to his place he wasn't there. She was told he was in hospital. When she got to the hospital she was told that he had been found wandering around the streets in a very bad state, because he had had an operation and been let out too soon.
>
> "But he's never had anything wrong with him, he's never been ill, so why did he need an operation?"
>
> "He's had a kidney removed."
>
> Apparently he met this attractive girl who took him back to her place, drugged him, and when he woke up he was in hospital, having had a kidney removed. Apparently she does this sort of thing. They made a beautiful job of the operation, but they let him out far too soon. Apparently this sort of thing is very common in the north.

Vickery then asked, "Where's 'the north'? North London?" and was told, "Ummm yes, North London. They sell the kidneys" ("Contemporary Legends").

"The north" was not the only place kidney thieves were said to be at work in the United Kingdom. The south coast too, it seems, was under threat. An August 1992 article in *Portsmouth and Southsea Streetlife* reported,

> Police are probing a terrible rumour they are praying is not true.
>
> It concerns young men being abducted by beautiful girls and having their organs removed. . . .
>
> Detective Superintendent Dave Watson, Commander of Southsea police, had so many reports that he felt he had to investigate.
>
> Detective Ian Mosely is on the case.
>
> He said: "I have investigated five different rumours that have been going round the city.
>
> "Each time I have come up against a brick wall.
>
> "But they all revolve round the same basic story which is very worrying.
>
> "Each story starts with a young man leaving a club on Southsea seafront with a beautiful girl then waking up in London, Liverpool or Bournemouth between two and four days later.
>
> "Often the victim believes he has been stabbed because of a wound in his back.
>
> "I spoke to doctors who [deal] with transplants who said it is highly unlikely that a fit man could possibly be walking round four days after having a transplant removed without having any treatment.
>
> "If this is happening in Portsmouth it would be horrific." (Barter)

The Irish version lacks a motif that is present in the English versions and seems to be more fully developed in stories from the United States at approximately the same time. This motif will be familiar from the chapter on AIDS Aggressors. In these narratives the man is lured to his fate by a beautiful woman, who removes his kidney on the spot. Danusha Goska quotes Jan Brunvand's version, supposedly from 1991, in "Waking up Less Than Whole":

> The story tells of a group of young men who went to New York City for a weekend of fun. One of them was attracted to a woman he met in a bar, and he told his buddies he was going to spend the night at her place and would get in touch with them later. They didn't hear from him until late the next day when he phoned to say, "I think I'm in such and such a hotel in room number so and so, but something is wrong with me and you'd better come and get me."
>
> When the friends arrived at the hotel room, they found their friend in bed and the sheets spattered with blood. He was very weak. When they helped him out of bed, they discovered a fresh surgical closure on his back and still more blood, so they rushed him to a hospital. There, the doctors discovered that the man had had one of his kidneys removed, and they concluded that he had been drugged so his kidneys could be taken for sale on the black market for human organs. (196–97)

By 1996, the story was even more elaborate and became even more like AIDS Aggressor stories as a result of the addition of a message left by the attacker. This version was e-mailed to Canadian folklorist Philip Hiscock by a California hairdresser in July of that year:

> [My co-worker] called me at home [a few months ago]. He said, "You are not going to believe what I heard, it really gives me the creeps, it actually has me freaked out." I said, "What?" An acquaintance of his had a nephew or cousin that went to Las Vegas for a little fun. While he was there he met a very friendly and attractive woman in the bar. They really hit it off, and after many hours drinking and

flirting, they went up to his room. He woke up some days later in the bathtub that still had some ice in it, naked. He found a note attached to him (how I don't remember) that said, "If you are reading this you have managed to survive. Call 911 immediately, stay calm and don't move out of the tub. Your kidneys have been surgically removed and you are in critical condition." (Footnote to Mazo)

The idea of the note was further elaborated in a version also sent from California to Jeff Mazo in London. (Mazo does not say when the message arrived, but it was presumably some time in 1996, when he published this account.)

This guy went out last Saturday night to a party. He was having a good time, had a couple of beers and some girl seemed to like him and invited him to go to another party. He quickly agreed and decided to go along with her. She took him to a party in some apartment and they continued to drink, and even got involved with some other drugs (unknown which).

The next thing he knew, he woke up completely naked in a bathtub filled with ice. He was still feeling the effects of the drugs, but looked round to see if he was alone.

He looked down at his chest, which had "CALL 911 OR YOU WILL DIE" written on it in lipstick. He saw a phone was on a stand next to the tub and dialled. He explained to the EMS operator what the situation was. . . She advised him to get out of the tub [and] look himself over in the mirror. . . [S]he told him to check his back. He did, only to find two 9-inch slits on his lower back. . . . [T]hey sent a rescue team over.

Mazo's correspondent went on to supply a lot of speculative rationalization. The drugs must have been medical rather than recreational; kidneys are worth ten thousand dollars each on the black market; the second party was a sham; "the people in it had to be at least medical students"; the victim is currently awaiting a tissue match for a transplant of his own. The message ends with a call for information to be sent to the Texas Rangers or University of Texas at Austin to help track down the perpetrators.

These versions show a clear progression from less to more elaborate and strongly suggest that by 1996 the story had been making the rounds for some time, especially in the United States, picking up motifs from other legends (especially AIDS Aggressor legends) as it went. The version told in Ireland, though undated, closely resembles the version circulating in Sweden in 1990 and is very vague and spare. The versions circulating in the United Kingdom in 1992 share some of the same motifs but are more elaborate and use an additional, very traditional, motif (a beautiful but perfidious woman), which we have already seen in action several times. The fourth one, from the United States, is even more formed and legendlike. It is much more dramatic and full of typical legend paraphernalia (not only a beautiful woman but also blood, drugs, and an emergency telephone call). The last ones from 1996 have all these features plus a motif that is a consistent part of the story from then on, the literally chilling detail of the ice-filled bathtub.

This motif features strongly in versions that started appearing in 1997, largely as the result of an e-mail warning, "Travellers Beware!!" that claimed that an organized gang of kidney thieves was operating in the United States, drugging business travelers, removing their kidneys, and selling them on the black market. One of the most interesting features of these versions is that they developed similarly to AIDS Aggressor legends. Mazo's version melded with mirror versions of AIDS Aggressor stories, but the e-mailed warnings dropped the party-and-beautiful-woman motif (and thereby the echoes of the poison and honey theme). The high-living partygoer was replaced by a weary "business traveler" whose innocent nightcap was drugged by local villains. Thus, the e-mailed warning exhibited a more generalized threat, similar to the casket and needle versions of AIDS Aggressor legends.

Web searches in August 2002 and March 2004 revealed that this version remained dominant, though a version with a female victim and a male decoy appeared in an online women's magazine (everything else in this version was the same as in Hiscock's version—perfidious seduction, ice-filled bathtub, note). The clue to the enormity that had been committed on the victim's body in this version was a tube sticking out of her back, a feature that is found as an alternative to the nine-inch suture in some other versions. The story also includes a bit of plot detail that gets over the implausibility of the conversation between the victim and EMS operator in Mazo's version: here it is said that the EMS operator was so used to such calls that she knew exactly what to ask the victim (www.happywomanmagazine.com).

The Debate: Issues and Interpretations

The folkloristic approach to these stories has met with resistance from some quarters. By treating stories of organ thefts as urban or contemporary legends, such critics imply, folklorists are ignoring or denying the evils created by a market in organs for transplantation and thus perhaps even adding to the problems.

This misapprehension about folklorists and their work probably had its beginnings in "baby parts" panics in South and Central America. In an attempt to dampen down the rumors and extricate the United States from some very nasty accusations, the U.S. Information Agency in Washington, D.C., initiated an investigation. In 1987, its "Program Officer for Countering Disinformation and Misinformation"—that is, its rumor buster—Todd Leventhal, began tracking rumors of child organ trafficking. In a report published in December 1994 he sought to defuse the rumors by comparing them to urban legends, citing prominent legend scholars Jan Harold Brunvand, Bengt af Klintberg, and Véronique

Campion-Vincent in support of his argument. Leventhal presented a conventional definition of urban legend as "a false story that is commonly believed despite the total lack of evidence for it because it encapsulates, in story form, widespread anxieties about modern life. . . . [T]hese myths achieve credibility because they give voice, form, and substance to unarticulated anxieties or suspicions" (2). As an example of an urban legend, he cited stories of pets exploding in microwaves and denied that there was "credible evidence that would indicate that trafficking in children's organs is a real phenomenon" (2). The implication that urban legends are always false and often trivial (as illustrated by the microwave story he gives as an example) and that rumors of a trade in organs could be dismissed as equally trivial enraged those who were trying to evaluate the evidence. Most vociferous among these has been a radical medical anthropologist from the University of California at Berkeley, Nancy Scheper-Hughes. A member of the Bellagio Task Force on Transplantation, Bodily Integrity, and the International Traffic in Organs set up by Columbia University in New York in 1995 and Organs Watch set up at Berkeley in 1999, Scheper-Hughes has committed herself to a thorough investigation of the nature and extent of organ trafficking. She is one of many academics, medics, and activists who have charted the rise of a global trade in organs that is deeply worrying and that appears to be yet another example of the ruthless exploitation of the Third World and its disadvantaged citizens.[11] In the paragraphs that follow, I shall look at the evidence that Scheper-Hughes and others have assembled about the organ trade and discuss her argument that organ-theft stories should not be regarded as urban legends.

TRADE IN ORGANS? THEFT OF ORGANS?

Unfortunately, it is true that there is and for a long time has been a trade in organs. There is little doubt that organs were sold or taken without consent for medical or other purposes in the past—the history of European scientific advance is littered with such instances—and disturbing evidence is emerging about experimentation on the brains of aboriginal people, the less able, social misfits, convicted criminals, and others.[12] There is troubling contemporary evidence, too, of the commodification of body parts for cash. Until recently, for example, at least one British hospital routinely provided thymus glands to a pharmaceutical company in return for cash donations (Bosely and Ward). Similarly, a story from CBS News (September 2002) alleged that genetic material had been taken from children and patented by Miami Children's hospital; it was further alleged that as early as the 1980s, doctors treating one patient at the University of California discovered that he "had spleen cells that could have special curative powers. So special, the university patented them and made millions selling the rights to a biotech company," all without the patient's consent. When the patient discovered what had happened, it was said, he took his case to the California Supreme Court, which found against him on the grounds that what had happened to him "might be unethical but it wasn't illegal. People, the court ruled, have no property rights to their own body."[13] More recently, there have been reports from California and New Orleans of the sale and misuse of bodies donated for medical research.[14]

There is also ample and growing evidence of a market in organs for transplantation.[15] In a 1998 article in the *New York Review*, David Rothman, the chair of the Bellagio Task Force on Transplantation, said that the "routes that would-be organ recipients follow are well known to both doctors and patients. Italians . . . travel to Belgium . . ., so do Israelis, who lately have also been going to rural Turkey and bringing their surgeons along with them. Residents of the Gulf States, Egyptians, Malaysians, and Bangladeshis mainly go to India for organs. In the Pacific, Koreans, Japanese, and Taiwanese, along with the residents of Hong Kong and Singapore, fly to China" (15). The suspicion is that these patients are paying not only for the skills of the surgeons but for the organs they receive, on many occasions from living donors. These living donors are overwhelmingly desperately poor people from the Third World, driven to self-mutilation by mounting debts and destitution. It also seems undoubtedly true that the donor system is corrupted in a number of ways: by trickery of various sorts, deception of donors, the intervention of brokers, and all the distortions to which greed, desperation, and inequalities of wealth lead.

It is relatively easy to find figures quoting the price of kidneys, to read newspaper stories of illicit operations and transactions[16] and to find advertisements offering to sell organs for cash (an online article about medical malpractice I accessed in August 2004 was accompanied by ads for hair implants and lung, liver, kidney, and pancreas replacements; an announcement of the "shortest waiting time for kidney transplantation"; and a "kidney needed" request). But although many people have offered many guesstimates, it is not easy to quantify this trade with any accuracy because it is a clandestine one. What is mostly lacking to date is a way of matching this largely anecdotal information to reliable figures that can show the extent of the practice.[17] The evidence, however, is that an illegal trade in organs (for research and transplantation) does exist and that it is a large and mounting problem on an international scale. It also a political process. As Scheper-Hughes says, "Organ transplantation now takes place in a trans-national space with both donors and recipients following the paths of capital and technology in the global economy. In general, the movement of donor organs follows modern routes of capital: from South to North, from the Third World to the First World, from poor to rich bodies, from black and brown to white bodies, from young to old bodies, productive to less productive, and female to male bodies" ("End").

No one would disagree that this is a matter of grave concern, but not everyone would wish to follow Scheper-Hughes's argument to the conclusion she draws, that this is part of "the increasing public hostility to the bodies, minds, children, and reproductive capacities of the urban poor" ("Min(d)ing" 33) and a "postmodern form of human sacrifice," a ritual scapegoating ("Min(d)ing" 52). Many people also would not want to conclude (as it appears she does) that because the existence of a market in organs for transplant has been proved, it follows that stories about organ thefts must be treated equally seriously. Documenting the history of organ transplantation has revealed that concerns about the objectification and commodification of the human body are justified, serious, and have enormous political significance, but it does not follow that stories about "cannibalizing kids" (Samper) have a similar status. Indeed, the Bellagio Task Force found "no reliable evidence to substantiate" allegations of kidnap and murder for organs, reporting, "Not one documented case exists of murder or kidnap or sale of children for their organs" (Rothman et al. 6–7 [online version]). Likewise, Rothman points out in the *New York Review*, "Although there have been sporadically reported stories of robberies of kidneys in India, I have not found a single documented case of abduction, mutilation, or murder for organs, whether in North or South America." In the same article he spells out why such reports must be intrinsically untrustworthy: "In truth medical realities make such kidnappings and murder highly unlikely. The rural villages and the urban apartments in which transplants are alleged to secretly take place do not have the sterile environment necessary to remove or implant an organ. Organs from children are too small to be used in adults. And however rapacious health care workers may seem, highly trained and medically sophisticated teams . . . are not likely to conspire to murder for organs or accept them off the street. Had they done so, at least one incident would have come to light in the last fifteen years" (16). Rothman thus effectively uncouples the trade in organs from rumors of organ theft and child abduction. I find these arguments convincing.

Consequently, I believe that the organ trade and stories about organ thefts are two separate issues, and it is important not to let one's sense of outrage lead one to believe that they must be inextricably linked or that one proves the other.

ORGAN THEFTS: URBAN LEGENDS?

But even if it is accepted that organ-theft stories have not been substantiated, perhaps we still need to discuss whether they are urban or contemporary legends rather than simple misinformation or understandable misconceptions. Part of the problem for those who deny the legendary nature of these reports is mistaken ideas about the genre. In this case, misconceptions seem to have been drawn principally from the pithy but simplistic definition in Leventhal's report (and its very unfortunate choice of examples). Other information seems to have come from a cursory reading of Brunvand's work, misquotation of Campion-Vincent's writings, and what sounds suspiciously like a misreading of Sandy Hobbs's "The Social Psychology of a 'Good' Story." Consequently, for many people, the term *urban legend* has become tainted with notions of falsity and triviality. Scheper-Hughes is undoubtedly right when she reacts with indignation to implications that these horrific stories are, as she puts it, "circulated and repeated because they are 'good to tell' [and] entertain by fright just like good ghost stories" ("Min(d)ing" 36). As the Bellagio Task Force report added in a rider to its statement about the lack of evidence for child organ stealing, "rumors of organs theft are not at one with tales of unidentified flying objects or of pets exploding in microwave ovens" (Rothman et al. 7 [online version]). But those of us who work in the field know that contemporary legends are much more than this, more serious and sometimes far more dangerous.

It's hard to know where to start unraveling the misapprehensions about the nature of contemporary legends contained in the statements I've quoted, but I shall focus on three aspects of the genre that may demonstrate why folklorists treat stories of organ thefts as urban or contemporary legends. First, Scheper-Hughes has repeated on many occasions that she finds that these stories express "the chronic state of emergency . . . experienced by desperately poor people living on the margins of the newly emerging global economy" ("Global" 200). "The organ-stealing rumors were told, remembered, and circulated," she says, "because they were true at that indeterminate level between the real, the surreal, and the uncanny. They expressed an intuitive sense that something was amiss" ("Min(d)ing" 36). They cannot therefore be "mere" urban legends: they must be "metaphorically true, operating by means of symbolic substitutions" (Rothman et al. 7, citing Scheper-Hughes). Yet this formulation comes remarkably close to what most contemporary legend scholars see as an almost ubiquitous characteristic of the genre: contemporary legends are usually thought of as stories that may not perhaps be factually true but that transmitting believers and believing hearers think *could* be true or even in some way *ought* to be true. An early essay by Georgina Boyes explored just this aspect of the genre in a typically lucid and insightful way. I don't agree with all the points Boyes makes in this essay, but most other legend scholars do, and her work is worth quoting because it demonstrates exactly what Scheper-Hughes means by metaphorical or symbolic truth and sets this out as an essential characteristic of the genre. In only her second paragraph, Boyes writes,

> The context in which rumour legends are performed is critical to the genre. These legends articulate, and to a great extent validate, wishes and fears. They are told because they express in a succinct and entertaining form what narrators wish to present as a truth about contemporary life and behaviour. These truths and the type of presentation associated with rumour legends are not, however,

arbitrary. The wishes and fears expressed through these legends are usually those of a particular social grouping. . . . *Any rumour legend performance, therefore, can be said to involve articulation and validation of a truth by and for a subculture.* (64, author's emphasis)

In this essay Boyes discusses the way a legend teller deals with challenges to the truth of the story being told, showing how the narrator moves from reaffirmation, to correction of minor details, to bringing in the accounts of other witnesses, to a "final reassertion of truth and refusal to accept that overall [the] legend does not represent the truth." She concludes, "Until the threat which the subculture perceives to be inherent in wider culture ceases to be a motive, narratives which articulate and validate the threat will be believed and communicated without question. Greater culture may suppress or deny these perceived truths, but the subculture 'knows' that they are a reality. *The* truth is a shifting concept, dependent on viewpoint and accidental presence at a place in time, *a* truth exists while ever it is perceived, and it is this actuality which generates and gives continued existence to rumour legends" (76, author's emphasis). As I understand it, this is also Scheper-Hughes's position. But instead of proving that organ-theft stories are not urban legends, as she thinks it does, it actually indicates that they are.

After the taint of "triviality" and "lies" is removed from the way contemporary legends are regarded, after it is recognized how serious and significant such stories can be, no one should be alarmed or outraged to find that others regard their stories as legends.

The second point I want to make is about the distribution of organ-theft stories. Though it is undoubtedly true that stories about, for example, children being abducted off the streets have had particular resonance in countries with poor records of civil rights and histories of violence toward street children and marginalized people, it is important to recognize that the match is not perfect. Stories of child abductions from public places for organ transplants or other violations of the body have been reported equally frequently from the United States and Western Europe as from Brazil or pre-Mandela South Africa (the countries Scheper-Hughes repeatedly cites), and such has been the case for several centuries, not only in the recent past. The same is true for stories of organ thefts from adults. For every story about the violation of the body of a disadvantaged person for the good of a privileged person, there is a story about the cannibalization of a privileged person's body by unscrupulous Others, Third World villains as well as the usual cast of madmen, social outcasts, murderers, crooked medics, and criminal gangs. (For another discussion, see Campion-Vincent's reply to Scheper-Hughes [Campion-Vincent, "On Organ Theft"].) The best correlation is, in fact, not between organ-theft stories and sociopolitical conditions but between one story and another and between organ-theft stories as a group and other stories of kidnap, theft, and the violation of the body. All of these tales rely on a shared reservoir of recurring themes, motifs, and narrative patterns, and like the latest AIDS Aggressor legends, they show *everyone* to be at risk.

This leads me to the significance of narrative patterning, especially recurrent motifs. As we have seen, in 1852 Benjamin Thorpe published a story in his *Northern Mythology* about "a wonderfully beautiful carriage" with a "richly clad" lady offering "sweetmeats and dainties" to children and then abducting them. More than a hundred years later, there were rumors in Eastern Europe about children being tempted into red or black cars and then abducted. In the 1990s there were persistent rumors in Britain and America about "killer clowns" bundling children into vans with pictures of clowns on the back, and there were stories in Italy about people dressed as nurses and carabinieri tricking children into ambulances and about young men being lured into trucks equipped as operating rooms. A virtually identical pattern can be found in stories reported to Scheper-Hughes in Brazil: "Residents of the ramshackle hillside *favela* of Alto da Cruzeiro, the primary site of my research, reported multiple sightings of large blue and yellow combi-vans (the so-called 'gypsy taxis' used by the poor the world over) driven by Americans or Japanese 'agents' said to be scouring poor neighbourhoods in search of stray young-sters" (Scheper-Hughes, "Min(d)ing" 34). Similarly, in South Africa, Scheper-Hughes heard "anxious rumors of luxury cars prowling squatter camps in search of children to steal" ("End"). Other recur-ring motifs are the warning messages or the notes said in some of the stories to be left on the mutilated body (a sort of coda to make sure the hearer gets the point), the "lure" motif (beautiful woman, "sweetmeats and dainties," gaily painted vans, and so on), suitcases full of eyes dripping telltale ice and bathtubs full of telltale blood, and the cast of stock characters (villainous foreign-ers, rapacious criminals, innocents abroad). Similarities of detail may seem a trivial thing to concentrate on given the seriousness of the content of the stories, but these recurring motifs are impor-tant pointers to the nature of the reports. Where these details occur, they are a pretty good indicator that one is in the pres-ence of folklore—they show that the account has been heard by many ears and told by many voices and in the process has been traditionalized.

There are two ways of interpreting recurring stories and repeated claims. The first is to believe, as Forteans believe of anomalous occurrences, that the multiplicity and similarity of the claims is evidence that such things really happen. The other is the folk-loristic approach, which sees recurring story patterns as evidence of the presence of folklore. I unashamedly take the folkloristic position: the more similar the pattern, the more closely I feel one should scrutinize the individual claims. I think it is impor-tant to bring the same standards of evidence to rumors, especially atrocity rumors, as to other information. If a story is patterned like a legend and travels like a legend and functions like a legend, then a legend is what it usually is, and it should be treated with caution if presented as news. News should be true and is assumed to *be* true; legends make no such promises.

DISSECTION

Introductory Remarks

At the heart of this debate lies what Donald Joralemon has called "an ideological war over the meaning of the human body in which organ transplantation is a major battlefield" (339). Concerns about organ transplants and legends of organ thefts very clearly bring into focus a range of related medical, cultural, ethical, and philosophical problems. These include the integrity of the body, the ownership of the body, the relationship of body and soul, the nature of the afterlife, and the definition of death. It is far beyond the scope of this book to explore these problems.[18] Here, I shall concentrate on a single aspect. The horror of organ-theft stories springs in great part from the sense that the victims' bodies are being both claimed and violated by others. Where the stories allege that children are being murdered for their body parts, the horror is intensified by the sense that the child is leaving this world not only claimed and violated by strangers but also mutilated and incomplete. Not only are cultural taboos being infringed, but so are powerful cultural boundaries; consequently, children are juxtaposed with death, medicine with crime, dying with commerce, concepts of the dead as "at rest" with bodies buried without all their parts. In the paragraphs that follow, I will explore this last juxtaposition as a way of contextualizing attitudes toward dissection and introducing the U.K. child-organ scandal that I will later discuss at some length.

The Material Dead

Though many—even perhaps most—people in the Christian world today would deny that they really believe in the resurrection of the body in a material heaven,[19] they continue to speak and act as if they did. Surrounded by images of the dead as material, how could it be otherwise? Churchgoers can see representations of the Day of Judgment with the reembodied dead getting out of their graves, being tumbled down to hell or raised up to heaven in material bodies plainly capable of pain or joy. Filmgoers may see the dead walking, talking, acting in the everyday world, not being recognized as ghosts and sometimes not even knowing they are dead (*Ghost, Sixth Sense, The Others*). Sharers of folklore can enjoy the legends of the "Guide of the Black Mountain," the "Ghost in Search of Help for a Dying Man," or the "Vanishing Hitchhiker," in all of which the dead are indistinguishable from the living.

The bereaved may be sent traditional consolation literature—"words against death" as British theologian and anthropologist Douglas Davies phrases it (2)—verses that insist that death is nothing at all and that the lost one has merely gone into another room. In this context, I would guess that the euphemisms *lost* or *gone before* are pretty accurate reflections of popular imagery of death. The term *dead* does not quite equate with "extinct" or even "nonexistent": its ramifications are less final and less absolute.

Those who have had a close shave with death but lived to tell the tale may report a near-death experience where they seem to pass through a tunnel, see an effulgent light or the gates of heaven, and converse with heavenly creatures or dead relatives. In her fascinating essay, "Letters to the Dead," Linda Dégh reports one particularly vivid experience: "During an episode of 'the Phil Donahue Show' that dealt with near-death experiences . . . a woman testified that she had met her brother of whose existence she had been unaware because he died as an infant before her birth. He appeared to her now in heaven as a young adult because the new body of the dead always remains a young grown-up" (165). The newly bereaved may see or hear, touch or smell the physical body of ones they have lost or may experience a sense of their presence (see Bennett and Bennett, *Presence*). Even the ghosts of literature and the past are remarkably material, though more obviously recognizable as ghosts. Banquo's ghost, the ghost of Hamlet's father, and the ghosts that came to taunt Richard III the night before battle are all very material entities. And so are many of those found in the classics and in the folklore compilations of the nineteenth century—the ghosts of the philosopher Athenodorus, the queen Anne Boleyn, or the highwayman Dick Turpin, for example.

This materiality is reinforced by the universal availability of photography: as Dégh says, "photos actually help keep the dead alive, fixing not only their ideal image but keeping them magically ageless for eternity, exactly as the family wants to see them in the hereafter" (175). Also, though the conventional service in the church or at the crematorium still focuses on the deceased as dead and on returning the corpse to the earth or the elements, the message is often undermined by the presence of a photograph of the deceased alive and well and by the participation of the mourners in creating a word picture of him/her as a living, breathing, acting person. So, although the formal rites may still emphasize dissolution and parting, the accretions the ceremony has acquired are adapted to the prevailing popular ways of imagining the dead as whole and indissoluble. The mourning that continues after the ceremony—the grave visiting and memorialization with verses, flowers, and photographs—also helps to reinforce these images of the dead, incorporating them into a surprisingly material and interactive otherworld where they are able to respond to the traumas of earthly life while they wait for the rest of the family to join them.

The materiality of the dead and the otherworld in popular imagery and imagination is nowhere more evident than in the "In Memoriam" column of the provincial newspapers about which Dégh has written. The practice is just as widespread in Britain as in the United States and takes almost identical forms—that is, a verse, usually based on a selection offered by the newspaper, gives the date of the death, celebrates the dead person's life, praises their virtues, and mourns their loss. These dead have been transported to a world almost as material as the mundane one and not very dissimilar. So the lost family member may be thought of as

> *Watching till we come home to him*
> *Anxious if we are late*
> *Watching from heaven's window*
> *Leaning on heaven's gate.*
>
> *Dégh 167*

Bodies as "Things"

All these reassuring popular conceptions, all these more or less unconscious cultural attitudes, are disturbed when the body of the lost loved one is cut up, excavated, considered a "thing" whose constituent parts may be "harvested" for use in a stranger's body or thrown away as useless rubbish. For such reasons, the families of people who had donated their bodies for medical research in the United States were outraged when it was recently discovered that universities were misusing the donated bodies. In February 2003, the willed-body program at the University of Texas medical branch at Galveston was suspended after the supervisor was allegedly found to have sold "nails from the fingers and toes of cadavers" for research between November 1999 and August 2001. "Officials" were said to have "also learnt that [he] allowed the ashes of dozens of cremated donated bodies to be mixed, making it impossible to return ashes to donors' families" ("Supervisor's"). The scandal led to an ongoing inquiry by the Federal Bureau of Investigation (Josefson).

In 2004, it was reported that the Tulane University in New Orleans had hired a New York-based company to "distribute" surplus corpses from the school's willed-body program, only to discover later that this company had sold seven bodies to the U.S. Army for up to thirty thousand dollars apiece to be blown up in land mine tests. The company was fired. Michael Meyer, professor of philosophy at Santa Clara University in California, is reported as saying, "Imagine if your mother had said all her life that she wanted her body to be used for science, and then her body was used to test landmines. There are some moral problems with deception here" (Buncombe, "Body Parts"). This is putting it too mildly, since the issue is not only an abstract ethical question but the physical horror endured by the bereaved.

Another scandal erupted at much the same time, in this instance involving the willed-body program at the University of California campuses at Los Angeles and Irvine. At Irvine, an audit of the program revealed a number of malpractices, including failing to return remains to families in accordance with their wishes. There were also various financial irregularities, including the sale of cadaver spines to a research group and the use of cadavers, without UCI's permission, in a private anatomy class run at UCI's morgue by a company belonging to an associate of the program supervisor (Charatan). At UCLA, the willed-body program was said to receive about 175 bodies each year donated for research and education; as at Tulane, this is far too many for the school's needs. It was claimed that the director of the program (catchily dubbed in one account the "Burke and Hare of Beverly Hills" ["Burke and Hare"]) had had an unofficial deal with another man for the private sale of 496 cadavers for $704,000. A special element of horror was added to this report by the information that the second man "was granted access to the university's freezers where he was allowed to saw off human knees, hands, torsos, heads, and other body parts."[20] It is not reported what the relatives thought of this practice, but the university is being sued and the numbers of bodies donated for research has since taken a dive. The scandal could well spread to other universities as more abuses come to light.[21]

The U.K. Child-Organ-Retention Scandal

We may guess how such a scandal could unroll because during the 1990s, the United Kingdom was rocked by a huge uproar about the illicit removal and storage of dead children's body parts at leading hospitals, often university hospitals. The affair rumbled on until 2004, resulting in the firing of researchers and hospital administrators and eventually in a change in the law.

These real-life stories help to contextualize the organ-theft legends we have discussed, indicating where the cultural pressures are and reinforcing analyses of popular attitudes toward the body. The details of the child organ scandal make the organ-theft legends seem both more real and more reasonable; conversely, the legends help one to understand the real-life scandal. Here, life echoes legend uncannily closely. In the rest of this chapter, I will try to bind all this together first by looking at the Anatomy Act that makes organ donation possible and second by charting the unfolding of the U.K. child-organ-retention scandal as a case study in popular attitudes. Though in discussing dissection I shall be looking at it from a British perspective, the act I discuss, the Anatomy Act of 1832, also forms the basis of U.S. law and procedures, so the legal situation in both countries is very similar (Ruth Richardson, personal communication, September 2003; see also Lock 67).

During 1999–2000, horrified parents of infants and small children who had died in various British hospitals found out that their children's body parts had been secretly removed and stored for medical research. Subsequent investigation revealed that it was common practice in hospital pathology departments when conducting autopsies to remove "tissue" and store it for future medical research or in some cases to sell it for profit to other medical or research establishments. Most distressingly, in many cases this tissue was not the slivers of flesh the term implies and to which many parents had given their consent but rather whole organs or complete body parts. In the most upsetting cases, heads had been removed or all the organs in the body taken out. (The organs must, of course, be removed and dissected to obtain tissue samples, but this was not made clear to the bereaved, whose consent therefore was far from informed.) What shocked parents was that these organs seemingly had been removed by stealth and that their children's little bodies had been treated with disrespect, regarded as "specimens" and stored in jars. The most shocking thing to the public as a whole was the discovery that the hospitals were, initially at least, surprised by the parents' outrage, for it appeared that the practice was commonplace, a regular part of hospital culture.

That culture owes much to the Anatomy Act, which permits the acquisition of unclaimed bodies for medical research. The measure was passed in 1832 but has never been repealed despite changes in cultural attitudes, social provision, and medical education. Though the Anatomy Act is more than 150 years old, it is important to understand its provisions and its enduring effects to comprehend both the attitude of hospitals to the retention of "tissue" and the depth of feeling that tampering with bodies, especially children's bodies, unleashes. My account of the Anatomy Act is taken from Ruth Richardson's marvelous book, *Death, Dissection, and the Destitute* (1988), which provides an in-depth analysis of the act, its political and social contexts, and its after-effects.[22]

THE ANATOMY ACT: THE "RAGE OF SCIENCE" VERSUS THE RAGE OF THE PEOPLE

Until the Renaissance, medical texts relied heavily on knowledge handed down by Galen (second century A.D.). However, during the Renaissance, the idea arose in enlightened circles that medical knowledge should be derived from the examination of actual bodies. In the sixteenth and seventeenth centuries, Italy led the world in medical and anatomical learning, especially at renowned centers such as Padua, and British anatomists often traveled there to study. By the mid-nineteenth century, however, London and Edinburgh had become leading cities for medical research and education, their reputation, too, having been built on expertise in anatomy, which had now become the most prestigious science of the day. In Scotland, dissection had received royal recognition and patronage from James IV (1473–1513), and in England Henry VIII (1491–1547) had granted the corpses of four hanged felons a year to the Company of Barbers and Surgeons for dissection. However, until 1663 the number of corpses legally available for dissection was only six. Between then and 1752, when an act of Parliament gave judges discretion to order dissection as an alternative to gibbeting as a postexecution punishment for murder, anatomists took it upon themselves to do deals for corpses.

In the eighteenth and early nineteenth centuries, medical education was transacted on a private basis: that and the growing prestige of anatomy as a science and an increased interest in the human body led to a black market in corpses. To maintain their reputation and ensure the profitability of their schools, anatomists needed corpses to dissect for private research and teaching purposes. Only a small number were available by legal means, so a trade in bodies arose. There is evidence that as early as the late seventeenth century, bodies were being stolen for dissection in Edinburgh. By the mid-1800s, it had become popular knowledge that corpses were being dug up and sold in many other cities in England and Scotland.

By the 1720s, the stealing of bodies from London graveyards was almost a commonplace, and it is clear "that the task was being undertaken by a new strata of entrepreneurs"—professional body snatchers, or "resurrection men." By 1800, corpses had become commodities, and in medical circles market terminology was being applied to human corpses (Richardson, *Death* 54–55). The demand was so great that every buried corpse in the country was vulnerable to being exhumed by body snatchers and sold. As an anonymous writer put it in 1829, "The husband, the wife, the off-spring, toothless age or toothless infancy, are marketable. Such is the march of intellect, such is the rage of science" ("An Address to the Public" [1829], quoted in Richardson, *Death* 52).

The epitome of the commodification of the body in nineteenth-century Britain was the career of the infamous body snatchers Burke and Hare. They more or less stumbled into the crime with which their names are synonymous. An old man died in Mrs. Hare's lodging house in Edinburgh owing his rent, and to cover the bill the two men decided to sell his body to the eminent surgeon Robert Knox. They were paid £7.10s (about five dollars) for the fresh corpse, which was then a large sum of money. Later, when another lodger fell ill, Burke and Hare made him drunk with whisky and smothered him. Thereafter all the bodies they sold to Knox, a further 15, were of people they had murdered. The seventeenth body was that of an old Irish woman, Mary Docherty, who had come to Edinburgh in search of her missing son. Burke noticed her begging outside a gin shop and invited her home for a meal. It happened that they were having a Halloween party that night. When the guests went home, Mary was killed, stripped, and hidden in the straw on Burke's bed until they could find a convenient time to take her corpse to the anatomy school. When the guests returned the next day, Burke seems to have panicked.

He became so agitated whenever one of the guests approached the bed that their suspicions were aroused, and they started enquiring after the old lady who had been so lively the night before. When a suitable opportunity presented itself, they searched the bed, and Mary's body was discovered. Hare turned queen's evidence, Burke was hanged in January 1829, and his body publicly dissected. It is generally thought that the Anatomy Act was passed in response to the crimes of Burke and Hare, but the report of the committee which recommended such an act had been published several months before (Richardson, *Death* 132–39). However, their crimes did speed up the process, and a new bill was introduced in Parliament and became law.

The Anatomy Act of 1832 allowed anatomists to claim the bodies of paupers who had died in workhouses or hospitals if those corpses were unclaimed for burial by their friends or relatives— effectively, if they were too poor to pay for a funeral.[23] Needless to say, this was an enormously unpopular piece of legislation. Dissection had previously been a punishment for serious crime, designed to be a "further terror and peculiar mark of infamy," as the 1752 act had described it (Richardson, *Death* 37). At a stroke, with the passing of the 1832 Anatomy Act, this dreaded fate became a punishment for poverty. Between 1832 and 1900, fifty thousand bodies of the poor were anatomized (Ruth Richardson in *The Victorian Way of Death*, BBC Channel 2, 4 May 2002). In this respect it is important to understand that part of the rationale for the 1752 act, which the 1832 act replaced, had been to deny the victim burial rites and a grave. Though the 1832 act specified that the remains should be buried after dissection, it still had the effect of denying the victim a decent send-off and the reassurance for the bereaved that their loved one had been laid to rest with due solemnity. The new law thus defied all popular norms of religious, social, and familial propriety.

The flouting of popular beliefs and practices was plainly the motivating force behind riots outside anatomy schools. In scenes that strongly mirror twentieth-century organ-theft panics, the cholera epidemics that swept Britain at this time often gave rise to street violence. In many cities, cholera victims were taken to isolation hospitals in special vans and confined there to try to stop the spread of the disease. So great was the fear and suspicion of the dissectors that people began to suspect that the healthy as well as the sick were being abducted in the vans and taken away for experimentation. Richardson says that during the 1832 cholera outbreak in Paisley, near Glasgow, Scotland, "Poor people doubted the existence of the disease . . . believing it to be . . . designed to permit coercion of the poor into hospitals for use in vivisection experiments, for dissection after death, or to keep down the population" (Richardson, *Death* 226). One of the worst of these riots took place during a cholera epidemic in Manchester, in northwest England, a few months after the Anatomy Act had been passed. Suspicions had been aroused when a three-year-old girl died in the cholera hospital. Her grandfather suspected that her body might have been interfered with but had allowed the funeral arrangements to go ahead. When his fears overcame him, he reopened the coffin. He found that her head had been removed and replaced with a brick. A crowd soon formed around the distraught old man, and the child's body was taken through the town to drum up support for an attack on the hospital. A rumor spread that the child had been murdered. About two thousand people rushed the hospital gates, broke all the windows at the front of the building, made a bonfire of the furniture, and destroyed the cholera van. Women went through the wards trying to liberate their friends. The child's head was eventually found in an apothecary's room and sewn back onto her body. The apothecary disappeared. The child was buried the following day in a ceremony attended by hundreds of people. The arrogance of the medical and political establishment was such that the riot was condemned as "lamentable ignorance" and was cited as further argument, should it be needed, against universal suffrage.

Throughout the agitation over dissection and body snatching both before and after the Anatomy Act was passed, rumors and legends traveled like wildfire. For example, sexual indecencies were rumored to take place in dissecting rooms; a contemporary cartoon showed a young woman on the Day of Resurrection demanding back her virginity, which had been lost on the dissecting table. It was also widely thought during the late eighteenth and early nineteenth centuries that anatomists fed used body parts to dogs. Antiquarian Francis Grose referred to rumors about "keepers of wild beasts" saving anatomists the trouble of burying bodies. Rumors were also rife that dissected bodies were made into soap and candles. Legends very similar to those circulating in modern times were also widely disseminated. Tales circulated that children were being stolen for dissection; some versions said that the children's bodies were being transported on the new steamships to be dissected abroad. Also highly reminiscent of modern legends are stories about anatomists who discover to their horror that the body they have purchased for dissection is that of a family member (Richardson, *Death* 94–97, 31).

The irony was that the Anatomy Act did not solve the problem of the illegal acquisition of bodies but simply moved it from grave robbers to corrupt public officials. After it became law, bodies were liable to be sold to anatomists by workhouse staff or sextons or spirited away by anatomists' agents posing as mourning relatives. Furthermore, the act institutionalized rather than broke the pernicious connection between medical education and dissection, encouraging hospital and medical school officials to believe that they had a right to bodies. Oddly, and perhaps significantly in light of recent events in the United Kingdom and elsewhere, the act left the status of body parts and "tissue" ambiguous. In particular, the measure did not address the question of whether the body and its separate parts were property of some sort, and if so whose. Most of all, the law flouted what Richardson calls the "tenacious belief that if due respect be given to the dead, both the future repose of the soul and the comfort of the mourners would be assured." As she poignantly puts it, "That part of Charlotte Atkins, of James Burwell, Eliza Brightman and her infant son, of Mark Rivett or of James Burdell, which had been washed and laid out, watched and waked, buried and wept over by bereaved families, was nominated by the anatomists a 'subject' and by the resurrectionists a 'thing.' No longer an object worthy of respect, the body of each of these people became a token of exchange, subject to commercial dealing, and then to the final objectification of the dissection room" (*Death* 72).

"There Are Parents Who Think They Have Put Their Children to Rest. . . . Now to Be Told This News Is Disgusting"

It was the same set of explicit or implicit beliefs and the same horror and disgust at the appropriation and objectification of a loved physical body, that led to the U.K. child-organ scandal at the turn of the twenty-first century.[24] The discovery that children's organs were being taken without proper consent (sometimes with no consent at all) and stored in hospital and university labs arose on the heels of a series of inquiries into the high death rate among children being operated on for heart defects in a large hospital in southwestern England. Since 1988, concerns had been raised within the hospital about the judgment and abilities of a surgeon who specialized in pediatric heart surgery there. In response to internal and public pressure, in 1998 the General Medical Council (the regulatory body for doctors in the United Kingdom) examined fifty-three operations on children in which more than 50 percent had died. Two surgeons and the hospital's chief executive were found guilty of serious professional misconduct: one of the surgeons and the chief executive were removed from the medical register, which effectively banned them from practicing medicine in Britain; the other doctor was banned from operating on children for three years. As soon as the General Medical Council announced its verdicts, the pressure for a government inquiry became irresistible. This investigation opened in Bristol in 1999 and reported its results in the summer of 2001.

Only weeks before the inquiry opened, a new scandal erupted. It was revealed that the hearts and other organs of more than 170 babies and children who had died during or after operations had been removed at the Bristol Infirmary heart unit and had been kept without the parents' consent. The reactions of the parents and the hospital were predictable and show the gulf that had grown up between medical culture and the cultural norms of the rest of the population:

> The latest revelation at the hospital has outraged parents. "We find it completely reprehensible and disgusting," said Trevor Jones, whose two-year-old daughter Bethany died after a heart operation in 1990. "Even if they are legally entitled to do this, morally they are not. There are parents who think they have put their children to rest and now to be told this news is disgusting."
>
> In a statement, the United Bristol Healthcare NHS Trust said it was routine practice for tissue to be retained after post mortems for education and audit purposes.
>
> The Trust said this procedure had always been standard practice throughout Britain and there was no legal requirement for them to obtain parental consent. (Wilson)

The contrast between these two statements could not be clearer. On the one hand, there is the parents' language of "disgust," morality, and putting their children "to rest"; on the other hand, there is the hospital's language of "tissue," "standard practice," and "education and audit" and its insistence that there was no legal requirement for them to consult relatives. Parents of children who had died from heart complaints at the Bristol Infirmary immediately started to demand information about the fate of their children's body parts, with the press right behind in pursuit of truth, justice, and a good story. As each case emerged, the medical establishment still tried to insist that it was an isolated incident and (contradictorily) that the removal and retention of organs after postmortems was standard practice and thus nothing to get upset about. The press, however, knew better and kept up a barrage of stories with headlines such as "Hospital Returned My Dead Son as an Empty Shell" (O'Neill, "Hospital").

The language and presentation of these reports are worth examining, both in themselves and because of the way they echo themes and motifs in organ-theft legends. Plainly, these organs are also thought to have been stolen and the body (though dead) mutilated and defiled just as a living body would be. Here, for example, are two stories from my local papers printed a few days after the disclosures. Typically, the journalists went in search of a local story and found a case where a child's heart had been taken by the Royal Manchester Children's Hospital, less than ten miles away. The first story is headlined, "They Stole My Baby's Heart" (Walker). The article is accompanied by a photograph of the family at the graveside; the emphasis is on the flower-bedecked grave and the abiding grief, and the text is full of words such as *horror, devastated, suspicious, bombshell,* and *heartache.* The family is quoted as saying, "Somebody's heart is the most important thing inside them and it feels like we are visiting an empty shell." The furor was nothing, however, compared to what was to come.

The disclosure that 170 hearts had been retained by Bristol Infirmary had come in February 1999; by September it was supposed that as many as 11,000 hearts had been stored nationwide for research purposes; by November the press was reporting that at Liverpool's Alder Hey children's hospital alone, 2,500 hearts had been retained since the 1950s, 850 of them in a single collection built up between 1988 and 1995 (Kelso). By the end of the year, the scandal was growing and overtaking other large teaching hospitals. In the spring of the following year, the National Committee relating to Organ Retention, a group set up by two bereaved mothers in December 1999, published a list of thirty-nine hospitals that had admitted taking and storing organs without properly informed consent, and forty-three other institutions where the practice was believed to be routine. One of the group's founders said, "We believe the practice occurred in every hospital with a pathology department" (O'Neill, "Arrogant").

By January 2000, the government's Chief Medical Officer, Professor Liam Donaldson, had completed an audit of "pathology holdings" in hospitals and medical schools in England. Published in January 2001, his report shocked British society, showing that 54,300 organs, body parts, and fetuses were held in pathology collections. The samples had been appropriated from 27,000 patients over almost thirty years; 44 percent were brains, 17 percent were hearts, and 13 percent were lungs; nearly 10,000 of these specimens had come from children, infants, and fetuses. Twenty-five hospitals were responsible for 88 percent of the holdings, with sixteen hospitals and medical schools each having 1,000 or more samples. Alder Hey held almost 7,000 organs, body parts, stillbirths, and fetuses; the famous London children's hospital at Great Ormond Street had almost 4,000; and Bristol, where the scandal began, had 1,400. In addition, the audit revealed that 50,000 organs and body parts and 480,600 samples of tissue were being kept in archives or museums set up prior to 1970. This gave a total of 584,900 bodies or bits of bodies, for one reason or another, left unburied and separated from the rest of the body. This figure was for England alone: it did not include hospitals, medical schools, archives, and museums in Scotland and Wales (Chief Medical Officer).[25]

Simultaneously with the publication of the Chief Medical Officer's audit, the Redfern Report into Alder Hey hospital was published. It confirmed the rumors about the extent of the hoarding of body parts, cataloging six collections of human remains and one of animal remains at various sites at the Liverpool National Health Service Trust as a whole. The report found a collection of 2,128 hearts, a collection of 188 eyes (taken from 97 fetuses and 12 newborns and children), and two collections of fetuses. A particularly grisly archive was revealed at the Institute of Child Health: 13 heads or parts of heads of children from a few days old and up, including that of an eleven-year-old boy; 22 heads of late-premature or full-term fetuses; and a container with the whole body of a child and a second container with the separated head. The labeling of these "specimens" was particularly shocking: one nine-week-old fetus was labeled "inflated monster, Humpty Dumpty." The real scandal of the report, however, was its disclosure of a large and grossly mismanaged collection of child organs and tissue stored in the hospital basement by one man—the Professor of Infant and Foetal Pathology at Liverpool University from 1988 to 1995, a leading authority on sudden infant death syndrome (crib death). When the report was published, the Secretary of State for Health announced in Parliament that the professor had "systematically ordered the unethical and illegal stripping of every organ from every child who had a post mortem. He ignored parents' wishes when they told him explicitly that they did not want a full post-mortem, let alone the retention of any of their child's organs. . . . He lied to parents. He lied to other doctors. He lied to hospital managers. He stole medical records. He falsified statistics and reports" (Milburn). The press went berserk.

Broadsheets and tabloids vied with each other for gruesome headlines and dramatic copy. So many of the motifs we have previously seen in legends are here implicitly or subliminally in the language of these reports—horror, betrayal, secrets, dirt, theft, butchery, and violation spiritual, psychological and physical. *The Independent*, a respected and usually level-headed quality paper, carried a huge banner headline on page 1, "The Basement of Horrors," lengthily subtitled, "The Organs of Hundreds of Children Were Hidden by Doctors in This Hospital Cellar. Yesterday Their Parents Learnt the Full Scale of a Terrible Betrayal." The first three paragraphs of the story told of the "horror" of what had happened, the "appalled" parents, the "shocked" members of Parliament, the "grisly secrets" that had been "revealed." The article spoke of body parts "removed without consent and kept in the dank cellar of a university laboratory . . . dirty and covered in thick black dust. . . . [S]ome of the organs were putrefying" (Laurance). "Get Doctor Frankenstein," screamed a headline in the tabloid *Sun*, showing a picture of the angry doctor fleeing the press cameras (Pascoe-Watson). The front page of the *Mirror*, one of the more restrained tabloids, had a large picture of the surgeon in the center with the headline, "The Baby Butcher," and an inset, "He Stole Their Hearts, Brains, Lungs, Kidneys, Livers, Eyes, Stomachs . . . EVERYTHING but their souls" (Palmer). The whole page was bordered with pictures of twenty-five babies. Six further pages inside were devoted to the stories.

An interim inquiry report, which had been published in May 2000, usefully summed up the cultural problem that was revealing itself. In the words of the chairman of the inquiry, Professor Ian Kennedy,

> The past was characterised by a type of professional arrogance which ignored, indeed did not acknowledge, the views and voice of parents. . . . The problem was that there was no real realisation that how [the doctors] saw it, their view of the world, might not be shared by others. . . . There was no conspiracy here; just a way of behaving. . . . For the parents of a recently deceased child, human material, certainly substantial specimens such as organs and parts of

organs and even smaller samples, are still thought of as an integral part of the child's body and, thus, are still the child. For the pathologist and clinician, the material is regarded as a specimen or an object. It is dehumanised. (O'Neill, "Arrogant")

These reflections certainly touch on one very important aspect of the scandal. Kennedy puts his finger on it exactly when he speaks of bereaved parents regarding the lost child's body parts as "still a part of the child's body and thus . . . still the child." Though this is never explicitly stated in any of the interviews with the parents, this perception is clearly the meaning of constant references in press reportage and in interviews with bereaved parents to children's bodies being returned to them as "an empty shell." It is also surely responsible for the horror with which the revelations were greeted. Sensational headlines proliferated, such as, "My Baby's Body Was on a Dirty Table in 36 Jars . . . I Put Them in a Bag and Ran Sobbing into the Street" (Russell and Storrar). For these parents, loss of bodily integrity in death was equivalent to the mutilation and defilement of the living and could not be borne.

In concentrating on the parents' emotional response to these discoveries, the press also implicitly highlighted the deep-seated cultural attitudes that informed the reactions. In "A Mother's Story," for example, journalist Julia Stuart freely quotes the words of one mother, whose memorable utterances include, "How could doctors put so little value on life? They had turned him into a jigsaw"; "[I] was invited into a hospital office and handed a cardboard box with the words 'Here you are. These are Oliver's testicles.' On the top was written 'packaging for post'"; "all the time I was horrified that they could think so little of life. This was a child I had held and kissed and part of him was in a cardboard box"; "in May last year [I] heard that tongues had also been retained. . . . I was horrified. . . . [T]o me, they had robbed him of his voice even in death." Here, in the words of this articulate woman, respecting the dead is seen as an integral part of valuing life, and being able to remember them alive entails that, in imagination at least, in death they are whole, as they were in life. This was emphasized time and again in the press coverage, which almost invariably set pictures of the whole and living child beside poignant stories of their death and dismemberment. Time and again, the parents said, "I won't bury my baby in two halves" (Christon); "If I had known that [my child's] heart had been taken out I would have insisted that it was put back in before she was buried. She came into this world with everything and I wanted her to go out of it complete" (O'Neill, "Hospital").[26]

These themes come together in a particularly poignant and horrifying story told by one mother who had lost her daughter twenty-one years earlier and had suffered trauma similar to that of the Alder Hey parents. When the little girl, Helenor, died, the husband had tried to comfort his wife with the words, "Don't torment yourself any more. Our daughter is at peace at last." "But," said the mother, "we found out later that she hadn't been left in peace at all." When Helenor was dying and on a life-support machine, the doctors asked for permission to take some brain tissue for tests, and the parents agreed. The life-support machine was switched off, and soon after that Helenor's body was returned to the parents for burial. The mother's suspicions were immediately aroused. "That's not her hair," she said. "What have they done?" The parents

had spotted that their daughter's head had been shaved and her hair replaced with a wig. It was the first signal that the surgery conducted on Helenor may have been much more extensive that they were led to believe. The surgeon (now dead) who carried out the biopsy contacted the couple after the inquest. . . . "He told us that the slivers of tissue he saw could only have been obtained by the removal of the whole of Helenor's brain. We could not believe it. We never gave permission for this." [The parents] remain convinced that this was done while their daughter was on the life-support machine. Years of relentless questioning failed to get answers. Then six weeks ago [the parents] received a letter [confirming that the brain had been removed but not retained at the hospital]. "We do not know where Helenor's brain is, or if it was destroyed," said [the mother] who took violets to the hospital every year for 17 years. . . . "I asked them please to put the violets wherever my daughter's brain is." (Ryle)

The child organ scandal rumbled on until the summer of 2004. In August of that year it was reported that burials had been taking place of "fifty nameless babies" whose bodies had been found at Alder Hey children's hospital. More funerals would follow "every Thursday for several months" until "at least 1,000 unidentified bodies, most of them foetuses less than 28 weeks old," were interred. The detail of these burials says it all. According to the reporter,

Each baby was dressed in a lemon or white gown, was covered in a "blanket of love," and laid in an oak casket bearing a plaque. . . . Mourners, many of them affected by the Alder Hey scandal, wept as the final casket was placed in the grave. . . . The 15-minute service was led by the Rev Ian Lovett, a chaplain at Liverpool's Aintree Hospital. The Alder Hey chaplain . . ., the Bishop of Liverpool . . . and representatives of the Roman Catholic, Muslim and Hindu faiths were also present. Dr Lovett said, . . . "May our gathering here today bring about a fitting conclusion to this time of pain." . . . At the end of the service, mourners lined up to scatter earth on the coffins. Flowers were laid at the graveside. The largest display, from the University, had a card which read; "At peace now." (Ward)

Nationally, the scandal resulted in the dismissal of a number of doctors, laboratory officers, and administrators. A full public apology was offered to the parents and an estimated £5 million was paid as compensation to 1,154 claimants. A new law is currently being debated in the U.K. Parliament under which hospitals and research facilities would face liability for failure to obtain proper consent for organ removal and retention and individual doctors would face unlimited fines and up to three years imprisonment for the same offense. The proposed law would also crack down on "transplant tourism."[27]

CONCLUSION

Helenor's story contains all the themes we have been discussing—horror at the appropriation and objectification of a loved physical body, dismemberment as defilement, the need for the body to be whole (in life and in death), the desire for "decent" funerals and a fitting "final resting place." The story also brings the wheel almost full circle back to legends of eye thefts. In Helenor's story there is the same pillage and desecration of the body of a child, the same cynicism, the same discarding of the part of the body that is no longer needed. In the parents' minds at least, Helenor was subjected to the removal of a vital organ while still breathing; to have her returned with a wig in a cynical and halfhearted attempt to make restitution has the same shock value as the note and cash in the pocket of the blinded South American child. Both Helenor's brain and the blinded children were acquired but then thrown away as garbage when their usefulness was over. Emotionally and in narrative terms, there is an equivalence between farming babies for spare parts and harvesting organs from dead children and storing them for display, education, and experiment or selling them for cash. There is a similar equivalence between abducting living children and commandeering the bodies of dead ones. In both cases, members of the press were major players, using their power to construct organ thefts as a social problem. Newspapers and other media were able simultaneously to project themselves as the social conscience of a nation, the voice of the people, and to fit the stories to themes they particularly love—corruption and betrayal, depravity and lies. These rumors, happenings, and legends had so much cultural clout that, with the press in full cry as major claims-makers, governments were forced to intervene.

NOTES

* Words attributed to anatomist John Hunter in Hilary Mantell's splendid novel *The Giant O'Brien*. The book presents an account of the relationship between the anatomist and the man whose body he craves to own and dissect. Both men really existed. Mantell's details are fictional, however.

1. My account is taken from the French edition. My discussions of "baby parts" and eye thefts draw extensively from this work. I thank the author for permission to quote this material.
2. Radford points out that four days later the boy retracted his story. After examining him, doctors found that his corneas were intact but that his eyes had been damaged by disease.
3. This story vividly recalls First World War atrocity legends in which Belgians were supposed to have torn eyes from German soldiers and particularly one story in which a child was said to have been discovered carrying a "bucket of eyes." According to David Jacobson (288), very similar rumors about tubs full of torn-out eyes circulated among crusaders during the First Crusade (1095–96). The Turks were then said to be the perpetrators.
4. Shonder; Radford 39; see also Pukas 16.
5. Cockney rhyming slang substitutes a rhyming phrase for the original term. For example, "trouble and strife" (wife), "whistle and flute" (suit), "apples and pears" (stairs), "dog and bone" (phone), "tit for tat" (hat).
6. Campion-Vincent, *Légende* 33–34, citing a September 1990 article in *Time* magazine.
7. For a detailed treatment of this legend as it appeared in Scotland, see Hobbs and Cornwell, "The Clowns"; Hobbs and Cornwell, "Clowns: Further Notes."
8. Clayton; Michell.
9. Dutroux was arrested in 1996 for the abduction of six little girls and the murder of four of them. Two survivors were rescued, near starvation, from the cellar of his house. He was not brought to trial until March 2004.

10. For England and Northern Ireland, see Barter; for Australia, see Moravec, "Organ Kidnap Stories," *Australian Folklore*, "Organ Kidnap Stories," *FOAFtale News*; for Germany, see Magin; for the United States, see Brunvand; Sieveking; for Sweden, see Klintberg; for Denmark, see Lassen.

11. See Scheper-Hughes, "Theft"; Scheper-Hughes, "End"; Scheper-Hughes, "Global"; Scheper-Hughes, "Min(d)ing"; Scheper-Hughes, "Keeping."

12. See, for example, Chamberlain; Millward; Hooper; McKie, "Brains"; McKie, "Scientists"; Rogers.

13. CBSNews.com, "Whose." For a chilling and insightful exploration of the problem of the ownership of genetic material, see Lock.

14. Buncombe, "Bodies"; Buncombe, "Body Parts"; CBSNews.com, "Body"; CBSNews.com, "UCLA."

15. Witness details revealed in "The Transplant Trade" broadcast in the United Kingdom on Channel 4 on 22 April 2004, during which a respected transplant surgeon, Professor Michael Friedlaender, expressed the opinion that it was "rampant" worldwide. See also Rothman.

16. See Price and Mackay, whose two-part article surveys the Human Transplants Act of 1989; Wallich and Mukerjee; BBC News, "Internet Organ Racket"; Rothman. Véronique Campion-Vincent also draws attention to the voluntary sale of organs by impoverished people throughout the world, particularly in China and India (see Campion-Vincent, *Légende* 10; Campion-Vincent, "Diffusion" 194).

17. It is claimed, for example, that by the early 1990s upward of two thousand kidney transplants with living donors were performed each year in India, but the figures do not show how many of these operations were commercial transactions. Similarly, though most researchers are convinced that organs are taken from executed prisoners in China in defiance of world opinion and in barbaric circumstances, it has not so far been possible to provide figures.

18. In addition to those cited in this discussion, I have found the following texts interesting: Breton; Cohen; Lock; Weiss; "Death in Japan"; Shinzo; Younger and O'Connell; Richardson, "Fearful"; Doniger.

19. According to a recent U.K. survey of popular attitudes to graves and burial, only 7.9 percent of 1,603 respondents said they believed in resurrection (Davies and Shaw 62).

20. Buncombe, "Bodies"; see also CBSNews.com, "UCLA"; CBSNews.com, "Body."

21. By August 2004, at least one regional newspaper had featured an article reporting previous irregularities in donor programs. See Zarembo and Garrison.

22. Unless otherwise states, all information about the Anatomy Act comes from this source. I thank the author for permission to quote from and refer to this

work. A much briefer consideration of the act and its context may be found in Lock 65–68.

23. Workhouses were institutions for the care of the destitute.

24. The afterword to Richardson's 2001 edition also has some reflections on the child-organ-retention scandal in the United Kingdom; see esp. 415–16, 418–21. On the comparisons between the dissection of the past and the transplants of the present, see Richardson, "Fearful."

25. As an example of the problem, the Hunterian collection at the Royal College of Surgeons in London includes "monstrous births . . . in bottles, the skeletons of physical freaks, a cast of the brain cavity of Dean Swift's skull, death masks, murderers' skeletons and relics, and all sorts and conditions of medical prodigies—feet, hands, internal organs—pickled or dyed to show their peculiarities to better effect" (Richardson, *Death* 64). The college still displays the skeleton of O'Brien, "The Irish Giant." When O'Brien died, there was quite a flurry of activity as rival anatomists bid for his corpse, though O'Brien himself, acutely aware of his novelty value (he was well over seven feet tall), had made elaborate preparations for his funeral and left instructions that he was to be buried at sea. John Hunter paid £500 (about $350) for his body, a vast sum in those days. See Mantell for a fictionalized account.

26. A comparison might be made with families of victims of 9/11. Writing from New York, for example, a British journalist spoke of the "grief that never ends for the family who buried their son five times" (see Usborne).

27. Press reports February–December 2003, esp. Topham; Meikle; Herbert.

KEY TEXTS

Campion-Vincent, Véronique. "The Baby-Parts Story: A New Latin American Legend." *Western Folklore* 49 (1990): 9–25.

———. "The Diffusion of Organ Theft Narratives." In *How Claims Spread: Cross-National Diffusion of Social Problems*, ed. Joel Best, 185–214. New York: de Gruyter, 2001.

———. *La Légende des Vols d'Organes*. Paris: Belles Lettres, 1997.

———. "Organ Theft Narratives." *Western Folklore* 56 (1997): 1–37.

———. "Organ Theft Narratives as Medical and Social Critique." *Journal of Folklore Research* 39 (January–April 2002): 33–50.

Goska, Danusha. "'Waking up Less Than Whole': The Female Perpetrator in Male-Victim Kidney-Theft Legends." *Southern Folklore* 54 (1997): 196–210.

Moravec, Mark. "Organ Kidnap Stories." *Australian Folklore* 8 (1993): 89–99.

Radford, Benjamin. "Bitter Harvest: The Organ-Snatching Urban Legends."
   Skeptical Inquirer 23 (May–June 1999): 34–39, 48.
Richardson, Ruth. *Death, Dissection, and the Destitute.* London Routledge,
   1988; London: Orion, 2001.
Samper, David. "Cannibalizing Kids: Rumor and Resistance in Latin America."
   Journal of Folklore Research 39 (January–April 2002): 1–32.
Shonder, John. "Organ Theft Rumors in Guatemala: Some Personal Observa-
   tions." *FOAFtale News* 35 (October 1994): 1–4.

REFERENCES CITED

Barter, Alan. "'Mugged for a Kidney' Probe." *Portsmouth and Southsea
   Streetlife,* 27 August 1992. Reprinted in *Dear Mr Thoms . . .* 28 (November
   1992): 32.
BBC News Online. "Egyptian Body Parts Scandal." 17 March 1999.
   http://news.bbc.co.uk/hi/english/world/middle-east/newsid-298000/
   298063.stm.
———. "Internet Organ Racket Uncovered." 9 October 1998.
   http://news.bbc.co.uk/hi/english/world/europe/newsid-189000/189961.stm.
Bennett, Gillian, and Kate Bennett. "The Presence of the Dead: An Empirical
   Study." *Mortality* 5, no. 2 (2000): 139–57.
Boseley, Sarah, and David Ward. "Cash for Body Parts Revelations Add to Trials
   of Children's Hospital." *Guardian* (London and Manchester), 27 January 2001, 3.
Boyes, Georgina. "Belief and Disbelief: An Exploration of Reactions to the Pre-
   sentation of Rumour Legends." In *Perspectives on Contemporary Legend:
   Proceedings of the Conference on Contemporary Legend, Sheffield, July 1982,*
   ed. Paul Smith, 84–78. Sheffield: CECTAL, University of Sheffield, 1984.
Breton, David Le. "Dissecting Grafts: The Anthropology of the Medical Uses of
   the Human Body." *Daedalus* 167 (1994): 95–111.
Brunvand, Jan Harold. *The Baby Train and Other Lusty Urban Legends.* New York
   and London: Norton, 1993.
Buncombe, Andrew. "Bodies Donated to New Orleans Medical School Were Sold
   to Army for Landmine Tests." *Independent* (London), 12 March 2004, 34.
———. "Body Parts 'Sold by Staff from Top US University.'" *Independent* (London),
   10 March 2004, 24.
"The Burke and Hare of Beverly Hills." NatWest News online.
   www.natwestinternational.com.
Campion-Vincent, Véronique. "The Diffusion of Organ Theft Narratives."
   In *How Claims Spread: Cross-National Diffusion of Social Problems,*
   ed. Joel Best, 185–214. New York: de Gruyter, 2001.

————. *La Légende des Vols d'Organes*. Paris: Belles Lettres, 1997 a.

————. "On Organ Theft Narratives." *Current Anthropology* 41 (2001): 555–57.

————. "Organ Theft Narratives." *Western Folklore* 56 (1997): 1–37.

CBSNews.com. "Body Parts Allegedly Sold." 8 March 2004.
http//:www.cbsnews.com/stories/2004/03/08/national/main604563.shtml.

————. "UCLA Sued in Body Parts Scandal." 9 March 2004.
http//:www.cbsnews.com/stories/2004/03/08/national/main604512.shtml.

————. "Whose Body Is It Anyway?" 18 September 2002. http//: www.cbsnews.
com/ stories/2002/09/18/eveningnews/main522429.shtml.

Chamberlain, Andrew. "Teaching Surgery and Breaking the Law: Dissection Was
Illegal until 1832, but It Was Done Anyway." *British Archaeology* 48 (1999): 6–7.

Chapman, Brian. "Body Parts in Bangkok." *FOAFtale News* 47 (October 2000): 14.

Charatan, Fred. "California Medical School Criticised for Improper Use of
Cadavers." *Student BMJ*, February 2001.
www.studentbmj.com/back_issues/0201/news/8a.html.

Chief Medical Officer. *Report of a Census of Organs and Tissues Retained by
Pathology Services in England, Conducted by the Chief Medical Officer.*
London: HMSO, 2001.

Christon, Ian. "I Won't Bury my Baby in Two Halves." *Stockport Express* (U.K.),
3 November 1999, 1.

Clayton, Alison. "Bogus Social Workers." *FOAFtale News* 37 (June 1995): 12.

Cohen, Lawrence. "The Other Kidney: Biopolitics beyond Recognition." *Body
and Society* 7, no. 2–3 (2001): 9–30.

"Contemporary Legends: Old? New?" *FLS News* 15 (July 1992): 6–7.

Czubala, Dionizjusz. "The 'Black Volga': Child Abduction Urban Legends in
Poland and Russia." *FOAFtale News* 21 (February 1991): 1–3.

Davies, Douglas J. *Death, Ritual, and Belief: The Rhetoric of Funerary Rites.*
London: Cassell, 1997.

Davies, Douglas J., and Alastair Shaw. *Reusing Old Graves: A Report on Popular
British Attitudes.* Crayford, Kent: Shaw, 1995.

"Death in Japan" (special issue). *Mortality* 9 (2004).

Dégh, Linda. "Letters to the Dead: Memoriams in Daily Papers." In *American
Folklore and the Mass Media*, 153–87. Bloomington: Indiana University Press,
1994.

Dimmick, Adrian. "Cannibals and Stolen Organs." *FLS News* 21 (June 1995): 10.

Doniger, Wendy. "Transplanting Myths of Organ Transplants." In *Organ Transplantation: Meaning and Realities*, ed. Stuart J Younger and Laurence
O'Connell, 194–221. Madison: University of Wisconsin Press, 1996.

Farge, Arlette, and Jacques Revel. *Logiques de la Foule*. Paris: Hachette, 1988.
Translated into English as *The Vanishing Children of Paris*. Trans. Claudia
Miéville. Cambridge: Harvard University Press, 1991.

Goska, Danusha. "'Waking up Less Than Whole': The Female Perpetrator in Male-Victim Kidney-Theft Legends." *Southern Folklore* 54 (1997): 196–210.

Herbert, Ian. "Alder Hey Doctor 'Failed to Investigate Organ Retention Claims.'" *Guardian* (London and Manchester), 16 December 2003, 16.

Hobbs, Sandy, and David Cornwell. "The Clowns." *Dear Mr Thoms . . .* 24 (January 1992): 2–9.

———. "The Clowns: Further Notes." *Dear Mr Thoms . . .* 31 (July 1993): 9–12.

Hooper, John. "The Dead Guerrillas, the Missing Brains and the Experiment." *Guardian* (London and Manchester), 18 November 2002, 17.

Jacobson, David J. *The Affairs of Dame Rumor*. New York: Rinehart, 1948.

Joralemon, Donald. "Organ Wars: The Battle for Body Parts." *Medical Anthropology Quarterly* 9 (1995): 335–56.

Josefson, Deborah. "Medical Centre Recalls Potentially Infected Body Parts." *BMJ News* 325 (17 August 2002): 356.

Kelso, Paul. "Inquiry over Child Organs." *Guardian* (London and Manchester), 4 December 1999: 1.

Klintberg, Bengt af. *Den Stulna Njuren: Sägner och Rykten i vår Tid*. Stockholm: Norstedts, 1994.

Köiva, Mare. "Bloodsuckers and Human Sausage Factories." *FOAFtale News* 43 (February 1998): 7–9.

Lassen, Henrik. "Kidney Thief in Denmark." *FOAFtale News* 40–41 (December 1996): 17.

Laurance, Jeremy. "The Basement of Horrors." *Independent* (London), 31 January 2001, 1.

Leventhal, Todd. *The Child Organ Trafficking Rumor: A Modern "Urban Legend."* Washington: U.S. Information Agency, 1994.

Lock, Margaret. "The Alienation of Body Tissue and the Biopolitics of Immortalized Cell Lines." *Body and Society* 7 (2001): 63–92.

Magin, Ulrich. "International Chronicles: Germany." *INFO Journal* 70 (January 1994): 45.

Mantell, Hilary. *The Giant O'Brien*. London: Fourth Estate, 1999.

Mazo, Jeff. "Melded Motif: Lipstick and Kidney." *FOAFtale News* 40–41 (December 1996): 18.

McKie, Robin. "Brains Removed in Organ Scandal." *Observer* (London), 11 May 2003, 7.

———. "Scientists Fight to Save Aboriginal Bone Bank." *Observer* (London), 28 September 2003, 14.

Meikle, James. "Jail Threat to Doctors in Organ Scandal." *Guardian* (London and Manchester), 5 December 2003, 8.

Michell, John. "Satanic Curses: Bogus Social Workers and Demonic Abductors." *Folklore Frontiers* 12 (1990): 4–9.

Milburn, Alan. Text of the Statement on the Royal Liverpool Children's Hospital Inquiry made to the House of Commons, January 2001. Press release, courtesy of the House of Commons Library.

Millward, David. "GP Struck Off over Plan to Trade Live Kidney." *Daily Telegraph* (London), 31 August 2002, 8.

Moravec, Mark. "Organ Kidnap Stories." *Australian Folklore* 8 (1993): 89–99.

———. "Organ Kidnap Stories." *FOAFtale News* 23 (September 1991): 6–7.

"More Organ Sale Rumours." *FOAFtale News* 38 (December 1995): 8.

O'Neill, Sean. "Arrogant Doctors May Be Prosecuted." *Daily Telegraph* (London), 11 May 2000, 9.

———. "Hospital 'Returned My Dead Son as an Empty Shell.'" *Daily Telegraph* (London), 30 September 1999, 14.

Palmer, Phil. "The Baby Butcher." *Mirror* (London), 31 January 2001, 1.

Pascoe-Watson, George. "Get Doctor Frankenstein." *Sun* (London), 31 January 2001, 4–5.

Price, David, and Ronnie Mackay. "The Trade in Human Organs, Part 1." *New Law Journal* (20 September 1991): 1272–73.

———. "The Trade in Human Organs, Part 2." *New Law Journal* (27 September 1991): 1307–9.

Pukas, Anna. "The Global Lie That Cannot be Silenced." *Folklore Frontiers* 27 (1995): 16–17.

Radford, Benjamin. "Bitter Harvest: The Organ-Snatching Urban Legends." *Skeptical Inquirer* 23 (May–June 1999): 34–39, 48.

Redfern, Michael, Q.C. *The Royal Liverpool Children's Hospital Inquiry: Summary and Recommendations.* London: HMSO, 2001.

Richardson, Ruth. *Death, Dissection, and the Destitute.* London: Routledge, 1988; London: Orion, 2001.

———. "Fearful Symmetry: Corpses for Anatomy, Organs for Transplantation." In *Organ Transplantation: Meaning and Realities,* ed. Stuart J. Younger and Laurence O'Connell, 66–100. Madison: University of Wisconsin Press, 1996.

Rogers, Lois. "Secret Tests on Brains of Serial Killers." *Sunday Times* (London), 4 April 2004, 4.

Rothman, David J. "The International Organ Traffic." *New York Review,* 26 March 1998, 14–17.

Rothman, David J., E. Rose, T. Awaya, B. Cohen, A. Daar, S. L. Dzemeshkevich, C. J. Lee, R. Munroe, H. Reyes, S. M. Rothman, K. F. Schoen, N. Scheper-Hughes, Z. Shapira, and H. Smit. "The Bellagio Task Force Report on Transplantation, Bodily Integrity, and the International Traffic in Organs." *Transplantation Proceedings* 29 (1997): 2739–45. sunsite.berkeley.edu/biotech/organswatch/pages.html

Russell, Andy, and Krissy Storrar. "My Baby's Body Was on a Dirty Table in Thirty-six Jars." *Sun* (London), 31 January 2001, 1, 3.

Ryle, Sarah. "'Human Abattoir' Fears of Parents Ignored for Twenty-one years." *Observer* (London), 5 December 1999, 5.

Samper, David. "Cannibalizing Kids: Rumor and Resistance in Latin America." *Journal of Folklore Research* 39 (January–April 2002): 1–32.

Scheper-Hughes, Nancy. "The End of the Body: The Global Traffic in Organs for Transplant Surgery." Essay based on 1998 Sidney Mintz Lecture. sunsite.berkeley.edu/biotech/organswatch/pages/cadraft.html.

———. "The Global Traffic in Human Organs." *Current Anthropology* 41 (April 2000): 191–224.

———. "Keeping an Eye on the Global Traffic in Human Organs." *Lancet* 361 no. 9369 (2003): 1645–48.

———. "Min(d)ing the Body: On the Trail of Organ-Stealing Rumors." In *Exotic No More: Anthropology on the Front Lines,* ed. Jeremy MacClanay, 33–63. Chicago: University of Chicago Press, 2002.

———. "Theft of Life: Organ Stealing Rumours." *Anthropology Today* 12 (1996): 3–11.

Schreiberg, David. "Dead Babies." *New Republic,* 24 December 1990, 12–13.

Shinzo, Kato. "Organ Transplants and Brain-Dead Donors." *Mortality* 9 (2004): 13–26.

Shonder, John. "Organ Theft Rumors in Guatemala: Some Personal Observations." *FOAFtale News* 35 (October 1994): 1–4.

Sieveking, Paul. "The Kidney Kidnappers." *Fortean Times* 65 (October–November 1992): 50–51.

Stilo, Guiseppe, and Paulo Toselli. "The Kidnappers and the Black Ambulance: Child Abduction Legends from Sicily." *FOAFtale News* 23 (September 1991): 5–6.

Stuart, Julia. "'I Feel I Failed to Protect Him in Life and Death': A Mother's Story." *Independent* (London), 31 January 2001, 5.

"Supervisor's Body-Donor Scam Wasn't up to Scratch." *Star* (London), 28 February 2003. www.thestar.co.za.

Thorpe, Benjamin. *Northern Mythology.* Vol. 3, *Netherlandish Traditions.* London: Edward Lumley, 1852.

Topham, Gwynn. "Alder Hey Parents Win Public Apology." *Guardian* (London and Manchester), 28 February 2003, 18.

Usborne, David. "A Grief That Never Ends for the Family Who Buried Their Son Five Times." *Independent* (London), 11 September 2003, 1.

Walker, Carl. "'They Stole My Baby's Heart.'" *Stockport Express* (U.K.), 17 February 1999, 1.

Wallich, Paul, and Madhursree Mukerjee. "Regulating the Body Business." *Scientific American* 274 (March 1996): 8–9.

Walsh, Nick Paton. "Doctors Plotted to Kill Man for Organs." *Guardian* (London and Manchester), 29 April 2004, 19.

Ward, David. "Nameless Victims of Hospital Scandal Are Laid to Rest." *Guardian* (London and Manchester), 6 August 2004, 11.

Weiss, Meira. "The Immigrating Body and the Body Politic." *Body and Society* 7 (2001): 93–110.

White, Luise. "Social Construction and Social Consequence: Rumor and Evidence." Paper presented at conference on the "Social Consequences of Rumor," Bellagio, April 2003.

Wilson, Jamie. "Scandal-Hit Hospital in Storm over Baby Hearts." 11 February 1999.
http://society.guardian.co.uk/bristolinquiry/story/0,10770,523081,00.html.

Younger, Stuart J., and Laurence O'Connell, eds. *Organ Transplantation: Meaning and Realities.* Madison: University of Wisconsin Press, 1996.

Zarembo, Alan, and Jessica Garrison. "Donated Bodies, Big Profits." *St. Paul Pioneer Press*, 14 March 2004.
www.twincities.com/mld/pioneerpress/news/world/8174864.htm.

BLOOD AND BABIES

Not only those who accuse should be believed.

—CARDINAL LORENZO GANGANELLI, 1759

A perennial theme in accusations brought against persecuted minorities is that they indulge in disgusting secret rituals involving any or all of the following: orgiastic sex, incest, baby sacrifice, consumption of human flesh or blood, and other breaches of bodily integrity such as the collection and use of stolen body parts. These rituals are very often seen as evidence of a conspiracy to overthrow the political, social, or religious order, to rule the world for personal gain or in the service of some dark lord. The documented history of such accusations can be traced over the best part of two thousand years, though the accusers and the victims vary. So in the year 177 A.D. in Lyons, France, the pagan majority accused the small Christian community of infanticide, cannibalism, orgies, and incest (Cohn 3–4); in 1466 in Italy, members of an ascetic Christian sect, the Fraticelli de Opinione, under torture "confessed" to rites including incestuous orgies and the sacrifice of a baby boy, then making his desiccated body into a powder and drinking it in wine (Cohn 42–54). In the fourteenth century, two elderly women confessed to the Inquisition at Toulouse that they had been in the service of Satan for about twenty years: "Frequently on Friday nights they have attended the Sabbath which is held sometimes in one place, sometimes in another. There, in company with other men and women who are equally sacrilegious, they commit all manner of excesses, whose details are too horrible to tell."[1] In Germany in 1891, Hermann Strack wrote in the preface to the third edition of his famous treatise, *The Jew and Human Sacrifice*, "Every year, especially about Easter-time, there is a revival of the accusation that the Jews . . . make use of the blood of Christians for purposes of ritual" (vii).

More recently, during an outbreak of religious and moral panic driven by Christian fundamentalists in the United Kingdom between 1989 and 1992, newspaper headlines spoke of children being forced into "sexual perversion, animal sacrifice and the drinking of blood" by parents caught up in satanic sects.[2] Similarly, in Germany in the winter of 2002–3, allegations arose that Satanists had killed, sliced up, and eaten babies (Boyes). In France during October 2003 the discovery of the dead bodies of four newborn babies led to the finger of suspicion being pointed at "satanists, gypsies and . . . eastern European prostitutes" amid claims of ritual abuse (Lichfield). In Zimbabwe it was alleged that supporters of Robert Mugabe had shot a white farmer and drunk his blood (Peta). More controversially—in a reference to Goya's famous painting, *Saturn Devouring One of His Children*—during the Israeli elections of 2003 the British newspaper the *Independent* printed a cartoon showing Ariel Sharon amid scenes of devastation eating the body of a child; a speech bubble came from his mouth, "What's wrong . . . You never seen a politician kissing babies?"[3]

Many attempts have been made to try to understand how such incredible rumors can flourish. Historian Norman Cohn tried to account for pagan accusations against early Christians as misunderstandings of religious texts and rites (8). Similarly, Strack, the scholar whose name is most closely associated with the debunking of the Blood Libel legend, has suggested that Christian accusations against Jews may be based on a misunderstanding of the rituals of Passover (H.L.S. 264). Strack has elsewhere suggested that Christian accusations against Jews are the result of a blood superstition in the majority community (*Jew* 276). Others have tried to understand these accusations by means of psychological or psychoanalytical concepts. Alan Dundes introduces some of these in his essay on ritual murder ("Ritual" 16 –17). His theory is that the explanation lies in "the Christian need for a scapegoat" to transfer religious guilt for central beliefs and practices such as the Eucharist. "Although Jews did not kill Jesus (. . . the Romans did)," Dundes writes, "Christian folklore insists that the Jews were Christ-killers. In this context the blood libel is simply another example of the same kind of Christian folklore. Christians blame Jews for something the Christians needed to have happened." Thus the Blood Libel legend can be understood through the psychoanalytical concept of "projective inversion," the accuser's trick of displacing his/her own fears and desires onto the accused (Dundes, "Ritual" 18).

I cannot accept the details of Dundes's argument, which seems to me to be based on some projective inversion of his own, but I do agree that there is no way of rationalizing this sort of accusation and that one should seek for an explanation in human psychology. In his review of Strack's *The Jew and Human Sacrifice*, Salomon Reinach quotes the words of a friend: "Note how uninventive human malignity is: it turns eternally in the same circle of accusations, human sacrifice, cannibalism, offenses against public decency." After listing several examples, he concludes in his own voice: "calumny, inspired by religious or national hatred, always turns in the same narrow circle and gorges itself on the same sustenance" (165, 166). It is this inevitable sameness that has to be taken account of and in which we may perhaps find a clue. In human sacrifice, cannibalism, the plundering of the human body, and depraved sexuality, we are dealing, I suggest, with the grossest images sick minds or sick imaginations can conjure up. Stories about such happenings are the welling up and narrativizing of images of ultimate bodily pollution.[4]

So potent are these images that once someone is suspected or accused of any of these things for any reason, the accusation takes on a life of its own. The first step is to believe that another person or group of people is defiled or defiling. It is noteworthy how many expressions of prejudice, especially ethnic prejudice, include the word *dirty* or terms that imply dirt. It is not a large step to imagine that such people do things that others consider dirty— eat dogs, for example. It may be a large step from there to imagine that they eat babies, but it is not inconsistent; it is driven by the same logic and is only a matter of degree.

Once the thought is uttered, the accusation has all the verisimilitude of horror ("it's too horrible to imagine, therefore it must be true"). It also has a sort of symbolic truth about it, in that the rumors accord with what prejudiced people fear or imagine certain others might do to them or to the social body. As Cohn says of the persecutions of Christians at Lyons in 177 A.D., "for many of the pagans these revelations confirmed their worst suspicions" (4). As soon as they enter the public domain, the images are narrativized as hearers and readers react to the rumors and as "victims" are encouraged to tell the tale of their sufferings. (As we shall see, accusations in the U.K. "satanic child abuse" cases had an apparently inexhaustible amount of colorful detail about men in black, rites in caves and tunnels, and all sorts of novelistic embellishments.) The "evidence" builds up via the lies of those with vested interests, the confessions of the accused (in the past usually collected via torture or the fear of torture), the testimony of "victims" (nowadays often obtained through pressure, influence, or suggestion), and the fondness of press and public for a sensational story. Before long, a major scare arises. If the rumors are then taken seriously by the judiciary, the Church, or the government, it is very difficult to call a halt to what has become an outright persecution. This was very evident in the "satanic ritual abuse" scare in the United Kingdom, which was halted just in the nick of time.

Images of pollution also come as a "bundle," as Reinach pointed out, so that an accusation of child sacrifice can trigger accusations of cannibalism, and accusations of cannibalism can trigger rumors of secret rites and orgies, and so on.[5] This works on a smaller scale, too; any of these claims may be made against fallen dictators and unpopular leaders (and will be believed); similar rumors spring up about serial killers and in times of war. Among well-known "cannibals" and takers of baby blood, we may count Napoleon Bonaparte,[6] Prince Rupert of the Rhine, the Cavalier faction in the English Civil War, Central African tyrant Jean-Bedel Bokassa (Nundy 15), Romanian dictator Nicolai Ceausescu (Simmons), and the British serial killers Frederick and Rosemary West (Chittenden 1, 2).

The early accounts studied by historians and folklorists include first-century accounts of the Catiline conspiracy against Rome, where Catiline is said to have mixed the blood of a man with wine and passed it around his followers: "when all had . . . drunk from the bowl, as is the custom in holy rites, he revealed his plan." Interestingly, this story was later expanded to include the details that Catiline and his followers had killed a boy, sworn an oath over his entrails, and then eaten the flesh (quoted in Cohn 6). There are also second-century cases of Christians charged with consuming sacrificial victims at nocturnal feasts;[7] throughout this time, Christians were also regularly supposed to indulge in indecent orgiastic rites.

Combinations of these types of accusations were also made against medieval Christian heretics. As Cohn explains, "centuries later . . . tales of erotic debauches, infanticide and cannibalism were revived and applied to various religious outgroups in medieval Christendom" (17). In this context, he discusses the persecution of Paulicians, the Bogomiles, the Waldensians, and the Fraticelli in continental Europe (16–59). Reinach also notes persecutions of the Albigensians and the Cathars founded on the same claims and points out that St. Augustine accused the Manichaeans of acts of which "one dare not even think, let alone . . . write about" (165). All were accused in pretty much the same terms.

A very similar set of accusations was later brought against the Knights Templar when it was decided that action must be taken to combat their increasing wealth, power, and influence. It is interesting to see that the summons for the Knights Templar to appear before the Estates General at Tours in 1308 is couched in terms of a plague threatening the cosmos itself: "Heaven and earth are agitated by the breath of so great a crime and the elements are disturbed. . . . Against so criminal a plague everything must rise up; laws, arms, every living thing, the four elements" (quoted in Cohn 93). At a later date, as Cohn shows in his discussion of the background to the European witch hunts of the sixteenth and seventeenth centuries, persons were regularly tried, convicted, and executed for the same imagined offenses, their accusers being convinced that the accused were not only a cancer in the body politic but a threat to the natural and supernatural order (225–55). In the paragraphs that follow I shall look at two examples of this pernicious folklore.

One strand of this tradition that folklorists have frequently studied is the Blood Libel legend (motif V361: "Christian child killed to furnish blood for Jewish rites"). In the passionate words of Haim Hillel Ben-Sasson writing in the *Encyclopaedia Judaica*, the Blood Libel legend is "a complex of deliberate lies, trumped-up accusations, and popular beliefs about the murder-lust of the Jews and their bloodthirstiness, based on the conception that Jews hate Christianity and mankind in general. It is combined with the delusion that Jews are in some way not human and must have recourse to special remedies and subterfuges in order to appear, at least outwardly, like other men" (1120). Ben-Sasson is here drawing attention to two interrelated threads of anti-Semitic folk belief—that Jews need blood for religious ceremonies and for cures for physical conditions as diverse as body odor and male menstruation. He is correct, I think, in seeing both as stemming from the anti-Semitic notion that Jews are polluted or polluting, "not like other men," haters of Christianity "and mankind in general." Similar attitudes seem to have informed Christian social workers and child-protection officers pursuing "Satanists" in the United Kingdom between 1989 and 1992. Literally incredible charges were brought against the parents and older relatives of children thought to be subjected to ritual abuse during satanic ceremonies. It was clear that the accused were indeed thought of as polluters and contaminators, not only of the children they had in their care but also of society in general. This affair reflects abuse accusations made a little earlier in the United States but is not identical and not as familiar; it thus complements and rounds out the picture of "blood and babies" folklore in our age.

These two examples of the utilization of demonizing folklore in the course of the defamation of those seen as enemies of God are the subject of this final chapter.

THE BLOOD LIBEL LEGEND AND ACCUSATIONS OF JEWISH RITUAL MURDER

Two things must be stressed at the outset of any discussion of the Blood Libel legend. First, I fully endorse Ben-Sasson's description of the libel as "a complex of deliberate lies, trumped-up accusations, and popular beliefs." All such cases that have come to trial have proved to be wholly unfounded, and many Christian writers and theologians, including a dozen popes, beginning with Gregory X in the thirteenth century, have refuted the ritual murder charge against the Jews (E. O. J. 830). It should not, in an ideal world, be necessary to make such personal statements, but when speaking of a subject that arouses such passions, it is better that it is understood right from the start that a discussion of anti-Semitic folklore does not mean an endorsement of it. Second, in spite of the impression given in some work on the legend (Dundes, "Ritual," for example), the Jews have not been the only people to have been thought of as "not like other men," not fully human harborers of grossness and pollution. It is true, however, that Jews have been particularly affected by these sorts of claims.[8] The history of the persecution of Jews for these imaginary offenses is a very long one; it is perhaps the oldest contemporary legend on record, dating from at least the twelfth century to the present day.

Scholars who try to construct a history of the Blood Libel often cite a second century B.C. case in which Jews were accused of fattening up a Greek every seven years for ritual sacrifice and consumption and a slightly more recent case in which it was alleged that about 415 A.D., the Jews of Inmestar in Syria staged a mock crucifixion of a boy, who later died from his injuries. However, even if these accounts were not fabricated, they do not constitute evidence of a continuous tradition of such accusations. Most scholars of the Blood Libel see the case of William of Norwich in 1144 as the occasion that led to the establishment of the sort of continuing folklore that makes the Blood Libel a legend rather than a series of related rumors.

Two Early Cases in England

WILLIAM OF NORWICH

"In [King Stephen's] time, the Jews of Norwich bought a Christian child before Easter and tortured him with all the tortures that our Lord was tortured with, and on Good Friday hanged him on a cross on account of our Lord, and then buried him. They expected it would be concealed, but our Lord made it plain that he was a holy martyr, and the monks took him and buried him with ceremony in the monastery, and through our Lord he works wonderful and varied miracles, and he is called St William" (Jacobs, *Jews* 19). Apart from this brief account in the final continuation of the *Anglo-Saxon Chronicle*, written in 1155 by the monks of Peterborough in the neighboring county of Cambridgeshire, the principal evidence for the William of Norwich affair comes from a seven-volume hagiographical work, *The Life and Miracles of St. William of Norwich*, by Thomas of Monmouth, probably begun in 1149 and completed in 1172–73. The only known copy of this work was discovered by British theologian, writer, and scholar Montague Rhodes James in 1889. Together with Canon Augustus Jessopp, James translated and edited the work and published it in 1896. Book 1, probably written between 1149 and 1150, is a straightforward hagiographical work covering William's conception, birth, and holy childhood, his martyrdom, and his early miracles. Book 2, probably written four or five years later, begins with a strident defense of book 1 and accounts of William's miracles and ends with a marshaling of "evidence" that supports the author's version of William's death. Books 3–6 followed shortly thereafter, book 7 was probably completed in 1172, and a prologue and dedication were added at that time.[9] It is Books 1 and 2 that chiefly interest us, for here the story and the evidence on which it is based are set out.

Reading book 1 of Thomas's *Life of William* is a shocking experience. The tone throughout is intemperate, and the gloating description of William's martyrdom quite sick. Then there is the vicious racism, shocking to modern minds. In Thomas's eyes, there is nothing that Jews will not stoop to, and they are constantly referred to as "our enemies." Thomas alleges that, in the spring of 1144, a twelve-year-old boy was abducted by Jews on the Monday before Good Friday, kept for a while in "the Jew's house," and on or around Wednesday was tortured and crucified by them. The body was kept until Good Friday when it was dumped in a wood on the other side of town. It was discovered on Easter Saturday. It had first been seen by a woman who had been led to it by a bright light; then a peasant reported to the forester that he had seen a body in the wood and led him to it. The forester wanted to bury it but, after consulting a priest, was persuaded to wait until after Easter Day. Nearly the whole town came out over the weekend to view the body, which was identified by William's aunt and uncle. According to Thomas, accusations that he had been murdered by Jews began almost immediately—the forester had thought so, William's aunt had had a prophetic dream, and so on. The whole town was in turmoil, he says, and there would have been a lynching had not the people been afraid of the sheriff, John de Chesney, who had been taking bribes from the Jews. The accusation was at length formally made by a priest, Godwin Sturt, William's uncle, at a meeting of the Church synod.

The story goes on, but let us turn to the torture and murder of William so lovingly documented by Thomas. The Jews begin by fixing William to what Thomas wants readers to think is a cross but is actually a structure of three posts with a crosspiece. William is tied against the central post, his left hand and foot nailed to the left-hand post and his right hand and foot bound to the right-hand post. They did it this way, Thomas says, "in case at any time he should be discovered it might not be supposed that he had been killed by Jews rather than Christians" (Jessopp and James 21–22)—in other words, the Jews deliberately botched the crucifixion to divert suspicion from themselves. Then they began torturing him. The tortures included gagging him with a teasle (a plant with a thorny seed-head used in the preparation of cloth), binding knotted cords tightly around his head and forehead and under his chin so that the knots pressed on his temples, the center of the forehead, and the Adam's apple in his throat. They shaved his head and stabbed it with thorns. The proceedings ended with a vicious stab wound to the left side, which penetrated the heart. Then they sent for boiling water, which they poured over him to stanch the flow of blood. This strange account is riddled with Christian symbolism to make it more like a recognizable crucifixion and to recall the events of Good Friday. The child is often referred to as a "lamb," the man accused of abducting the child is "the imitator in almost everything of the traitor Judas," and William's death is described as "his awful passion."

Let us now return to Thomas's story at the point where Godwin Sturt formally accuses the Jews of murder. This is rather interesting because Thomas actually disposes of the accusation quite quickly. Godwin is made to accuse the Jews of murder at some length but to only briefly hint at some sort of ritual and to stop short of alleging that the child was crucified (Jessopp and James 43–45). We must remember that Thomas cannot put words in the mouth of anyone who was actually at the synod and therefore would be in a position to challenge his account: he can suppress some things and twist the meaning of others, but he cannot lie too blatantly. So Godwin is made to speak about "wounds," "punishment," and "practices which the Jews are bound to carry out on the days specified"—that's all. The bishop, Eborard, is skeptical (as Thomas cannot disguise) but three times asks members of the Jewish community to attend the synod to answer the charge. They appeal to Sheriff John, who tells them that the synod has no jurisdiction over them and does not allow them to appear until Eborard threatens them with summary justice in their absence. At this meeting, Godwin challenges them to undergo trial by ordeal, an offer they decline. As a compromise, John suggests that the Jews agree to submit to the ordeal at a later date. When this compromise is also refused, he hurries the Jews away and keeps them in the royal castle until the king can be consulted. (At this point, Thomas implies that the king, too, will be bribed to take the Jews' side in this dispute.) The king declares in favor of the Jews, the bishop drops the case, and the Jews return home, a result that Thomas attributes to a conspiracy of Jews, Sheriff, and King to pervert the course of justice.

At all times Thomas writes as if he was either an eyewitness or had special access to the deeds, thoughts, and motives of the principal players. We know that this could not have been the case, since he did not arrive in Norwich until 1146 or even later. At best, where his account is not wholly fictive, it is based on memories and hearsay evidence collected some years after the events. Crucial contributors to this story are William's aunt, who identified the body; the monks who washed the boy's body prior to its reburial in the monks' cemetery about a month after his death; a Christian woman who was working in "the Jew's house"; a prominent citizen called Ælward Ded; and a monk, Theobald of Cambridge, who was a convert from Judaism.

These "witnesses" and their "evidence" have been subjected to a great deal of scholarly analysis and criticism, which I won't discuss in any detail here. Suffice it to say that the testimony sounds much like the sort of rumor, gossip, and hearsay that might have been swapped in a rumor flap and subsequently expanded, emended, and narrativized. In addition to the very strange crucifixion and the tale of the crooked law enforcer and the bribable king, there is a story about a sacrifice and another about an encounter with murderers in a wood. The detail of these testimonies, taken out of the context of Thomas's vivid storytelling, is frankly laughable.

Take, for example, Ælward Ded's encounter with the murderers in the wood. On his deathbed—so Thomas was told by a friend of a friend—Ælward confessed to having suppressed vital evidence about the murder of the boy—to wit, that he had encountered a group of local Jews in the wood where William was killed just before Easter 1144. A sack was slung over the back of the horse on which of one of them was riding. When Ælward touched it, he was sure he felt a human body inside. When he challenged them, the Jews sped off into the thickest part of the wood, where—so Ælward later heard—they hung the body from a tree by "a thin flaxen cord" (though a line or two later we are told that the body was found "lying in the open" under an oak tree). Strangely enough, having apparently detected a serious crime, Ælward did not follow the suspects but calmly resumed his devotional meditations and walked on. Nor did he report the incident when he got home, since by then, according to Thomas, the Jews had panicked and "run to Sheriff John" to ask what could be done. For another substantial bribe, John pressured Ælward not to reveal what had happened. Ælward was as good as his word or better, since he remained quiet for three years after the sheriff's death.

The testimony of the Christian servant—or the inference Thomas derives from it—is no more believable, yet it is from her evidence that his strange description of William's death is concocted. Her story is that she heard a commotion and was sent for boiling water. Through a chink in the door, she saw a boy tied to a post. This is not much of a story, so afterward—Thomas says—she took him to the house to back up her account by showing him the visible evidence of the crime. Once again, it is thin sort of evidence. I would guess that what she showed him were nail holes on part of the paneled screen commonly found in the better class of English medieval house between the hall (the public part of the house) and the solar (the private quarters). Hence the cross with three uprights. I'd also guess that Thomas could find only two nail holes in appropriate places so had to assume that only two of the boy's limbs had been nailed and that the other two had somehow been tied. Hence the crucifixion that was not a crucifixion and the cross that was not a cross. The boiling water the servant says she was sent to fetch is fitted into Thomas's story somehow by supposing that it was needed to stanch the flow of blood from the boy's tortured body. Again, the witness suppressed her evidence. This time, according to Thomas, it was because, as the only Christian person working for Jews, she feared for her life. If this was the best evidence of the murder that could be found, Thomas would have been better omitting it. It hardly makes a credible picture.

Finally, there is Theobald's testimony. Thomas claims that Theobald said that "in the ancient writings of his fathers it was written that the Jews without the shedding of human blood, could never obtain their freedom, nor could they ever return to their fatherland. Hence it was laid down . . . that every year they must sacrifice a Christian . . . to the Most High God in scorn and contempt so they might avenge their sufferings on them" (Jessopp and James 93). This accusation is of course familiar to folklorists and historians but was novel at the time. With the benefit of hindsight, we now see how it fits into the picture of Jewish religious crime that Thomas was trying to build up, but one wonders whether his allegations appeared to be credible and relevant to contemporary readers or whether they seemed to be just another wild accusation.[10] He presents no evidence for his statement except some unprovable stuff about "ancient writings." Indeed, there is no independent evidence even for Theobald's existence, and nothing in Thomas's text to indicate that he did not make the whole thing up. Again with hindsight, we can guess that Thomas must have heard this claim from some source or another since it later became a staple of ritual murder accusations. Even so, Theobald's strange testimony does not serve Thomas's purposes very well. Thomas wants to prove that the Jews crucified William and did so in mockery of Jesus, so that something of the sanctity of Jesus would rub off onto the boy and make him a useful (and profitable) saint for his cathedral. But this is not what Theobald alleges. His story does not match Thomas's. Whereas Thomas alleges that the boy was crucified but nowhere says this act was committed as a sacrifice, Theobald alleges that the Jews perform annual sacrifices but nowhere mentions a crucifixion.

Thomas's story is in general so full of holes and absurdities that much of the scholarship on this subject has involved speculation about what might really have happened at Norwich in 1144. Reinterpretations have been many and varied depending how much of Thomas's evidence the interpreter has been prepared to believe. In his chapter on "The Legend" in the introduction to his and Jessopp's edition of the *Life*, M. R. James puts forward four possibilities: that this was a genuine ritual murder by the Jews of Norwich; that William was killed by a Christian who threw the blame on the Jews; that William was killed by a person or persons unknown and the rest of the story was invented; and that William might indeed have been killed by Jews—or a Jew—or in the Jewish Quarter and the rest of the story then invented. James's own— controversial—conclusion was that the answer lay somewhere between the last two hypotheses, though in the latter case he would assume that it was either an accident or the work of a lone madman. In a critical review, Joseph Jacobs proposed instead that William was crucified by his relatives. William's family was ignorant and fanatical enough, he argued, to think that a mock crucifixion (stopping just short of death) would sanctify the boy and call down blessings on his family. Poor William was so traumatized by this procedure that he suffered a cataleptic fit, which his relatives took for death. He was then transported to the wood, where his body was lightly covered with earth and leaves. When his family was later called to the scene to identify him, they buried him and thus ensured his real death.[11] The family threw the blame on the Jews because they needed a scapegoat and hated Jews.

Other interpretations have ranged from the cataleptic fit theory minus the Christian crucifixion detail (Roth, *Ritual* 15; H.L.S.) to the suggestion that some dangerous and perhaps fatal horseplay might have occurred in Norwich during the celebration of Purim a month earlier and that dark rumors were abroad about Jewish practices. As a boy friendly toward Jews, William was taken to the house to be questioned about these rumors. When he got frightened and refused to answer questions, the Jews turned to torture to extract the information and from there to crucifixion (Anderson 100–5). Another commentator, V. D. Lipman, has suggested that this was a case of abduction and sexual abuse, probably by a Christian (56). This argument is based on Thomas's description of the child being found "dressed in his jacket and shoes" (Jessopp and James 32–33).[12] One of the most recent commentators, Gavin Langmuir, has declined to enter into debates about what "really happened" but makes it quite plain that he is unwilling to believe any of Thomas's evidence. He contends that Thomas made up all or almost all of the story or relied on fabulations created after the event by William's Jew-hating priestly family.

But perhaps what stands out most for the historian of defamatory folklore is that none of the participants in the original drama accused the Jews of a crucifixion—not the forester who found the body, not William's aunt, not Godwin Sturt. At this point, the accusation was only of child murder, with the stated or implied corollary that the Jews must be the murderers since no Christian would do such a dreadful deed. It is Thomas himself who accuses the Jews of crucifying the boy, but he cannot depict a recognizable crucifixion. In any case, he seems to allege that the act was committed only as an afterthought. While the Jews were "rioting in a spirit of malignity around" the boy, Thomas says, "some of those present" encouraged the others to string the boy up in mockery of Jesus and "as though they would say 'Even as we condemned the Christ to a shameful death, so let us condemn the Christian'" (Jessopp and James 21). Thus, Thomas's own account shows that the crucifixion was not premeditated, there has been no prior or universal agreement about the purpose of the proceedings, and there was no suggestion of a ritual. The crucifixion was a spur-of-the-moment thing inspired by a desire to give Christians a taste of their own medicine. Moreover, even when Thomas is portraying the child as a "lamb," he does not suggest that the procedures were part of a sacrifice or ceremony of any kind. The claim that the Jews did indeed kill Christians in an annual ceremony was not added until five years after the first account, when Thomas put it into the mouth of Theobald of Cambridge in book 2 of the *Life*. All this, plus the detail that the Jews of Norwich sent for boiling water to stanch the flow of the murdered boy's blood, makes this a very strange candidate for the first blood libel accusation.

HUGH OF LINCOLN

Nine or ten accusations of Jewish child murder surfaced in England between the Norwich case and 1290, when the Jews were expelled from the country. They may have been copycat accusations, but the records are too scant to be certain: as far as we can judge, three more involved crucifixion, while the others were accusations of child abduction and murder; none involved exsanguination.[13]

The most famous subsequent English case is that of Hugh of Lincoln in 1255. This accusation and the way it is recorded seem almost certainly to have been drawn from Thomas of Monmouth's *Life* of William of Norwich. Most certainly, too, this is a recognizable ritual murder accusation in all its particulars. The extract below is taken from the account by medieval English chronicler Matthew Paris:

This year [1255] about the feast of the apostles Peter and Paul
[27 July], the Jews of Lincoln stole a boy called Hugh, who was about
eight years old. After shutting him up in a secret chamber, where
they fed him on milk and other childish food, they sent to almost all

the cities of England in which there were Jews, and summoned some of their sect from each city to be present at a sacrifice to take place at Lincoln, in contumely and insult of Jesus Christ. For, as they said, they had a boy concealed for the purpose of being crucified; so a great number of them assembled at Lincoln, and then they appointed a Jew of Lincoln judge, to take the place of Pilate, by whose sentence, and with the concurrence of all, the boy was subjected to various tortures. They scourged him till the blood flowed, they crowned him with thorns, mocked him, and spat upon him; each of them also pierced him with a knife, and they made him drink gall, and scoffed at him with blasphemous insults, and kept gnashing their teeth and calling him Jesus, the false prophet. And after tormenting him in divers ways they crucified him, and pierced him to the heart with a spear. When the boy was dead, they took the body down from the cross, and for some reason disemboweled it; it is said for the purpose of their magic arts. (Jacobs, "Little," in *Blood Libel* 43–46)

Apart from the disemboweling, which is a new feature, and the date (July rather than Easter), the rest of this sounds very much like Thomas's account of the death of William: the abduction of a young boy, the torture, the ghoulish antics of the Jews around the suffering child (this time "gnashing their teeth"), the crucifixion, the wound to the heart, and so on. But there is one important difference: at Lincoln the accusation against the Jews has seamlessly incorporated the annual sacrifice motif that Thomas tacked on in book 2 of his narrative and put in the mouth of Theobald.

The story goes on to tell of the mother's anguished search for her child. It was reported that he had last been seen going into a Jew's house, then the body is discovered in a well, a fact which is later explained by saying that the Jews had first tried to bury it but the earth cast it back up again. (At Norwich, too, the earth refused to let the body stay buried.) Here, however, another significant divergence between the Norwich and the Lincoln stories occurs. Instead of being received with some skepticism, the Lincoln accusation is at once believed in toto, and instead of the Jews being sheltered by the king and his sheriff, the king is one of the persecutors. So the story ends with the arrest and interrogation of a local Jew, his "confession" and terrible death, the removal of ninety-one Jews to London, and their imprisonment there. This ending is a sign of the times. Thanks to Norwich and copycat accusations elsewhere, and thanks to increasing hostility to Jews from the populace, the monarch, and the secular authorities, the story cannot have a happy ending.[14]

An interesting aspect of both these cases is one man's role in turning the death of a local boy into a Jewish murder. At Norwich, the perpetrator was Thomas of Monmouth; in Lincoln, it was John of Lexington, who, according to Matthew Paris, was "a man of learning, wise and prudent." Happening to be present at the discovery of the boy's body, John immediately interpreted the scene for all the bystanders: "We have heard sometimes that Jews have dared to attempt such things in insult of our crucified Lord Jesus Christ" (Jacobs, "Little," in *Blood Libel*, 44). Quite who Lexington was is not clear, but he was plainly a man with some authority. He was able, for example, to offer immunity to the poor Jewish man who had been arrested (on no better grounds than that the child's body had been found in his well) if he would "expose . . . all that has been done in this matter." According to Paris, the man immediately confessed that, "What the Christians say is true. Almost every year the Jews crucify a boy in injury and insult to Jesus. But one is not found every year, for they do this privately and in remote and secret places. This boy, whom they call Hugh, our Jews crucified without mercy." When death was imminent (the king having overturned John's offer of immunity), the man further confessed, "I will tell the truth to you all. Nearly all the Jews in England agreed to the death of this boy, and from nearly every English city where Jews live some were chosen to be present at this sacrifice as a Paschal offering" (Jacobs, "Little," in *Blood Libel*, 45). The timing of this confession pretty obviously indicates that it was made (if it *was* made) under torture or the threat of torture or in hope of a reprieve.

I find this confession interesting because it does suggest the search in Christian folklore for an explanatory framework that could answer the obvious question in all of these accusations: Why would anyone, Jew or Christian, do such horrible things? In the written accounts, the explanation is always that of course Christians would not, but Jews might. But the question still remains—*why* might they do it? Is it possible that all the elaborate stories about sacrifices at certain dates and places, the baking of blood into Passover bread, the need for blood for medicinal purposes, and so on stem from the need to find some sort of logical framework to bolster up the central accusation and that these various "explanations" were beaten out of the accused during brutal interrogations? In this way, the creation of the full-blown Blood Libel legend would mirror the way the stereotype of witches and witchcraft was later built up in Europe during the fifteenth to seventeenth centuries.

Cases in Continental Europe: From Fulda to Iampol, 1235–1756

Let us now leave accusations that Jews crucified Christian children and look at how the "blood libel" proper—the idea that Jews used Christian blood for ritual purposes—emerged on the European continent. The case that is generally reckoned to be the first to feature an accusation of exsanguination is the one that led to the execution of thirty-four Jews at Fulda in Germany in 1235. Here is Hermann Strack's account of this episode taken from the Erfurt Annals: "In this year on 28 December, at Fulda, 34 Jews of both sexes were put to the sword by crusaders, because two of the

Jews had, on Holy Christmas Day, cruelly killed the five sons of a miller who lived outside the city walls, and was at the time at church with his wife; they had collected their blood in bags smeared with wax and had then, after they had set fire to them, gone away" (quoted in Strack 178). Unlike the case of Hugh of Lincoln, at Fulda there is no claim that these are sacrifices unless the emphasis put on the events occurring on Holy Christmas Day can be taken as implying this. The accusations speak only of the blood being needed for curative purposes. The emperor, Frederick II, set up an inquiry into these rumors and concluded that there was no substance whatever to them. He announced that he "fully acquitted the Jews of Fulda of the crime attributed to them, and the rest of the Jews of Germany of such a serious charge" (Strack 179). Pope Innocent IV likewise came out strongly against there being any truth in such accusations. It was too late, however, to help Fulda's Jews: they had already been tortured into confessions and executed.

Cases in which Jews were accused of obtaining Christian blood began to proliferate across Europe. At Valréas, France, in 1247, multiple wounds were found on a two-year-old girl; local Jews were accused and tortured, and here it was alleged that Christian blood was used "quasi sacrificium." In Germany, at Pforzheim in 1261, Jews were said to have inflicted multiple wounds on a seven-year-old girl, collected her blood on a piece of folded cloth, and then thrown the body into the river. At Weissenburg in 1270, local Jews were accused of hanging a seven-year-old boy up by the legs and opening his veins to extract all his blood. Similar sorts of accusations continued to be made throughout the rest of the century. The accusations varied, sometimes being no more than that the local Jews had kidnapped a child or that someone had sold a child to the Jews for nefarious purposes. Only one of these accusations (at least as reported by Strack) follows the classic ritual pattern of murder plus cannibalistic feast or exsanguination. This is a 1329 case at Savoy where a local Jew "confessed" that he had kidnapped five children and sold them to two coreligionists who had killed the children to make a salve out of their heads and entrails for use in Passover ceremonies every sixth year instead of a sacrifice (Strack 190). Again, the secular authority, in this case, Count Edward of Savoy, undertook a thorough investigation of the claims and concluded that they were the deliberate lies of people who hoped to gain the property of those they accused.

At a conservative estimate, at least thirty-eight trials of Jews for murder of Christians took place in the countries of Western Europe between 1144 and the end of the fourteenth century (Hsia 2–3).[15] The trials would have been only the tip of the iceberg. That there was, by the mid-thirteenth century, a considerable folklore on the subject is evidenced by the number of papal bulls and bulls of protection issued by Popes between 1247 and 1447 (thirteen in all) (Strack 236–37). The 1272 bull issued by Gregory X confirms the existence of the folklore and highlights its nature at that time. The use that the majority community made of that folklore is also apparent: "It sometimes happens that certain Christians lose their Christian children. The charge is then made against the Jews by their enemies that they have stolen and slain these children in secret, and have sacrificed the heart and blood. The fathers of the said children, or other Christians who are envious of the Jews, even hide their children in order to have a pretext to molest the Jews, and to extort money from them" (quoted in Roth, *Ritual* 22).[16]

Many of the cases of that time continued to exhibit considerable vagueness about what the Jews were supposed to be doing with the blood of Christians. Later accusations tend to be much more specific, though extremely varied, giving the distinct impression of a legend in search of a story. At Trent (modern day Trento, Italy) in 1475 on Maundy Thursday (the day before Good Friday), a two-and-a-half-year-old child was murdered. The local

Jews were accused of killing him so that they could use his blood for their Passover bread and wine. The confessions, obtained through horrible torture, confirmed that respected members of the Jewish community had strangled the child because they were obliged to have fresh Christian blood for their ceremonies that year "as in a year of jubilee" (Strack 194).[17] The child, Simon, was beatified. At Tyrnau in 1494 the accusations were of murder and exsanguination, but the "confessions" gave four rather distinct reasons for Jews needing Christian blood: it was useful in treating the wound of circumcision; it could be used as a love potion; it was a specific against male menstruation (from which Jews were said to suffer); and it was needed for ritual purposes. In the latter case, the old folklore of lots being cast to decide where the sacrifice should occur was revived: "they had an ancient but secret ordinance by which they are under obligation to shed Christian blood in honour of God in daily sacrifices in some spot or other; they said it happened in this way that the lot for the present year had fallen on the Tyrnau Jews" (Strack 202; Trachtenburg 149). In Pösing, Hungary, in 1529, Jews were "persuaded" to confess that they had murdered a child and then sucked its blood out with quills and small reeds. Persons of quality supposedly smeared themselves with the blood at wedding feasts. And so it went on. In the fifteenth and sixteenth centuries, at least fifty accusations of the same sort (and this is probably a conservative estimate) were brought against Jews in Italy, Poland, Hungary, and the German-speaking countries. The only reason that such charges were not made in England, France, Portugal, and Spain during this period is that Jews had already been expelled from these countries.

The expulsion of Jews from Spain in 1492 resulted in large measure from a high-visibility case "uncovered" by the Inquisition. This was the case of "El Santo Niño de La Guardia," which has received detailed attention from Isidore Loeb and H. C. Lea. The Inquisition became convinced—on what evidence is not clear—that in 1488 a Christian child had been subjected to a Jewish ritual murder. Eleven people were thought to be responsible, six of them Christians and five of them second-generation Jewish Christians, sons of converts from Judaism to Christianity. Three of the latter were dead at the time of the arrests in 1490; when they were found guilty of the crime in 1491, they were burned in effigy. The eight living suspects were subjected to torture or threats of torture and "confessed" to the most bizarre crimes. Though the confessions were full of gaps and inconsistencies, the outline of the story extracted from them was as follows.

They had gathered at some time or other in a cave somewhere or other to crucify a child. His arms and legs were stretched out on two pieces of wood like a cross. He was whipped, pinched, and spat on; thorns were pushed into his head, his shoulders, and the soles of his feet; a vein was opened in his arm and the blood was drained into a cauldron, bowl, or an earthenware pot; his side was pierced with a knife and his heart was removed. All this was done as an insult to Jesus and accompanied by vile imprecations addressed to him in the person of the child. After the child died in a thousand torments, he was taken down from the cross and buried the same night in a secret place. Several days later, the same gang reassembled secretly in the same cave to cast a spell with the stolen heart and a consecrated wafer. Their intention was to cause the death of the Inquisition and all other Christians, to destroy the Catholic faith, and to restore Mosaic law. When the group's spells did not appear to be working, the members assembled a third time in another place, and one of them was sent with the heart and the wafer to a learned rabbi in the town so that the spells could be done again.

Loeb subjects the evidence amassed by the Inquisition to a rigorous appraisal, concluding (1) that the testimonies were obtained by torture or the fear of torture; that they are full of contradictions, improbabilities, and outright impossibilities; (2) that the judges did nothing whatever to discover the truth of the allegations, not even the minimum necessary; (3) that the accusers were unable to say when the crime had occurred and there was no evidence that a child had disappeared (no corpse or remains); (4) that the child never existed (Loeb, "Enfant"). Lea adds that when the site of the supposed grave was examined, there was no evidence of a corpse or of a severed head, nails, wood, or any other implements of a crucifixion. These were said to have been taken up to heaven so that they would not fall into the hands of idolaters. He goes on to follow the growth of the subsequent cult through the miracles witnessed at the site of the supposed grave, through the legends and sacred plays about the child saint, and through the place the legend held in Spanish literature until the date of writing (1889). Even though the crime was almost certainly imaginary in every respect, the accused were found guilty and burned at the stake (Lea, "Santo Niño"). Within a year, the Inquisition was able to persuade the monarchy to expel the Jews from Spain.

At least in Germany, the number of trials began to diminish in the post-Reformation period. Ronald Po-chia Hsia notes that two complementary forces were at work: the endeavor of Emperor Frederick III to suppress any charges arising in local courts; and the secularization of the discourse of child murders. "One of the manifestations of this transformation," Hsia writes, "was the greater emphasis of ritual child murders in witchcraft discourses of the late sixteenth century, as witches seemed to have replaced Jews as the most dangerous enemies of Christian society" (228). Accusations elsewhere continued unabated throughout the seventeenth and eighteenth centuries, including, to mention only a few, at Verona in 1603, Venice in 1705, Viterbo in 1705, and Ancona in 1711 (Loeb, "Mémoire"); throughout Poland from about 1650 to 1780 (Roth, *Ritual*); and in Hungary and Transylvania between 1764 and 1791 (Strack).

The accusations in Poland led to the publication of one of the most famous denunciations of the Blood Libel legend. After ten years of persecution and numerous rumors of ritual murder, the accusation surfaced at Iampol in 1756. A Christian child was murdered, and local Jews were immediately accused of having killed him to use his blood in their Passover bread. Both the bishop of the Iampol Diocese and the bishop of Kiev were implicated in the pogrom that followed. To try to protect themselves, the Jews of Iampol sent a representative to Rome toward the end of 1757 to present a petition to Pope Benedict XIV. The following year, Cardinal Lorenzo Ganganelli was instructed to investigate the rumors. In his report, presented in March 1758 and adopted in September or December 1759, Ganganelli considered fifteen previous cases and concluded that the charges were unfounded and incredible in all but two of them. These cases—the murders of Simon of Trent in 1475 and André (or Andreas) de Rinn in 1462— were obviously difficult for him to repudiate since both boys had been elevated to the status of saints and martyrs with the authorization of the Pope. The papal nuncios for Poland were duly instructed to do all they could to protect the Jews from the accusations, and in 1763 the king, Augustus III, issued a decree exonerating the Jews from all charges and taking them under his protection.

The Nineteenth Century to the Present: Damascus and Back Again

THE NINETEENTH CENTURY

If anything, accusations increased during the nineteenth century. Writing about the "ritual murder canard" under the heading "Human Sacrifice" in the fourteenth edition of the *Encyclopaedia Britannica*, British folklorist and literary scholar E. O. James notes that forty-two charges of ritual murder are recorded in that century (E. O. J. 830). (The figure is probably higher since Cecil

Roth notes that twenty-two cases were "more or less formally raised in Europe" in 1887–91 alone [*Ritual* 16], and Dundes reports that fifty were reported between 1870 and 1935 ["Ritual" 9]). Among the most notorious of these were charges brought at Damascus, Syria, in 1840 where "confessions" were extorted by tortures of medieval ferocity, prompting the president of the United States, Martin Van Buren, to speak of "heart-rending scenes which took place at Damascus" and to instruct the U.S. chargé d'affaires "to interpose his good offices" on behalf of the Jews of Damascus (Jacob 141). Outlining the political background to this case, Joseph Jacobs suggests that it was the beginning of Zionism in that it focused the attention of Jews worldwide on nationality as well as religion ("Damascus").

In the later part of the century, accusations arose in Turkey (Landau 198) and elsewhere in the Middle East, particularly in Egypt. Jacob Landau discusses fifteen previously unstudied documents relating to Blood Libel accusations activated by the Greek community of Alexandria from May 1870 to April 1892. He points out that although the accusations arose among poor Greeks, the Egyptian intelligentsia were just as prejudiced against Jews and firmly believed that Christian blood was used in the baking of the Passover bread (202). Nearly all these child deaths turned out to be accidental, but the accusations gave rise to riots on a considerable scale, so that in March 1881, for example, the Italian consul general in Cairo expressed the fear that the thirteen thousand troops and policemen available would not be sufficient to control the mob (201). Accusations were raised somewhere almost every year in the 1890s: in France and Romania in 1892; in Moravia, Bulgaria, Czechoslovakia, Poland, and Germany in 1893; in Prussia in 1894; and again in Germany in 1896.

Among the most notorious European cases of the time were those brought at Tisza-Eszlár, Hungary, in 1882 (Wright; Handler); Corfu in 1891 (Strack 213–15); Xanten, Rhenish Prussia, in 1891

(Strack 215–18) (a case of particular interest for students of the Blood Libel legend because it is one of the first to suggest that the wounds on the dead child were identical to those a *schachter* [Jewish ritual butcher] would make); and Polna, Czechoslovakia, in 1899 (Červinka). Russia experienced particularly fierce pogroms against Jews as a result of the Blood Libel legend, starting in April 1881 with a charge brought at Yelisavetgrad, which, in the words of Cecil Roth, "stained the last years of the old Russian Empire, constituting one of the greatest tragedies of the sort in the recent history of the human race" (*Ritual* 16).

Throughout the latter half of the nineteenth century, the publication of tracts and articles alleging the truth of the Blood Libel legend whipped up European anti-Jewish feeling. The writings of Konstantin Cholewa de Pawlikowski (1866), Geza von Onody (1883), Canon August Rohling (1883), and the Abbé Desportes (1890) as well as a series of forty-four articles in Milan's *Osservatore Cattolico* (March–April 1892) were particularly influential and dangerous in spreading the myth. By the end of the nineteenth century, Rohling's writings had been taken up by the Austrian Ministry of Education and widely disseminated. In the famous case brought against Leopold Hilsner in Polna, Czechoslovakia, in 1899, Rohling offered to give evidence to prove that Jews really did employ human sacrifice. He was challenged by Strack, who publicly accused Rohling of "perjury and gross forgeries," and by Josef Samuel Bloch, who accused him of fabricating data and disputed his academic competence. Rohling did not reply to Strack but instituted a libel action against Bloch, which he later decided to withdraw, thus tacitly admitting the justice of Bloch's accusations (Dundes, Headnote to Červinka 136).

Strack's monograph offers a passionate denunciation of all these works and a detailed deconstruction of the articles in the *Osservatore Cattolico* (169–74). I will concentrate, however, on the claims made by Abbé Desportes as quoted by Raoul Girardet in a section entitled "L'Empire des Ténèbres" (the empire of darkness) in "La Conspiration" (conspiracy), a chapter of his book on political myths and mythologies (41–48). Desportes's work, "Le Mystère du Sang Chez les Juifs de Tous les Temps" (the blood rite among the Jews throughout the ages) was published as recently as 1889, but it could easily be mistaken for the work of a medieval witch-hunter. Girardet quotes extensively from it in discussing the way images of the enemy within become conflated with images of defiled and voracious beasts lurking in the shadows (as Girardet calls it, "a bestiary of conspiracy"). Desportes's work makes repellent reading but is worth dwelling on because it so clearly shows the unreasoning prejudice that fuels the Blood Libel legend. According to Desportes, Jews have periodic ceremonies for which they choose a very young boy (or, failing that, a young girl) as a sacrifice, meticulously planning the abduction beforehand. The children have to be without sin or stain, their blood pure and free from any polluting contact. The Jews open up the child's veins by inflicting multiple wounds so that the blood spurts out like water out of a sponge. The blood is collected in an urn, shared among those present, and drunk amid wild chants. Some of the precious liquid is sometimes used for the Passover bread, and sometimes a little of it is put aside so that those present can use it later as a libation. As Girardet comments, Desportes is inviting his readers to a "veritable feast of vampires." But the blood drinking is no accident or whimsy on the part of any individual, says Desportes, it is a biological imperative without which Jews could not survive. Moreover, not content with taking blood, the Jews use their victims to gratify depraved sexual tastes. Having drained the blood, they flog their victim until the flesh is tender and rosy and (if the victim is a boy) defile, tear, and destroy his genitals. The marks left on the body by this emasculation are a sure indication that a Jewish ritual murder has been committed, says Desportes.[18]

Although Desportes's tract is disgusting reading, it has a special interest for the historian of traditional slanders. In addition to continuing the idea that the deeds are done by the *schachter* (see the continuing references to "le couteau rabbinique" and "le couteau de la synagogue"), Desportes introduces a motif that, as far as I am aware, had not until then been appropriated by the Blood Libel legend but that any historian of slander would have been expecting. This is the notion of depraved sexuality.

As we have seen, this motif was present alongside accusations of cannibalism and ritual murder in charges brought against the early Christians and later against Christian heretics. Both accusations were later brought against the Knights Templar in the fourteenth century. Both were consistently made during witchcraft trials from the fourteenth to seventeenth centuries, and they surfaced together in the British satanic ritual abuse scares of the 1980s and early 1990s. As A. H. Rose says in his review of Roth's *The Ritual Murder Libel and the Jew* in *Folklore*, "the two go together, sadism with sexual aberration" (93). Yet as far as I am aware, until Desportes, Jews were accused of ritual murder and exsanguination or (occasionally) cannibalism but not of sexual defilement. True, stories in popular tradition about Jews needing fresh blood for ailments such as male menstruation hint that, sexually, Jews are not like other men, but the orgiastic feast motif seems not to have previously appeared as a regular part of the folklore of Jewish depravity. Thus, this despicable work set a trend and was more readily believable because it completed the stereotype of the ritual excesses of the bestial enemy within.

THE TWENTIETH CENTURY AND TODAY

Blood accusations continued into the twentieth century, famously the Beilis (or Kiev) case from the Ukraine in 1911–13. This case shows to perfection how such accusations played out in real life;

how the Blood Libel legend not only feeds on ignorance, superstition, and prejudice but can be exploited for personal and political gain, sometimes by the humblest and least educated people, sometimes by the government itself. Like the Damascus case, the events in the Ukraine shook the world and brought protests from British, German, and French churchmen and intellectuals and from large sections of the Russian population (see Roth, *Ritual* app. C). It was sensational stuff. A detailed and chilling contemporary report by George Kennan laid out the evidence relating to the murder of a thirteen-year-old boy for which Mendel Beilis, a poor Jew and ex-soldier, was being prosecuted. There was no evidence at all against him—he merely had the bad luck to work in a nearby factory and to be Jewish. What evidence there was clearly pointed to the murder being committed by a criminal gang that exploited the folklore of Jewish ritual murder to avoid prosecution. The ritual murder claim was taken up by Kiev's anti-Semitic factions and eventually by the czar himself to serve political purposes. During the course of the investigation, two honest detectives were fired, defamed, and persecuted for the crime of being on the right track. Beilis was acquitted two years after being charged.

Even more notorious, of course, was the use of the myth by the Nazis in Germany. Alan Dundes quotes a chilling May 1943 letter from Heinrich Himmler to Berlin's chief of police: "We will organize . . . several trials for this category of crime. The problem of ritual murder ought to be treated by experts in such countries as Rumania, Hungary and Bulgaria. I have the idea that we could pass on these ritual murder cases to the press in order to facilitate the evacuation of Jews from these countries. . . . In short I am of the opinion that we could give anti-Semitism an incredible virulence with the help of anti-Semitic propaganda in English and perhaps even Russian by giving huge publicity to these ritual murders" ("Ritual" 15).

If these two examples illustrate the lies that this sort of folk-lore breeds, the next examples are clear instances of the hysteria and histrionics such tales engender and feed on. As a tribute to Rabbi Joseph Lookstein of New York, Abraham Duker published eight newspaper reports from the United States in the second decade of the twentieth century. The first was from *Forverts* (5 February 1913) and told how when Jacob Miller, a Jew from Pennsylvania, had a son, the family wanted to have a large cele-bration for the occasion. The woman in charge of the catering arrangements, Mrs. Stein, could not cope with the work and called in the Millers' Christian servant girl to help her. Seeing Mrs. Stein sharpening a knife to cut up chickens, the girl imag-ined that she was about to become a ritual sacrifice. She became hysterical when Mrs. Stein tried to take her hand to calm her and ran about shouting that the Jews were trying to murder her. The neighbors heard her and soon the whole town arrived in the street. Meanwhile, the girl had hidden herself. When she could not be found, the crowd began to shout that the Jews had killed her. The Millers lived through a terrible night, and the town qui-eted down only when the girl was found safe and well the follow-ing morning (Duker 98–99).

The second case occurred in New York and was reported in *Forverts* on 21 April 1913 under the headline "Polish Goye Mur-ders Her Husband Because of a Blood Libel. Shocking Murder on Pitt Street—Young Woman Makes Accusation against Her Hus-band That He Sold Her Only Child to Jews for Passover and She Kills Him for It" (Duker 99–101). The third and fourth reports come from Fall River, Massachusetts, in 1919. The report in the 22 April 1919 *Fall River Evening Herald* is headlined "Boy's Tongue Is Slashed by Men. Below-the-Hill Mother Tells Police That Blood from Her Son Was Taken for Use in Religious Rites" (Duker 102–4). The fifth article reports a court case brought against Polish immigrants who sought to stir up anti-Jewish riots in Chicago in July 1917. They claimed that a Jewish businessman, Mr. H. Kohn, had enticed a small Polish boy into his shop and had killed him and taken his blood for religious purposes. The ringleader, Casimir Lata, had attacked Mr. Kohn, shouting "Return our child to us!" and "the Zhids should be killed!"[19] The next two reports relate to an October 1919 incident in Pittsfield, Massachusetts, in which a seven-year-old boy who had fallen out of a tree onto a sharp stick claimed that he got his leg wound when he was dragged to the basement of a synagogue and cut with a knife. His story caused local uproar, but he later confessed that he had made the tale up (Duker 104–6).

Duker's last document is another newspaper report from Pittsfield, this one printed in *Der Tog* on 15 November 1919.

Polish Blood Libel against Jews in America

Little Polish Boy in Pittsfield, Mass, Tells That Jews Have Locked Him Up in the Synagogue and Extracted from Him Two Bottles of Blood; a Local Paper Writes about It. A Springfield Newspaper Reprints It.—A Policeman Comes to the Synagogue, Subjects the Hebrew Teacher to a Hearing and Discovers Blood Stains on the Cellar Wall.—An Investigation Reveals That It Is Blood of a Chicken,—The Boy Confesses That He Had Invented a Lie. Jews Demand an Investigation. (Duker 106)

Saul Friedman has described an incident in the United States in 1928 with a less fortunate outcome, and trouble arose in Poland in 1918 and again in 1928, in Lithuania in 1929, and in Bulgaria in 1934.[20] Anonymous leaflets alleging the reality of Jewish ritual murder were distributed in California in 1933 (Roth, "Blood" 327). The libel resurfaced again in Poland in 1946, where an anti-Semitic rising was well organized and led to killings and mass exodus of Jews. (For a detailed treatment of this pogrom, see Czubala and Milerska.) The Blood Libel legend was reactivated in Soviet Dagestan, Uzbekistan, Georgia, and Lithuania between 1961 and 1963. It was used by Muslim states in agitations against Israel, Jews, and Judaism, with this sort of propaganda appearing in Egypt, Lebanon, and Iraq between 1967 and 1978 (Duker 86–88).

In the summer of 1990, a group calling itself the Campaign for a Gentile-Jewish Reconciliation circulated a scurrilous leaflet in Britain. The pamphlet drew attention to an obscure investigation that had taken place during the previous spring at a synagogue in East London where police had been digging up the parking lot, supposedly in search of a child's body. According to the leaflet, after two months the police reported that they had found only some animal bones and that they were not taking their investigations any further. Referring explicitly to the case of William of Norwich, the writer of the leaflet preferred to interpret this as a Jewish ritual murder followed by a police cover-up, and linked Jews to the pornography industry and pedophile rings. The author saw this as another instance of the massive, secret, and subversive influence of Jews in Europe, "a power monopoly sanctified in a cloud of 'Holohoax' mythology" (Another "Blood Libel"). In 1991, the Dowager Lady Birdwood was prosecuted under U.K. race-relations legislation for distributing anti-Semitic literature (leaflets containing the blood libel) (Steele 3). In 2002, Sandy Hobbs drew attention to an article in a Saudi newspaper alleging that Jews use the blood of Christian or Muslim children in pastries during Purim; the columnist was fired ("Blood Libel"). To bring us full circle back to Damascus, in July 2003 a British member of Parliament claimed that the Blood Libel legend was still believed by the Syrian administration. As evidence, she referred to a Web site that quoted passages from a 1986 book by the Syrian minister of defense in which this infamous affair was treated as a genuine Jewish crime.[21]

This truly horrifying catalog of prejudice and unreason indicates that the history of this ancient slander has not yet ended.

THE BRITISH CHILD RITUAL ABUSE SCANDAL

> In the evening, when the candles are lit . . . they bring together, in a house appointed for the purpose, young girls whom they have initiated in their rites. Then they extinguish the candles, so the light shall not be witness to their abominable deeds, and throw themselves lasciviously on the girls, each one on whomever first falls into his hands, no matter whether she be his sister, his daughter or his mother. For they think they are doing something that greatly pleases the demons by transgressing God's law. . . . When this rite has been completed, each goes home; and after waiting nine months, until the time has come for these unnatural children to be born, they come together again at the same place. Then, on the third day after the birth, they tear the miserable babies from their mothers' arms. They cut their tender flesh all over with sharp knives and catch the stream of blood in basins. They throw the babies, still breathing and gasping, on to the fire, to be burned to ashes. After which, they mix the ashes with the blood in the basins and so make an abominable drink. . . . Finally they partake together of these foodstuffs. (Cohn 19)

This testimony was brought against a dissident Christian sect, the Bogomiles, in the mid-eleventh century. One can immediately see how it relates to the Blood Libel legend and to the defamatory accusations with which this chapter began. But could similar sorts of things be claimed—and believed—in the scientific age? Unfortunately, the answer is yes. Debbie Nathan, Bill Ellis, James Hicks, Jeffrey Victor, and others have detailed these sorts of accusations as they arose in America at the end of the twentieth century.[22] As the British version of these panics may be less familiar to readers, this chapter will conclude with a description of the way a similar panic unfolded during the late twentieth century on the other side of the Atlantic Ocean.

Between February 1989 and October 1996, I collected somewhere in the region of 150 reports from quality newspapers in the United Kingdom concerning claims of satanic or ritual abuse of children (for a selection, see Bennett, "Sex"), and Bill Ellis, Sandy Hobbs, and I monitored roughly 225 more accounts between the early months of 1991 and the end of 1992 (see Ellis, Bennett, and Hobbs). All of the outrageous accusations leveled against the Bogomiles can be found somewhere in this database. Judge for yourself.

My story begins with an article published in the *Independent on Sunday* in October 1990:

In darkness, the Rock cemetery in Mansfield Road, Nottingham is a frightening place. Silhouettes of the occasional person can be seen but these are difficult to distinguish from large, often crumbling, Victorian graves, which stretch across acres of graveyard skirted by main roads and avenues of trees. . . .

Paths dip and weave away from the traffic into silence until suddenly one comes to a five-foot wall. The land plunges 100 feet. This is the "Coliseum," a sunken graveyard surrounded by vaulted archways which are draped with greenery.

Down a winding path, children have brought foster parents and social workers to show them a metal grid shrouded with ivy, beyond which, they say, they were sexually abused and degraded at night in satanic ceremonies. Beyond that grid is a sandstone tunnel. . . . Local tradition says that condemned prisoners were taken through the tunnel. (O'Sullivan, "Dispute")

The ceremonies supposedly performed in this "tunnel of the condemned" in 1989–90 were said to include drinking blood, sacrificing animals, and killing and eating babies or cooking them in microwave ovens. By 1991, the accusations made by hunters of satanic abuse included settings such as haunted castles, skeleton-ridden cemeteries (and most bizarrely, a hot-air balloon over the River Clyde) as well as such practices as dressing up as clowns or wearing hoods, cloaks, and masks; drinking urine; smearing children with excrement (Waterhouse, "Secret Bungalow"[23]); drugs; torture; rape; and bestiality (Phillips). During 1989–90, allegations of witchcraft, satanism, and black magic featured in fourteen wardship cases involving forty-one children removed from their parents and taken into local authority care. It was reported that the official solicitor and his staff had begun "to notice a new and shocking element in the growing number of sexual abuse cases they were dealing with—bizarre stories worthy of Dennis Wheatley or Stephen King novels" (Waterhouse, Kingman, and Cuffe). In March 1990, the leading child-protection agency in England and Wales,[24] the National Society for the Prevention of Cruelty to Children (NSPCC), announced that seven of its child-protection teams were working with child victims of what was called "ritualistic abuse." Reports began to circulate orally and via the press (especially the tabloids) of bizarre and sadistic practices, of children made to eat part of a human heart and of a baby seen in a microwave oven and another in a freezer. Other newspapers followed up with stories about "Sabbaths" and confessions of young girls being used as brood mares, with abortions induced at five months so that the fetuses could be used for sacrifice (Waterhouse, Kingman, and Cuffe).

It seems very likely that what was to become a full-blown panic had spread to the United Kingdom from the United States (like so many other cultural products, good and bad). The phenomenon invaded Britain early in 1988 through various channels, including books and testimonies from the American religious right and American "experts" who spread the message by means of the media and conference circuits. As soon as it reached the

United Kingdom, the cause was taken up by a variety of individuals and organizations including "survivors," antioccult campaigners, Christian organizations, social workers' groups, and—perhaps most importantly—the NSPCC, which began advising its officers and the police to be on the watch for satanic or ritual abuse. A pivotal moment seems to have been a seminar that took place in September 1988 in Reading, in southern England. (Two others followed in April and September of the following year.) The testimony at the first seminar included that of a police officer who told of a baby cooked in a microwave oven as part of a satanic ceremony. A rash of satanic abuse allegations followed—in the county of Kent, at Congleton in Cheshire, and most notably in Nottingham, in central England.

In February 1989, amid claims of satanic involvement, eight members of a multigenerational extended family from Nottingham and their friends were jailed on fifty-three charges of incest and abuse against twenty-three children ("Social Workers and the Police"). At one of the seminars on ritual abuse, a social worker claimed that the children said they had been "tortured and repeatedly penetrated orally and anally by adults in strange costumes. They were forced to watch their brothers and sisters similarly abused. They were also forced to eat excreta and drink the blood of animals sacrificed in front of them" (Waterhouse, Kingman, and Cuffe). The Chief Constable of Nottinghamshire, the senior police officer for the county, and the director of social services launched an inquiry into these and similar claims. The resulting report stated that no evidence of abuse had been found (only evidence of some very dubious interview techniques, to which I will return later). The Chief Constable went so far as to issue a stark warning to the government that similar rumors should be "killed off" before more damage was done.

But it was already too late. By September 1989, claims were being investigated in Manchester, in northwest England. The case began with two girls, aged seven and four, who were taken into care after allegations of child abuse (a baby born subsequently to the same mother was also removed from her care at birth). Shortly before Christmas, after three months of interviews with the NSPCC, the girls began telling strange stories and naming eleven other children as victims. Once again, no evidence of ritual abuse was found; nevertheless, the children were kept in local authority care and denied any contact with their parents, and the social workers remained convinced that all fourteen children had been involved in satanic ceremonies in which animal sacrifices had been performed, blood drunk, and babies killed. By March 1990, similar satanic claims were surfacing in nearby Rochdale. Over a six-month period, twenty children from six Rochdale families were taken from parents ("snatched from their beds in dawn raids," according to the press [Miles]), placed on the child-protection register, and made wards of court. Fifteen of these children remained in council care or in foster homes in the late autumn of that year. By this time, thirty other cases of potential satanic abuse had come to light in the city. The Rochdale trial was moved to London in September 1990, and an inquiry was launched. As at Nottingham, this resulted in severe criticisms of the way social services had handled cases and conducted interviews (O'Sullivan, "Council").

This period of general credulity gradually gave way to a period of skepticism in which divisions started opening up between social workers committed to the idea of satanic child abuse and the police, who became increasingly reluctant to follow up claims such as these or to open proceedings against supposed perpetrators. Especially significant was the skeptical stance taken by the then Chief Constable of Manchester, James Anderton, a man not otherwise known for liberal views or enlightened attitudes on social and moral issues. Four days later Merseyside (Liverpool) police also dropped charges of satanic abuse that they had been investigating. Through the end of 1990, press coverage in England showed an increasing hostility to such claims, as evidenced by such headlines as "Rochdale Criticised" (*Financial Times*, 20 September); "Twisting the Truth to Fit a Ghoulish Fantasy" (*Sunday Times*, 23 September); "Police Chief Warns of Ducking Stool Justice" (*Independent*, 4 October); "Police and Council Deny Claim of Child Satanic Rituals at Cemetery" (*Guardian*, 4 October); "Abuse Case Care Staff Criticised by Judge" (*Independent on Sunday*, 18 December).

However, though belief in such horrors was waning in England, the same was not true of Scotland. Indeed, the fiercest and most distressing battles were fought there. In Ayrshire in the spring of 1991, ten children, the youngest only sixteen months old, were removed from their homes in cases involving twenty-eight children and twenty-four adults. The stories that emerged during this investigation were the usual wild stuff: "One devil worshipper could apparently use telepathic powers to cast a spell on a child 15 miles away and make her legs sore, while Big Jim . . . could, on occasion, turn into a spider and a mouse. One woman was said to have been murdered as a sacrificial offering after intercourse with a Satanist" (Waterhouse, "Secret Bungalow").

By far the most serious outbreak of satanic hysteria occurred in the Orkneys, a group of remote islands off the northeast coast of Scotland. As early as July 1989, the Royal Scottish Society for the Prevention of Cruelty to Children (RSSPCC) had become convinced that a family being investigated for child abuse had been involved in satanic practices. In November 1990, three children's allegations against four local families were taken seriously enough for three weeks of dawn raids to follow and for nine children to be taken from their parents in February of the following year and placed in foster homes on the mainland. A "cloud of suspicion" reportedly fell over the community at St. Margaret's Hope on the island of South Ronaldsay, with islanders "living in fear of [a] knock on the door," as rumors flew that there was a secret list with the names of twenty more children on it.[25] Incredibly, the chief suspect as the island's resident devil worshipper was a sixty-four-year-old Presbyterian minister. After being repeatedly questioned by social workers and RSSPCC officers, the children alleged that the clergyman had been masked and dressed as a turtle or had been dressed in a long black cloak with a hood. They called him "The Master." He had hooked them with a crook while they danced in a circle to satanic music at night in a disused quarry on the outskirts of the village. Anyone he caught was sexually abused (Cusick, "Community"). More details were later added, such as that the children were sometimes costumed as Brownies or members of the Boys' Brigade and that the minister also made love to their mothers while they were dressed as cowboys or "the white ghost" (Introduction to Ellis, Bennett, and Hobbs 2). The case came to court in April; after only one day of evidence, Sheriff Kelbie, the presiding judge, dismissed the case as fatally flawed, and the children were allowed to return home.

However, an appeal was lodged against this judgment, and in June it was unanimously overturned on the grounds that the sheriff had "allowed himself to form views about the contents [of the social workers' evidence that] would have made it impossible for him to bring a fair and balanced judgment to the issues" (Introduction to Ellis, Bennett, and Hobbs 2). Controversy continued and led to the setting up of an official inquiry in August 1991. After investigating for nine months and spending £6 million, the inquiry published its report in October 1992, describing the dismissal of the first judgment as "most unfortunate" and sharply criticizing all those involved—the social workers, the police, and the Orkney Islands Council. Social workers' training, methods, and judgment came in for special condemnation. As far as the concept of "ritual abuse" was concerned, the report argued, "the use of [this term] is not only unwarrantable at present but may affect the objectivity of practitioners and parents" (Introduction to Ellis, Bennett, and Hobbs 5). The effect of the affair on the families of those accused and on Orkney islanders in general was incalculable. As late as the autumn of 1996, one boy was still reliving the horror of those days and fighting to clear his parents' names (Brown and Woods).

So how were such things possible in the twentieth century in a country whose people are noted for being reserved and phlegmatic? Looked at now, roughly ten years later, one cannot imagine that anyone could believe, let alone act on, stories of ministers dressed as turtles (Ninja turtles?), teenage "brood mares," microwaved babies, forbidden sex in hot-air balloons and tunnels under graveyards, and outdoor midnight orgies in one of the coldest and most northerly parts the country. It is hard to explain, but I would guess that the initial impetus was the sudden convergence of a number of cultural trends. A new pattern emerged that, though incredible as a whole, was not entirely disbelieved because parts of it confirmed the experiences, beliefs, and prejudices of various interests and professional groups. This happened at a time when the country had been "softened up" by a prior highly publicized child sex scandal and when American evangelicals were on hand to interpret events. I shall leave the latter point aside for the moment, for the pernicious effects of the American-led seminars on ritual abuse have been well covered in the work of Bill Ellis and in some of the journalism I shall be mentioning (see esp. Ellis's introduction to Ellis, Bennett, and Hobbs). Instead, I shall briefly look at a child sex scandal that immediately preceded the emergence of claims of ritual or satanic abuse.

"Here we go again, only more so," said one commentator on the Rochdale affair as she began her discussion with a reference to the earlier "Cleveland affair" (Phillips). This scandal had only just concluded—after months of anguish, claims and counterclaims, demonstrations and counterdemonstrations—with the revision of guidelines issued to social workers and child-protection teams.

A high-flying pediatrician had claimed that she had found a new diagnostic tool that allowed easy identification of the anal sexual abuse of young children. Using this diagnostic tool, she tested children presenting with nonaccidental and other injuries at the Accident and Emergency Department of a hospital in the northeastern county of Cleveland, where she practiced as a consultant. Large numbers of these children were identified as having suffered sexual abuse. National figures for child sex abuse immediately shot up to unprecedented heights, and the press spent happy hours bemoaning the depravity of an age where such dreadful crimes against children were apparently so commonplace. As in the case of Rochdale and other towns, a large number of children were taken from their homes amid acrimony, incrimination, and heartrending scenes, only to be returned in due course when the pediatrician's work was discredited and she lost her job. Although fears that there had been child abuse on a massive scale were eventually quieted, the sexual abuse of children nevertheless became a highly visible issue. The majority of the early press reports of the Nottingham and Rochdale ritual abuse cases referred back to the Cleveland affair, and most of the official inquiries were geared more toward discovering whether the post-Cleveland guidelines had been properly followed than to finding out the truth about the claims. The press, the public, and, most importantly, the child-protection agencies had become sensitized to concerns about children and sex.

The ritual abuse seminars played to these sensitivities, to fears about paganism and the occult that had been increasing in some Christian circles, and to the child-centered approaches to family problems that had been growing in strength among social workers in Britain since the 1960s. It is not coincidental, for example, that the leading social worker on South Ronaldsay had been influenced by the work of American psychiatrist Roland Summit, who served on the advisory board of a U.S. pressure group, Believe the Children. The seminars imported a complete culture that validated these attitudes and fitted the supernatural worldview of many of those present—a complete and satisfying answer to the central puzzle of why adults should want to abuse children and to the problem of evil in general. To quote the title of an article by Debbie Nathan, "the devil made them do it."

The belief in ritual child abuse was a cultural product, and it grew in strength and consistency as various bodies bought into it, networked, and circulated informational material. Chief among this literature was the now-infamous list of "satanic indicators" widely circulated to NSPCC staff, police, child-care professionals, and council social workers in a national campaign (for details, see Strickland and Waterhouse). Classic signs and symptoms were said to include clingy behavior, aggressive play, nightmares, bed-wetting, preoccupation with feces and urine, fear of ghosts and monsters, the recitation of nursery rhymes with obscene over-tones, blowing raspberries, and laughing uproariously when any-one broke wind. (Parents and grandparents will note that the last group of symptoms sound pretty much like the regular behavior of any three-year-old.) The Nottingham inquiry team specifically mentioned the satanic indicators as one factor in the production of the stereotype of ritual abuse. Other factors the investigators believed had contributed to the panic were the introduction by a NSPCC officer of symbols suggesting witchcraft, unreliable testi-mony from adult witnesses, the spreading of stories among chil-dren while in local authority care, and above all social workers' interview techniques.

The justice of the penultimate of these observations will be immediately evident to any folklorist or children's play specialist and should have been evident to anyone who had regular contact with young children. Consider the supposed setting for these "crimes" (graveyards, tunnels, haunted castles, disused quarries), the characters involved (masked, robed, and hooded figures; Ninja turtles; killer clowns; skeletons; ghosts; ghouls; monsters; and "the Master," presumably Dr. Who's immortal adversary in the television series), and the accessories (darkness, severed body parts, excreta, urine, horrible things to eat, and "ritualistic music," which, as Sheriff Kelbie said, "could be anything from Kylie Minogue to Andrew Lloyd Webber" [Cusick, "Orkney"]). These elements pretty much represent the content of the average schoolchild's "scary story" session. Then there are the patently urban legend components—microwaved babies, cannibalism, and the all-too-familiar paraphernalia of blood libels and body-part rumors, which might have been contributed by older children and teenagers. Folklore, all of it, and immediately recognizable as such by any dispassionate observer. Professor Elizabeth Newson, who with her husband, Professor John Newson, is a leading child-development expert, was certainly quick to spot it, saying, "We have to consider that what is operating may be professional hysteria. There is a sort of excitement about ritual abuse. I'm wondering whether these are professional myths, like urban myths" (Waterhouse, "Children's Games").

However, the inside observers were not dispassionate. They had bought into what the Chief Constable of Nottinghamshire during an October 1990 interview called "an orthodoxy of belief" that was "spreading like an epidemic across Britain" (Waterhouse, "Satanic Inquisitors"). While the police began to distance themselves from such beliefs, social workers closed ranks, and a gap opened up between the two groups. In such a climate, it became unthinkable for child-protection teams not to believe the children and treachery to challenge colleagues' evidence. In addition, so it seemed to insiders, the evidence was mounting and was serious and convincing.

To outsiders and to those with hindsight, on the other hand, the evidence was flawed. It was based on the a priori assumption that (satanic) crimes were indeed being committed, perhaps on a large scale. Significantly, the stereotype for such crimes was already also fixed. The satanic panics in the United States had followed on the 1980 publication of *Michelle Remembers*, a book devoted to the personal testimony of a supposed survivor of satanic abuse (Smith and Pazder). This book almost certainly was not only the precursor but the cause of the panics. Numerous seminars on incest and abuse that took place in the United Kingdom in 1988 and 1989 were influenced by, organized by, or infiltrated by American antisatanic activists. Thus, the stereotypes created by *Michelle Remembers* and expanded during the course of satanic panics in the United States were imported to the United Kingdom, ready-made and ready to use as a forensic tool.

What Michelle had supposedly remembered, during intensive therapy, was years of appalling physical, sexual, and psychological abuse at the hands of a coven of satanists, including her own mother. She had witnessed debauchery, murder, the sacrifice of babies, the mutilation of animals, and the drinking of blood. At conferences and seminars in Britain, Michelle's stereotype of abuse was confirmed and expanded. "Survivors" testified that human fetuses had been eaten by members of British satanic sex rings, that children were hung up by their feet and suspended over chain saws, that fetuses were bred specially for sacrifices. Anthropologist Sherrill Mulhern, who has studied psychotherapists and survivor testimony, told journalist Rosie Waterhouse, "*Michelle Remembers* crystallised the satanic abuse legend among psychotherapists. [They] began networking with one another and with child therapists. I think the majority of adult survivors' accounts are the result of the interaction between the therapist, the patient and the surrounding satanic cult stories" (Waterhouse, "Making"). It was only after many years that the concept of submerged memories was discredited through the work of Mulhern and others and was replaced with its opposite, the false memory syndrome. In the interim, however, "submerged memories" caused immeasurable suffering.

One corollary of the satanic stereotype was the conviction that the perpetrators of such crimes (being satanists) were necessarily wicked and would naturally tell lies. The consequence of this was that some very dubious interview techniques were used to get at the "truth." "The truth was out there," but it would have to be sought against stiff resistance from the victims (signed up, as they were—though innocently—to the demonic agenda). Time and again, inquiries concluded that agencies' and social workers' interview techniques involved intimidation and leading questions. In dismissing the Orkney case in April 1991, Sheriff Kelbie complained that the children had been deprived of their rights as persons, coached into giving statements, and repeatedly "subjected to what could only be described as cross-examination designed to break them down and admit to being abused" (Waterhouse, "Secret Bungalow").

The usual practice was to remove children from their homes and to forbid any parental contact. The Orkney children, for example, had been taken far away to the mainland on short notice and had not been allowed to take any toys or personal items with them. (The rationale for this cruel behavior was that the parents might try to influence the children either directly or by imprinting satanic signs and symbols on the toys.) Interviews took place in what was thought of as a secure and neutral space but which actually had the effect of alienating and isolating the children, and they were repeatedly questioned, sometimes over a period of several months. In the Ayrshire case, the four children in one family were interviewed sixty-eight times in only five months.

Then there was the use of leading questions. Incredibly, the Nottingham inquiry team found that the NSPCC officers had asked children questions such as "Did you kill three or four babies?" "Did you sexually abuse the little boy before you were made to kill it?" "Who ate it?" and "What parts did you eat?"

Unsurprisingly, the adviser to the inquiry, Professor John Newson, head of the Child Development Research Unit at Nottingham University, called this "tantamount to brainwashing." In the report he observed that one seventeen-year-old girl was "led to confabulate a story that she had taken part in satanic sacrifices. The girl later said the story was totally untrue and that the only knowledge that she had, had come from the social workers, that she had been pressurized, that the social worker would not take no for an answer." The report concludes, "The social workers who already believed in satanic abuse could by this method convince a child that she was a murderer and that she was guilty of cannibalism and devil worship. . . . It is a sobering thought that in the 17th century she could have been burnt as a witch with inquisitors using identical methods" (Waterhouse, "Satanic Inquisitors").

This comparison is very just. The methods do indeed in some respects resemble those used in the European witchcraft trials of the fourteenth through seventeenth centuries, and so do the consequences. Just as in witchcraft interrogations, in order to stop the tortures, those accused of witchcraft turned to folklore to find suitably bizarre experiences to confess, the child victims of NSPCC officers' and social workers' intimidatory interview techniques offered their tormentors whatever bits of child lore came to mind and seemed to please their tormentors. And just as any evidence the accused could produce in the witchcraft trials seemed adequate and could be made to fit somewhere into the overall scheme of things, so the strangest things were considered to be evidence enough in the U.K. abuse hearings. In contrast to the Orkneys' Sheriff Kelbie, the Ayrshire judge was convinced that there had been "systematic sexual abuse and corruption of a number of young children" and was considering publishing his findings "to alert the public to the extreme depravities and the appalling practices which have been disclosed to me in the evidence in this case." The Ayrshire police were said to have impounded a pair of goatskin ski boots, two "Postman Pat" children's videos, and a copy of a John Wayne film (Strickland and Waterhouse).

The consequences, too, of this blinkered approach to truth finding was the same in both cases. A vicious circle of self-proving "proofs" was built up—an endless cycle of accusation → interrogation → confession → construct followed by construct → interrogation → confession → confirmation of construct followed by further accusations and the repetition of the cycle. The result is a seemingly indisputable edifice that is continually being confirmed and enhanced. As in witchcraft accusations, it becomes impossible to challenge the evidence: one is forced to challenge the construct itself and argue that, whatever the evidence, it is just not possible. The British judicial system is not well adapted to such a process; hence, when individuals such as Sheriff Kelbie do reject everything outright, an appeal is inevitable and will probably be upheld.

In retrospect now, it all seems as odd as it was frightening. At times, one could almost believe that the accusers were familiar with the witchcraft accusations of the medieval and early modern periods. At other times, especially in the children's testimony, the claims seemed to be clearly based on representations of witches in popular culture—television, children's scary stories, and comics. At times the testimony, especially that of adult "survivors," was reminiscent of accusations made against the early Christians. At other times it was very Aubrey Beardsley and Dennis Wheatley.

But although it was all folklore in one sense or another, the panic was for a time capable of putting people in great danger and inflicting great damage, not only on individuals but on whole communities. A useful guide to the interpretation of contemporary legends might be, "If it's true, it's important." Here is another example where nobody doubted it was important but there was considerable conflict about whether it was true.

NOTES

1. Depositions in the archive of the Inquisition at Toulouse, quoted in Kors and Peters 93. Very similarly worded accusations about wild sexual orgies were made in the 1950s against "Holy Rollers" in the United States: "We were accused of hypnotizing one another and falling into trances. It was widely reported that we turned out the lights to conduct wild sex orgies and engage in wife-swapping" (quoted in Ellis, "Sectarian" 11–12).

2. *Independent on Sunday* (London), 18 March 1990, quoted in Bennett, "Sex," 40.

3. The cartoon caused a considerable outcry. The paper later had to devote three full pages of its review section to defending the cartoonist. See *Independent Review*, 27 January 2003, 4–6.

4. In January 2000, the U.K. broadsheet *The Daily Telegraph* printed a fascinating personal account of postoperative hallucinations. While lying close to death and heavily drugged, the writer experienced horrific and apparently "real" visions of body stealers, devilish priest-surgeons with broken scissors strapped like logos to their chests, bodies lying beside him packed in layers of pork, hospital wards "littered with bodies" and draped with the paraphernalia of drug abuse (McAlpine). Likewise a (now deceased) acquaintance told me of the appalling visionary experiences he endured after brain surgery. The most horrible of these was a Goyaesque episode in which he ate his own children.

5. See also Rose 93; Girardet 41–48; Campion-Vincent, esp. 126.

6. According to Joseph Jacobs, novelist William Makepeace Thackeray saw Napoleon on St. Helena and was told, "That is Bonaparte; he eats three sheep every day and all the little children he can put his hands on" (Jacobs, "Little" 199).

7. E. O. J.; Ellis, *"De Legendis"* 201–3; Cohn 1–3.

8. And other forms of defamation. For a list of Jewish "crimes" compiled by an anti-Semite, see Burton 120–29. Burton's list includes, alongside the Blood Libel, accusations of the kidnapping, assault, torture, and murder of children, poisoning wells, and desecrating the Host used in Catholic masses. For a balanced exposition of accusations of Host desecration, see Despina, "Accusations" pts. 1 and 2.

9. Langmuir 26–28. See also the discussion of Langmuir's dating in Bennett, "William."

10. Other scurrilous rumors may have arisen about the Norwich Jews. For example, when the accusation first came to John de Chesney's ears, he sent an indignant message to Bishop Eborard that the Jews should not answer *"such inventions* of the Christians" (emphasis added; the word *such* implies that this was one of several similar "inventions").

11. Interestingly, Thomas reports that Godwin thought that the child might still be alive because witnesses noted small movements of the earth that lay over the body. When the earth moved for a second time, "the priest bade them make haste, for he believed that he would find him still alive" (Jessopp and James 39). This was later interpreted by Thomas as the first of the boy "saint's" miracles.

12. This seems quite likely. At any rate it is possible that the child was subjected to some sort of abuse. However, I am not convinced that Thomas meant to imply that the child was dressed *only* in jacket and shoes: he might have meant that he was dressed in his outdoor clothes. In favor of Lipman's hypothesis, it should be noted that Thomas uses exactly the same phrase when describing how the monks wash the body before reburying it in the monks' cemetery. He says that they took off his "jacket and shoes," not "his clothes" as one would expect were he fully dressed.

13. Figures compiled from Strack 173, 177; Jessopp and James lxiv–lxvi. James dismisses one of these cases, that of Herbert of Huntingdon (1181), because Jews were not specifically accused.

14. Popular hostility seems to have arisen chiefly as a side effect of enthusiasm for the crusades; the hostility of the monarchs arose from changes in the financial relationship between the kings and the Jews. See Bennett, "William."

15. Hsia's figure is drawn solely from secondary sources. It probably underestimates the numbers. Hsia says that there is evidence of at least seven more such trials from the twelfth century.

16. Similarly, Martin V in 1422 stigmatized accusations that Jews mingle blood with their Passover bread as "a charge brought unjustly." In 1540, Pope Paul III said, "We have heard with displeasure from the complaints of the Jews of [Central Europe] how for some years past, certain magistrates and other officials, bitter and mortal enemies of the Jews, *blinded by hate or envy, or as is more probable by cupidity*, pretend . . . that Jews kill little children and drink their blood" (quoted in Roth, *Ritual* 22–23; emphasis added).

17. The timing alone made that accusation ridiculous, as Strack points out: in 1475 Passover and Maundy Thursday fell on the same day, 23 March; Passover celebrations would have started the previous evening, when the child was still safe at home with his parents.

18. "Une autre blessure se rencontre fréquemment dans les assassinats talmudiques, c'est celle qui consiste à souiller, à déchirer et à dévaster les parties viriles de la victime. Quand on trouve un cadavre d'enfant avec ce stigmate, on peut presque toujours conclure que le couteau de la synagogue s'est acharné sur ces restes sanglants" (quoted in Girardet 46).

19. *Jidisher Courier*, 7 July 1919, in Duker 103–4.

20. Friedman; Newall 113; Roth, "Blood" 327.

21. *Hansard* (official record of British Parliamentary debates), 2 July 2003, pt. 3.
22. See, among others, Nathan, "Devil"; Nathan, "Ritual"; Ellis, *Aliens*; Hicks; Victor. See also Richardson, Best, and Bromley.
23. Rosie Waterhouse began as a believer but soon changed her mind and became one of the very few journalists who courageously refused to engage in satanic speculation. In a series of well-researched, authoritative, and level-headed articles, she devoted her energies to debunking current fears. The *Independent* remains the leading newspaper published in England and Wales for quality (left-leaning) investigative journalism. My account is largely built from Waterhouse's articles in the *Independent* over a two-year period. Unless otherwise stated, all references are to her articles. See esp. "Children's Games"; "Making"; "NSPCC"; "Police Chief"; "Satanic Cults"; "Satanic Inquisitors"; and "Secret Bungalow."
24. Even before devolution, Scotland had its own jurisdiction and agencies. Scotland's child protection agency is the Royal Scottish Society for the Prevention of Cruelty to Children.
25. Respectively, *Times* (London), 3 March 1991; *Glasgow Herald*, 4 March 1991, Hinton 18.

KEY TEXTS

Bennett, Gillian. "'St.' William of Norwich and the Blood Libel: Revaluating the Legend." *Folklore* 116 (2005): 119–39.

Ben-Sasson, Haim Hillel. "Blood Libel." In *Encyclopaedia Judaica*, 4 :1120–31. Jerusalem: Keter, 1971.

Dundes, Alan. *The Blood Libel Legend: A Casebook in Anti-Semitic Folklore.* Madison: University of Wisconsin Press, 1991.

James, Montague Rhodes. "The Legend." Chap. 6 of the introduction to Augustus Jessopp and Montague Rhodes James, eds. and trans., *The Life and Miracles of St. William of Norwich by Thomas of Monmouth*, lxii–lxxix. Cambridge: Cambridge University Press, 1896.

Jessopp, Augustus. "St. William of Norwich." *Nineteenth Century* 33 (1893): 749–66.

Richardson, James T., Joel Best, and David G. Bromley, eds. *The Satanism Scare.* New York: de Gruyter, 1991.

Roth, Cecil, ed. *The Ritual Murder Libel and the Jew: The Report by Cardinal Lorenzo Ganganelli (Pope Clement XIV).* London: Woburn, 1935.

Strack, Hermann L. *The Jew and Human Sacrifice (Human Blood and Jewish Ritual): An Historical and Sociological Inquiry.* Trans. Henry Blanchamp. London: Cope and Fenwick, 1909.

REFERENCES CITED

Anderson, M. D. *A Saint at Stake: The Strange Death of William of Norwich.* London: Faber, 1964.

Another "Blood Libel" . . . *or Ritual Murder?* N.p.: Campaign for Gentile-Jewish Reconciliation, 1990.

Bennett, Gillian. "Sex and Cannibalism in the Service of Satan: A Checklist of Articles about Satanic Abuse in the British Quality Press, February 1989 to October 1990." *Dear Mr Thoms* . . . 20 (April 1991): 36–44.

———. "'St.' William of Norwich and the Blood Libel: Revaluating the Legend." *Folklore* 116 (2005): 119–39.

Ben-Sasson, Haim Hillel. "Blood Libel." In *Encyclopaedia Judaica,* 4 :1120–31. Jerusalem: Keter, 1971.

"Blood Libel." *Letters to Ambrose Merton* 28 (Summer 2002): 7.

Boyes, Roger. "German Satanists 'Ate Babies.'" *Times* (London) 17 January 2003, 11

Brown, Allan, and Richard Woods. "Boy Fights to Clear Parents of Sex Abuse." *Sunday Times* (London), 20 October 1996, 10.

Burton, Richard. *The Jew, the Gypsy and el Islam.* London: Hutchinson, 1898.

Campion-Vincent, Véronique. "Démonologies dans les Légendes et Paniques Contemporaines." *Ethnologie Française* 23 (1993): 120–30.

Červinka, František. "The Hilsner Affair." In *The Blood Libel Legend: A Casebook in Anti-Semitic Folklore,* ed. Alan Dundes, 135–61. Madison: University of Wisconsin Press, 1991.

Chittenden, Maurice, and Adrian Lee. "Wests: Evidence of Cannibalism." *Sunday Times* (London), 26 November 1995, 1, 2.

Cohn, Norman. *Europe's Inner Demons.* 1975; St Albans: Paladin, 1976.

Cusick, James. "Community Where Ancient Traditions Live On." *Independent* (London), 1 April 1991, 5.

———. "Orkney Children Home as Abuse Case Collapses." *Independent* (London), 5 April 1991, 1.

Czubala, Dionizjusz, and Anna Milerska. "Myths and Rumors Surrounding the Last (1946) Pogrom of the Jews in Poland." Paper presented at the conference of the International Society for Contemporary Legend Research, Newfoundland, June 1999.

Despina, Marie. "Les Accusations de Profanation d'Hosties Portées contre les Juifs (Part 1)." *Rencontre—Chrétiens et Juifs* 5 (1971): 150–70.

———. "Les Accusations de Profanation d'Hosties Portées contre les Juifs (Part 2)." *Rencontre—Chrétiens et Juifs* 5 (1971): 179–91.

Duker, Abraham G. "Twentieth-Century Blood Libels in the United States." In *Rabbi Joseph M. Lookstein Memorial Volume,* ed. Leo Landerman, 85–109.

New York: KTAV, 1980. Reprinted in *The Blood Libel Legend: A Casebook in Anti-Semitic Folklore*, ed. Alan Dundes, 233–60. Madison: University of Wisconsin Press, 1991.

Dundes, Alan. "The Ritual Murder or Blood Libel Legend: A Study of Anti-Semitic Victimization through Projective Inversion." *Temenos* 25 (1989): 7–32. Reprinted in *The Blood Libel Legend: A Casebook in Anti-Semitic Folklore*, ed. Dundes, 336–78. Madison: University of Wisconsin Press, 1991.

———. Headnote to František Červinka, "The Hilsner Affair," in *The Blood Libel Legend: A Casebook in Anti-Semitic Folklore*, 136. Madison: University of Wisconsin Press, 1991.

Ellis, Bill. *Aliens, Cults, and Ghosts: Legends We Live*. Jackson: University Press of Mississippi, 2003.

———. "*De Legendis Urbis*: Modern Legends in Ancient Rome." *Journal of American Folklore* 96 (1983): 200–208.

———. "Sectarian Libels." *FLS News* 16 (November 1992): 11–12.

Ellis, Bill, Gillian Bennett, and Sandy Hobbs. *The Orkney Island SRA Case: A Checklist of British Newspaper Reports*. ISCLR Occasional Publications 1. 1993. Introduction by Bill Ellis.

E.O.J. [E. O. James]. "Human Sacrifice (Ritual Murder Canard)." *Encyclopaedia Brittanica*, 14 th ed. 1973.

Friedman, Saul S. *The Incident at Massena: The Blood Libel in America*. New York: Stein and Day, 1978.

Girardet, Raoul. "La Conspiration." Chap. in *Mythes et Mythologies Politiques*, 22–62. Paris: Seuil, 1986.

Handler, Andrew. *Blood Libel at Tiszaeszlár*. New York: Columbia University Press, 1980.

Hicks, Robert D. *In Pursuit of Satan: The Police and the Occult*. Buffalo, N.Y.: Prometheus, 1991.

Hinton, Isabel. "Fear and Loathing in St. Margaret's Hope." *Independent* (London), 15 April 1991, 18.

H.L.S. [Hermann L. Strack]. "Blood Accusation." In *The Jewish Encyclopedia*, ed. Isidore Singer, 260–67. New York: Funk and Wagnall, 1925.

Hsia, R. Po-chia. *The Myth of Ritual Murder: Jews and Magic in Reformation Germany*. New Haven: Yale University Press, 1988.

Jacob, Ezekiel. "Persecution of the Jews in 1840." *Publications of the American Jewish Historical Society* 8 (1900): 141–45.

Jacobs, Joseph. "The Damascus Affair and the Jews of America." *Publications of the American Jewish Historical Society* 10 (1902): 119–28.

———. *The Jews of Angevin England: Documents and Records*. London: Nutt, 1893.

———. "Little St. Hugh of Lincoln: Researches in History, Archaeology, and Legend." In *Jewish Ideals and Other Essays*, 191–224. London: Nutt, 1896.

Reprinted in *The Blood Libel Legend: A Casebook in Anti-Semitic Folklore*, ed. Alan Dundes, 41–71. Madison: University of Wisconsin Press, 1991.

———. Review of *The Life and Miracles of St. William of Norwich, by Thomas of Monmouth*, ed. A. Jessopp and M. R. James. *Jewish Quarterly* 9 (1897): 748–55.

Jessopp, Augustus, and Montague Rhodes James, trans. and eds. *The Life and Miracles of St. William of Norwich by Thomas of Monmouth*. Cambridge: Cambridge University Press, 1896.

Kennan, George. "The 'Ritual Murder' Case in Kiev." *Outlook* 105 (1913): 529–35.

Kors, Alan C., and Edward Peters. *Witchcraft in Europe, 1100–1700 : A Documentary History*. Philadelphia: University of Pennsylvania Press, 1972.

Landau, Jacob M. "Ritual Murder Accusations in Nineteenth-Century Egypt." In *The Blood Libel Legend: A Casebook in Anti-Semitic Folklore*, ed. Alan Dundes, 197–232. Madison: University of Wisconsin Press, 1991.

Langmuir, Gavin I. "Thomas of Monmouth: Detector of Ritual Murder." In *The Blood Libel Legend: A Casebook in Anti-Semitic Folklore*, ed. Alan Dundes, 3–40. Madison: University of Wisconsin Press, 1991.

Lea, Henry C. "El Santo Niño de la Guardia." *English Historical Review* 4 (1889): 229–50.

Lichfield, John. "French Baby Killings Lead to Rumours of Satanic Ritual Abuse." *Independent* (London), 31 October 2003, 13.

Lipman, V. D. *The Jews of Medieval Norwich*. London: Jewish Historical Society of England, 1967.

Loeb, Isidore. "Un Mémoire de Laurent Ganganelli sur la Calomnie du Meurtre Rituel." *Revue des Études Juives* 18 (1889): 179–85.

———. "Le Saint Enfant de La Guardia." *Revue des Études Juives* 15 (1887): 203–32.

McAlpine, Alistair. "Hallucinations? I Swear I Saw It All." *Daily Telegraph* (London), 12 January 2000, 17.

Miles, Tim. "Minister to Act on Rise in Ritual Child Abuse." *Guardian* (London and Manchester), 11 November 1990, 3.

Nathan, Debbie. "The Devil Made Them Do It." *In These Times*, 24 July–6 August 1991, 12.

———. "The Ritual Sex Abuse Hoax." *Village Voice*, 12 June 1990, 36–44.

Newall, Venetia. "The Jew as a Witch Figure." In *The Witch Figure: Folklore Essays by a Group of Scholars in England Honouring the Seventy-fifth Birthday of Katharine M. Briggs*, ed. Venetia Newall, 95–124. London: Routledge and Kegan Paul, 1973.

Nundy, Julian. " 'Cannibal' Emperor Bokassa Is Offered Forgiveness in Death." *Daily Telegraph* (London), 5 November 1996, 15.

O'Sullivan, Jack. "Council Criticized over Child Abuse Cases." *Independent on Sunday* (London), 13 November 1990, 3.

———. "Dispute over Ritual Child Abuse Divides City: 'Tunnel of the Condemned' under a Sunken Graveyard." *Independent* (London), 4 October 1990, 3.

Peta, Basildon. "Mugabe Men 'Shot White Farmer and Drank His Blood.'" *Independent* (London), 25 October 2002, 15.

Phillips, Melanie. "Satanic Cloak Hides the Real Horror." *Guardian* (London and Manchester), 21 September 1990, 23.

Reinach, Salomon. "L'Accusation du Meurtre Rituel." *Revue des Études Juives* 25 (1892): 161–80.

Richardson, James T., Joel Best, and David G. Bromley, eds. *The Satanism Scare.* New York: de Gruyter, 1991.

Rose, A. H. Review of *The Ritual Murder Libel and the Jews: The Report by Cardinal Lorenzo Ganganelli (Pope Clement XIV)*, ed. Cecil Roth. *Folk-Lore* 46 (1935): 93–94.

Roth, Cecil. "Blood Libel." In *The Standard Jewish Encyclopedia.* London: Allen, 1959.

———, ed. *The Ritual Murder Libel and the Jew: The Report by Cardinal Lorenzo Ganganelli (Pope Clement XIV).* London: Woburn, 1935.

Simmons, Michael. "Two Generations Suffer Ceausescu's Fertility Fetish." *Guardian* (London and Manchester), 10 January 1990; reprinted in *Dear Mr Thoms . . .* 15 (April 1990): 22.

Smith, Michelle, and Lawrence Pazder. *Michelle Remembers.* New York: Congdon and Lattes, 1980.

"Social Workers and the Police." Leading article *Independent* (London), 5 October 1990, 20.

Steele, John. "Dowager Convicted in Race Hate Case." *Daily Telegraph* (London), 17 October 1991, 3.

Strack, Hermann L. *The Jew and Human Sacrifice (Human Blood and Jewish Ritual): An Historical and Sociological Inquiry.* Trans. Henry Blanchamp. London: Cope and Fenwick, 1909.

Strickland, Sarah, and Rosie Waterhouse. "Witch-Hunt Is Launched over Books and TV." *Independent on Sunday* (London), 28 October 1990, 3.

Victor, Jeffrey. *Satanic Panic: The Creation of a Contemporary Legend.* Chicago: Open Court, 1993.

Waterhouse, Rosie. "Children's Games That Bred Alarm over 'Satanism.'" *Independent on Sunday* (London), 23 September 1990), 6.

———. "The Making of a Satanic Myth." *Independent on Sunday* (London), 12 August 1990, 8.

———. "NSPCC Faces Sack over Satanic Abuse." *Independent on Sunday* (London), 23 September 1990, 1.

———. "Police Chief to 'Kill off' Abuse Stories." *Independent on Sunday* (London), 7 October 1990, 1.

———. "Satanic Cults: How the Hysteria Swept Britain." *Independent on Sunday* (London), 16 September 1990, 3.

———. "Satanic Inquisitors from the Town Hall." *Independent on Sunday* (London), 7 October 1990, 6.

———. "The Secret Bungalow of Child Interrogation." *Independent on Sunday* (London), 14 April 1991, 4.

Waterhouse, Rosie, Sharon Kingman, and Jenny Cuffe. "A Satanic Litany of Children's Suffering." *Independent on Sunday* (London), 19 March 1990, 5.

Wright, Charles H. H. "The Jews and the Malicious Charge of Human Sacrifice." *Nineteenth Century* 14 (1883): 753–78.

AFTERWORD

The study of contemporary legend has been bedeviled by two widely followed but almost contradictory approaches. The first is the assumption that contemporary legends are false (hence the popular term for the genre, *urban myths*). The second is that contemporary legends are cautionary tales or at least reflections of the fears of modern society. These claims sit badly together, yet scholars have often managed to adopt both of them: while themselves believing the stories to be untrue, scholars have claimed that such tales are worth studying because other people believe them and therefore the shrewd observer can use them to decipher what is going on in the social subconscious. I want to use the final pages of this book to look at this academic folklore and relate it to the legends I have been discussing.

The assumption that legends (and their cousins, rumors) are false is often implicit, merely an undercurrent to the researchers' work, but at other times it can be quite explicit. Jan Brunvand offers a typical phraseology: "urban legends are folklore, not history. . . . To some degree urban legends must be considered false" (xii).

Sometimes the assumption is half implicit and half explicit, as in Gordon W. Allport and Leo Postman's well-known definition of rumors as lacking secure standards of evidence, a definition that is often carried over to contemporary legends. In addition, there is often another, wholly implicit, assumption that rumors and legends are things that *other people* pass along and/or believe in. It is therefore the duty of those who "know better" to debunk them. Though, of course, you only have to be round folklorists for ten minutes to realize that they are major transmitters themselves.

It is an irony that folklorists, whose work stems from an interest in what other people do and think and say and believe, rarely support popular worldviews. Their first impulse seems to be to disbelieve. Often without stopping to consider the evidence, they rush to disallow/delegitimize popular conceptions. Thus, they risk becoming "thought police" for the establishment view. The unfortunate effect is to cause them to forget that this worldview is also a form of folklore (Hufford).

It is perhaps because folklorists have thus implicitly belittled the materials of folklore that the history of the discipline is full of attempts to find an excuse for studying it. Since its inception, folkloristics has been a subject in search of academic legitimacy and intellectual significance. As George Laurence Gomme, a founding member of the (British) Folklore Society, put it in 1880, folklore is "somewhat unmeaning to the realism of the present age: and the question that seems to present itself to the popular mind is, what have grown-up men and ripe scholars to do with all this?" (13). Thanks to Wallace, Huxley, Lamarck, and most importantly Darwin, early folklorists found their raison d'être in evolutionary theory. In particular, they seized on the concept of cultural evolution sponsored by Edward Burnet Tylor and developed it into a "science of history" that enabled the previously fragmented and diverse materials of folklore to be systematized and to contribute to the foremost intellectual challenge of the age, the construction of a prehistory of humanity. This approach thus transformed folk-lorists' trivial pursuit into a part of the most exciting endeavor of the age and, in the words of John Campbell of Islay, "raised up a pastime for children to be a study for the energies of grown men and to all the dignity of a science" (ii). Folklorists have been searching for a good theory ever since.

This is where the psychosocial approach to contemporary legends comes in. This approach is attractive to scholars because it gives them an important social, political, and intellectual role to play. As specialist documenters and interpreters of current scares and stories, they can claim unique insights. Their expertise enables them to open a window on contemporary culture by revealing its hidden fears and coded messages and thus to interpret the culture to itself. Folklorists' skills allow them to hold their intellectual own against the well-regarded claims of sociologists and psychol-ogists, and by debunking as well as interpreting modern legends to earn "Brownie points" as good citizens too.

This worries me. If we, as folklorists and legend scholars, are to set ourselves up as "good citizens," then we have to be confident not only that our information is adequate but that our judgment is sound. The central issues of legend study thus become exactly those things which legend theory has so often tripped up on—the nature of "evidence" and "truth" and the way they are constructed. These are not simple problems. Truth is a notoriously difficult concept (it defeated Socrates), but even if we abandon "truth" and fall back on "evidence," the problem does not go away, for we come right back to the questions "What is 'evidence'?" and "Who decides what 'evidence' is?" And even if we can agree on what constitutes evidence, and even if we agree that the evidence is adequate, we can still be wrong. History is littered with ex-truths. Truth keeps changing, and yesterday's sure knowledge becomes today's folklore and legend. So a little caution is called for. Though it cannot be that all rumors and legends are false (though most of those I have discussed in this book are indeed false or at least debatable), the converse does not hold true either. Not all of them are harmless alternatives to the common view or "just good stories." Troublingly, we may not always be able to spot the difference.

Speaking personally, I have never been embarrassed by being a folklorist, and I see no need to apologize for it or to justify my interest in contemporary legends by claiming to know what the truth is or to be able to decode the hidden messages of modern society. I think the stories speak for themselves, though in different voices at different times. In studying them we are dealing with phenomena that, for good or ill, spring from the human psyche (unfortunately too often for ill, as in the legends in this book). We don't need a theory to explain them or to explain ourselves to others. The stories are enough in themselves.

The legends I have looked at in this book are dangerous and inflammable stuff, but theories don't help us to understand them. I believe that describing their spread is enough to reveal their nature. Plainly, they have staying power. None of them is trivial in any sense of the word, and documenting the way they have been presented and used is not a trivial pursuit.

The Bosom Serpent stories with which I began, despite their fantastic-seeming details, have had enough resonance through the ages to function as discourses of knowledge and power, to incorporate past understandings of the body, past diseases and past cures, and past debates about who owns the body and who is entitled to know what's wrong with it. Fear of sex allied to distrust of women and their charms—expressed through the skin-gift-death/sex-gift-suffering transmutations of the poison and honey theme—runs like a thread from ancient times through the misogyny of the medieval priesthood into modern times via dresses worn to attract a mate but contaminated by the touch of death. AIDS Aggressor stories have both reflected and helped to shape public discourse about disease and infection at both popular and governmental levels.

In many ways, the story that seems to have gone temporarily underground (to use Bill Ellis's concept of a "diving" legend), "Killing the Prodigal Son," is the most typical contemporary legend. It has had a huge influence in both popular and elite literature and a documented history from the early seventeenth century onward. In its tragic yet thrilling plot, writers have found the medium to express views of the human condition, human relationships, and the relationships of God to humans—poignant or bleak, according to their personality or philosophy. It waits now to emerge again into the modern world to dramatize and critique the agony of war.

In the final two chapters I have attempted to show how legends are part of life, not merely reflectors of life but shapers of life views and instigators of political action. For me personally, the legends examined in these two chapters are the blackest and most disturbing stories I have looked at. No way are they trivial, and no way are they merely warnings, cautionary tales, or indicators of social fears and pressures. They are fear itself and have led to fearful actions—crime, suffering, agony of mind and body, and persecution on a frightening scale and at the highest level.

So as I approach the last words of a project that has occupied almost eight years of my life, a personal declaration seems appropriate. Though I am not sure that I particularly want folklore to be raised, in Campbell's words, "to all the dignity of a science," I am sure that it is not in any way, nor ever has been, "a pastime for children." I hope the stories I have discussed here are ample proof of that.

REFERENCES CITED

Allport, Gordon W., and Leo Postman. *The Psychology of Rumor*. New York: Holt, 1947.

Brunvand, Jan Harold. *The Vanishing Hitchhiker: American Urban Legends and Their Meanings.* New York and London: Norton, 1981.

Campbell, J. F. *Popular Tales of the West Highlands.* 4 vols. Edinburgh: Edmonston and Douglas, 1860.

Gomme, George Laurence. "Folklore and the Folk-Lore Society." *The Antiquary* 1 (1880): 13–15.

Hufford, David. "Traditions of Disbelief." *New York Folklore* 8, nos. 3–4 (1982): 47–55.

INDEX